Beginning
Reading

Date Due

DEC − 8 2006			
APR 2	2008		

Beginning
Reading

a balanced approach to
teaching literacy during
the first three years at school

Yola Center

continuum
LONDON • NEW YORK

Cover Art by arrangement with Special Forever: An environmental communications project, Murray-Darling Basin Commission and Primary English Teaching Association.

Continuum International Publishing Group
The Tower Building   15 East 26th Street
11 York Road   New York, NY 10010
London
SE1 7NX

First published in 2005 by Allen & Unwin
83 Alexandra Street, Crows Nest NSW 2065, Australia

British Library Cataloguing-in-Publication Data
A catalogue record for this book is available from the British Library.

ISBN: 08264 8875 7 (paperback)

Library of Congress Cataloguing-in-Publication Data
A catalogue record for this book is available from the Library of Congress.

Typeset by Midland Typesetters, Australia
Printed by South Wind Production, Singapore

Contents

Preface

This book is dedicated to everyone who is interested in research-based data about effective literacy instruction for all children, especially those in their first three years of school. It is intended primarily for those involved with beginning reading in regular classrooms, which typically contain a small but significant number of at-risk literacy learners. I hope, therefore, that it will prove of interest to teacher–educators, practising classroom and resource teachers, literacy consultants, student teachers, policy makers, parents and any others who are concerned with early reading processes and practice in primary/elementary classrooms.

Acknowledgements

There are always acknowledgements to be made, whenever any book is written. However, when a book like this is written, which attempts to synthesise the best research and practice of other people, the debt is enormous and can never be adequately acknowledged.

Thus I begin by expressing my gratitude to all the researchers and practitioners whose work is recorded in this text. While they are too numerous to be acknowledged individually, I would like to single out Professor Brian Byrne, Dr Marion de Lemos, Professor Linnea Ehri, Professor Tom Nicholson and Professor William Tunmer for their professional and personal encouragement.

Perhaps my greatest debt is to Dr Robert Slavin and his colleagues from Johns Hopkins University, Dr Nancy Madden, Dr Barbara Wasik, Dr Nancy Karweit and all the members of the Success for All team in Baltimore, Maryland. They started me on my adventure in beginning reading, and have remained unfailingly generous with their friendship, time and assistance.

Closer to home, I wish to thank my many colleagues at Macquarie University, Associate Professor Sandra Bochner, Associate Professor Donna Gibbs, Dr Judy Goyen, Dr Lynne Outhred and Moira Pieterse, without whose encouragement and assistance this book would never have been written or published.

In particular, I would like to thank my close associate, Louella Freeman, who was with me at the beginning of the journey and, amazingly, is still there to give advice.

I would also like to extend my appreciation to Louise Kobler and to Sue McLain, who proofread the document for style and content, and were never afraid to give their opinion.

My publisher, Elizabeth Weiss from Allen & Unwin, deserves a special mention and possibly a citation for courage. I am extremely indebted to her for her attention and suggestions throughout the publication process, as I am also to Joanne Holliman, senior editor at Allen and Unwin.

Finally, but most importantly, I would like to thank my family, who are the first to suffer in an undertaking like this: my children, Jackie, Nicky and Richard and their partners, who were consistently encouraging, and my husband Steve who, as always, gave me unconditional assistance, support, and the most severe but constructive criticism.

Yola Center, 2005

To the memory of my parents,
Maksymilian and Madeleine Glass

How to use this book

I have written this text on teaching literacy in the first three years of school because I firmly believe that effective instruction depends on knowledge of theory derived from converging research. Thus, each section contains comprehensive review of relevant theoretical literacy concepts, followed by a suggested program of literacy practice.

In the first section I outline the rationale for writing this reading instruction. Sections 2 and 3 are concerned with teaching literacy skills and strategies in the first school year, while sections 4 and 5 deal with literacy theory and practice in the second and third school years, respectively. Appropriate group and individual literacy assessments and intervention procedures for each school year, as well as research pertaining to individual intervention, are presented in section 6. Materials for the suggested programs outlined in the chapters can be found in the Appendix.

As this book concentrates on literacy theory and practice associated with the first three years of school, the theoretical rationale of beginning reading is provided in some detail. Some readers, of course, may not be interested in all the theory sections, while others, with a more theoretical orientation, may wish to omit some of the curriculum sections dealing with teaching practice. For the convenience of all readers, therefore, the theoretical sections are clearly differentiated, whenever possible, from those sections in which practical issues are discussed.

The practical sections of this text attempt to cover the reading outcomes and indicators for Early Stage 1 and Stage 1 of the English K-6 Syllabus in Australia, which are similar to those articulated in New Zealand, the US and the UK. However, visual literacy, as defined in the syllabus in the first three years of school, is restricted to visual representations in the form of semantic maps and simple flow charts. For reasons of economy, the use of computers in the classroom has not been addressed in this text.

While there can never be a 'one size fits all' text for teaching literacy, I hope that this synthesis of effective research and classroom practice enables teachers to provide high quality beginning reading instruction to all their students.

WHO NEEDS another book on *reading* instruction?

Introduction

It is a truism that most children learn to read, irrespective of the mode of instruction, and (dare one say it?) sometimes despite the mode of instruction. However, it is also clear that a significant minority of children in regular classes in regular schools will have trouble with the literacy process.

While it is always dangerous to quote figures, and these will fluctuate according to geographical area, various overseas estimates suggest that about 20–25 per cent of the school population will be at-risk of literacy failure (Stedman & Kaestle, 1987). More recently in the United States, Snow et al. (1998, p. 98) have suggested that 'the educational careers of 25–40 per cent of American children are imperilled because they do not read well enough, quickly enough, or easily enough to ensure comprehension in their content courses in middle and secondary schools'.

The Australian estimate is somewhat more conservative, with between 10 and 20 per cent of primary/elementary school children considered to have persistent and significant problems in learning to read (House of Representatives Standing Committee on Employment, Education and Training, 1992; Waring et al., 1996). A recent review of public school education in NSW, Australia, also revealed that while the best readers in this state performed well in comparison with students from other OECD (Organisation for Economic Cooperation and Development) member countries, children in the lowest achievement band compared extremely poorly (Vinson Report, 2001).

During classroom observations and in conversation with many teachers, I have frequently heard them express deep frustration with this group of 'at-risk' or 'reluctant' readers. The teachers with whom I have been associated, both experienced and novice, have often confided that their pre-service training had not equipped them to assist struggling readers satisfactorily.

So much is currently required of a student teacher in a teacher training program that the time devoted to effective literacy instruction for all learners is, of necessity, far too brief.

It is quite apparent that teacher concern with students having literacy difficulties in regular classes exceeds national boundaries. A recent US study of elementary reading instruction practices reported by teachers and administrators (Baumann et al., 2000) indicated that accommodating struggling or underachieving students in regular classrooms was their greatest challenge. The comforting adage issued to teachers (and parents) a generation ago, that children would grow out of their reading problems, proved to be incorrect. As far back as 1988, Connie Juel had found that there was almost a 90 per cent chance that children who were poor readers at the end of first grade would continue to be poor readers throughout the primary/elementary grades (Juel, 1994). She cites the example of a child called Anna, who did not read well in first class. By the fourth grade, Anna was declaring quite unequivocally that 'she'd rather clean her room than read'.

All those concerned with a child's education will readily understand the opportunities that will be denied to a child like Anna. It is primarily to teachers of such children in regular classes everywhere that this book is dedicated. While teachers have always had access to many outstanding theoretical books on early literacy, and recourse to many well-researched commercial programs, there has been a dearth of early literacy books with an evidence-based approach to instructional practice. I hope that this text will fill this void by grounding early literacy classroom procedures within the most current research data. I also hope that such a book will prove useful to teacher educators, student teachers, policy makers, parents and others interested in the process of children's reading acquisition and the practices that are designed to foster it most effectively.

1 Speaking and reading

If you don't need to teach speaking, why do you need to teach reading/writing?

This chapter highlights the similarities and differences between speaking and reading, in order to explain why some children who have no difficulties with the former may still experience problems with the latter.

All parents, and all elementary/ primary teachers who are parents, know that pre-school children acquire oral language without receiving explicit instruction in it. Indeed, parental attempts at such explicit instruction generally have little effect at all on the way young children speak. As a typical concerned grandmother of a grandson aged 17 months, who communicated only in a series of grunts, squeaks and gestures, I wondered about the need for some early language intervention. The day I decided to pluck up courage and suggest to his mother that she consult a speech pathologist, he greeted me with a perfectly constructed, if less than perfectly articulated, three-word sentence. It was my turn to be speechless.

Foorman (1995) also gives an interesting example of the ease with which nearly all children in all societies develop a language, even when the environmental trigger to their language acquisition is only minimal. She writes (p. 378) that children who grow up in societies where their parents speak an ad hoc communication of the marketplace, called a 'pidgin', create and transmit their own language, called a 'creole'. A pidgin has a small vocabulary and a borrowed, inconsistent grammar from the speaker's native language. Unlike a pidgin, a creole is a language in its own right—with its own grammar, vocabulary and sound system. Children who speak Cajun, a creole language that developed out of the French and English linguistic environments of Louisiana, have acquired a language different from the pidgin spoken by their parents. It appears that children are biologically programmed to construct grammar in spite of the contrived linguistic input surrounding them. However, they are most unlikely to develop literacy in a similarly non-conducive environment.

To immigrants who arrive in their new country at adolescence or later, the dissimilarities between speech and reading/writing are, regretfully, only too obvious. My father, who arrived in Australia in his early thirties, became an extremely proficient reader of English (as good as he was of Polish) because his word recognition skills carried him through once he had acquired a working vocabulary in English. However, unlike his daughter, who arrived at the age of three and adopted the accent of the marketplace, he was never able to become a proficient English speaker, to the extent that he was never able to lose the Eastern European accent of his native land.

I have another interesting example of the ease with which children acquire new vocabulary, culled from my young grandson during regular baby-sitting sessions. He is now very aware of noises in his environment for which he demands continual explanation. When I told him that a particular noise was that of a window creaking, he looked at me intently and repeated 'window cweaking'. When his mother arrived to pick him up, and the wind and window began their usual orchestration, he remarked to his mother that it was only the window cweaking. Imagine reading the word 'creaking' correctly after only one print exposure.

Examples such as these have led Barbara Foorman to comment on the profound discrepancy between the development of language and that of literacy. To say that they merely emerge as part of a common developmental pathway is to rob speech of its biologically driven nature (Foorman, 1995) and to impute to literacy a natural spontaneity that cannot be supported in fact or theory.

The reason for the development of speech, without explicit instruction, in all normally developing infants, is that speech is a product of biological evolution. It stands as the most obvious, and arguably the most important, of our species-typical behaviours. Reading/writing, on the other hand, did not evolve biologically, but rather developed (and then, only in some cultures) as a secondary response to that which evolution had already produced. A consequence of this is that we are biologically destined to speak, but not to read and write (Liberman, 1997, p. 5).

As Liberman (1997) also remarks, language has been around for 200 000 years or more, and articulate speech for perhaps 75 000 years (Corballis, 2004), while the idea that it could be rendered alphabetically only occurred about 4000 years ago, suggesting that it is far more difficult to transcribe our thoughts on paper than it is to produce them orally. Furthermore, while all cultures have an oral tradition, only some find it necessary to translate that tradition into print.

To clinch the argument, we know, as teachers, that we will experience an unfortunate number of reluctant readers in our classrooms. However, we are less likely to experience the luxury of even a few reluctant speakers. Speech may have to be learned, but it does not have to be taught. On the other hand, reading and writing, for most people, will not be learned unless it is taught, and for some people, it will not be learned unless it is taught well. It is *important* for teachers to understand the dissimilarities as well as the similarities that exist between speaking and reading/writing. *Without this understanding*, they could easily underestimate the difficulties some children will have in acquiring literacy.

The aim of this book, therefore, is to give teachers in inclusive settings access to theory and research-based programs that have a generally preventive effect during the early school years in reducing the literacy problems of many at-risk learners.

What is the real relationship between speaking and reading/writing?

Having established, pragmatically and intuitively, that speaking a language does not necessarily entail reading or writing that language, we still need to know why this divergence exists.

Essentially, reading involves two basic processes (Gough & Tunmer, 1986; Hoover & Gough, 1990). One process is learning how to decipher print and the other is understanding what the print means. Or, as expanded by Torgesen (2000, p. 56), 'To comprehend written material, children need to be able to identify the words used to convey meaning, and they must be able to construct meaning once they have identified the individual words in print.'

Teaching these two processes in a complementary fashion guarantees a balanced approach to reading instruction. Michael Pressley, when making the case for a balanced perspective on reading instruction, has this to say: 'Balanced-literacy teachers combine the strengths of whole language and skills instruction, and in doing so, create instruction that is more than the sum of its parts' (1998, p. 1). The strengths of a whole-language approach, as I see it, are its insistence on a print-rich environment to stimulate a child's desire for reading. The strengths of a skills approach are its insistence on the explicit instruction of sound–symbol associations, both in isolation and in context to foster a child's word recognition ability.

It is this latter precept that has aroused the greatest controversy, despite overwhelming evidence that expert readers are extremely proficient at word-level processes (Pressley, 1998, p. 56). The need to include explicit decoding instruction when teaching beginners to read arises because difficulties at the word level often prevent children (particularly those at-risk) from becoming competent and interested readers. This is largely because speaking (and even speaking well) does not automatically translate into being able to decipher print. However, having a good command of a language will certainly enable children to understand the language written down, once they have learnt to decipher the print.

Another of my grandsons is just over four years of age and lives in a non-English-speaking country. From time to time, I send him tapes of books that I read aloud in English. He has no trouble listening to the tapes and under-standing the stories on them, provided that they are pitched at a four-year old's level of comprehension. Furthermore, being bilingual he can readily understand appropriate stories that are read to him in his native tongue. However, if he were given the same books to read by himself, in either language, he would not yet be able to decipher the print and, apart from the pictures, these books would remain meaningless to him.

Another interesting example of the same phenomenon is the apocryphal story of the poet Milton (Gough et al., 1996). As his eyesight faded, he would ask his daughters to read him books in his beloved Latin. Although he could no longer decipher the print (he was blind), he could still enjoy the text because of his mastery of the Latin language. His daughters, not being blind, could decipher the print, but no doubt found the reading process rather tiresome as neither of them could understand Latin.

So just what is the relationship between speaking and reading that prevents the majority of pre-school children from actually reading a story that is totally comprehensible when it is read to them? To answer this question, we should really examine all our options.

➤➤   Is reading easier than speaking?
➤➤   Is reading equivalent to speaking?
➤➤   Is reading harder than speaking?

In view of what I've already said, and from what experience as parents and teachers has taught us, the first option sounds a little bizarre. Still, let's look at the arguments set out by a speech theorist, Alvin Liberman (1997, p. 9), to examine this proposition more closely.

He suggests that on the surface, reading/writing appear to be easier than talking. The medium of reading/writing is print and is much clearer to observe than the speech signal, which is transient, and leaves much to be desired from a physical point of view. Furthermore, if you compare the effectors—fingers for writing, tongue for speaking—the skilfulness of the former far outweighs the clumsiness of the latter. Apart from licking lollipops and stamps, there is a limit to what the tongue can actually do. Finally, if you examine the receptors—the eye for reading, the ear for listening—you would have to agree that as a channel for transmission the eye is more effective than the ear. For example, in how many households does the radio hold sway over the television?

Nothing Liberman has said so far can be effectively denied. However, if the proposition that reading was easier than speaking were true, we would be seeing more children in our schools with speech difficulties than with reading/writing difficulties. We also wouldn't have to read books to four-year-old children whose reading abilities would exceed the surprisingly sophisticated speech we know that they possess at this age. In such a utopia, caregivers could concentrate on their own interests while pre-schoolers sat in silence, reading to themselves! Unfortunately, it seems patently obvious that reading presents a greater challenge than speaking.

Let's now examine the second option, that reading/writing and talking are equivalent. We have all heard arguments that reading and speech are similar in acquisition and that, as a consequence, reading/writing need no more explicit instruction than does speaking. This, after all, is the premise on which some whole language theorists base their approach to early reading instruction (for example, Goodman, 1986). While we know, through our experience with the reading disabled rather than with the language disabled, that equating the ease of speech acquisition with that of reading acquisition is a tenuous proposition, its non-equivalence can also be demonstrated theoretically.

The biological primacy of speech has already been addressed and we know that all communities of humans have a fully developed spoken language, while only a minority possesses its written equivalent. Furthermore, speech in all languages employs a single, universal strategy for constructing utterances by combining and permuting a few dozen consonants and vowels (Liberman & Liberman, 1992).

Scripts, on the other hand, are a cultural construction and are not represented in the same form universally. Just think of the difference between the English, Hebrew and Chinese writing systems.

Thus it would seem that we must also reject the second option, that reading and speaking are equivalent. We would then be forced to acknowledge that an approach to early reading instruction based on the equivalence of reading and speech has a questionable theoretical foundation.

What about our third option, that reading could be harder than speaking? This, of course, makes intuitive sense. Furthermore, it makes biological sense. While Liberman's elegant theorising is diverting when it implies that, logically, speech should be harder than reading, neither he nor most contemporary reading researchers support that first option. Liberman goes on to say that speech, in a triumph of evolution over engineering, has found a way around the limitations of the tongue and ear in a way that reading/writing have not managed with the finger and eye (Liberman, 1997, p. 9).

When we process spoken language, we actually use central phonological structures in the brain, rather than 'end' organs such as our ears (Ehri, 1998). Processing speech is not a matter of processing sounds but instead a matter of processing combinations of rapidly executed, coarticulated,[1] motoric gestures that are controlled by central processes in the brain (Ehri, 1998, p. 5).

We now know that speech processing is well beyond the limits of the ear. The critical phonemic segments that speakers and listeners process reside in the brain and are detected successfully by speakers and listeners because both possess the same biological equipment (Ehri, 1998, p. 5). In other words, the brain is specially designed for processing spoken language but it has no special central equipment for processing written language. In order to read and write, or to decipher and produce print, written symbols also need to be processed by the central equipment that biologically accommodates itself to speech. For this to happen, written language must penetrate and gain a foothold in the central equipment used to process speech. Letters (graphemes) must become attached to phonemes (sounds), so that sight words[2] are established in memory (Ehri, 1998, p. 5), before the central

---

1 Coarticulation is the overlapping of the articulatory gestures involved in the different phonemes within a word. Thus when we say /d/ at the beginning of a word, we are already anticipating the shape of the following vowel. Consequently, how we say /d/ in 'dog' will be different from how we pronounce /d/ in 'den'. This merging permits us to speak much faster than if we had to say each phoneme individually, as in the overt spelling of a word like 'd/o/g' (Byrne, 2002, p. 35).

2 Ehri's definition of 'sight words' is one that involves the automatic retrieval of words from memory—these have been read many times before and no longer need decoding; that is, the automatic access to most written words that literate adult readers possess. Sight words in this context do not refer to those words that children, early in their school career, learn to recognise from flash cards through visual cues rather than through a process of decoding (commonly referrred to as sight word reading by primary/elementary teachers).

processor can do its work. Or, to put it more simply, the symbols of print must be translated into identifiable spoken words that are readily accessible to the central processor. For this to happen, children have to learn first that words consist of sequences of sounds that can be manipulated (phonemic awareness) and then learn the symbols that correspond to these sounds (phonics or cracking the alphabetic code).

It is this phonemic analysis of spoken language, necessary for beginning readers, that is difficult and unnatural because speech is seamless on the surface with no breaks signalling phonemic units. Furthermore, there is no need to deconstruct speech sounds consciously as a listener because, as is true of all biological modules, their processes are not available to conscious inspection (Liberman, 1997, p. 12). So the psychologically real unit, the phoneme, is part of an automatic and unconscious process and (to compound the difficulty) is buried in the speech signal as a result of coarticulation (Byrne, 2002, p. 36).

What's more, obtaining meaning from speech, the ultimate aim of a conversation, requires no analysis of underlying phonological structures. Readers, on the other hand, need to analyse written language consciously in order to turn it into the signals that will permeate the central processor. That is precisely why a growing child learns speech effortlessly on mere exposure, but why many children need directed teaching experiences to learn to read and write. And that is why teachers need to know the differences as well as the similarities between the process of speech acquisition and the process of deciphering print.

At this point, a simple summary may clarify the preceding discussion.

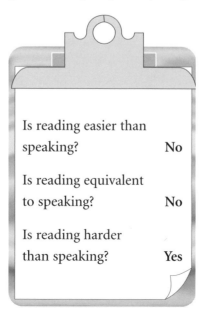

Is reading easier than
speaking?   No

Is reading equivalent
to speaking?   No

Is reading harder
than speaking?   Yes

Teachers must be aware that reading and writing skills will only develop if written language (or print) also gains entry to the central equipment used to process speech through the establishment of sight words in memory (Ehri, 1998, p. 12). Therefore one of their primary tasks is to transfer the wonders of phonology from speech to script by showing children that words are distinguished from each other by the phonological structure that the alphabet represents (Liberman & Liberman, 1992, p. 349).

While this is a critical task for teachers in the first two to three years of school, they must, at the same time, foster and extend both the receptive and expressive speech skills that children bring to school to enable their pupils to derive meaning from print at an increasingly challenging level. Children must be taught to develop their vocabulary skills, their knowledge of content areas, their appreciation of text structure, their thinking and reasoning skills and comprehension strategies in addition to word reading ability (Torgesen, 2000, p. 57). This, of course, is the essence of a balanced approach to reading instruction that is required of the beginning reading teacher.

Summary

In this chapter, the similarities and differences between speaking and reading were highlighted in order to explain why we find a significant minority of reading-disabled children in regular classrooms, but very few speaking-disabled youngsters. In putting forward the case for a balanced approach to beginning reading instruction, I have also indicated that the greatest impediment to skilled reading is difficulty at the word level which can be prevented, to a large extent, by explicit instruction in word recognition. However, I have also emphasised the importance of a print-rich classroom and the need for comprehension instruction in order to foster children's love of reading and writing.

In the next section, instruction at both the meaning and word level at the start of the school year will be examined.

STARTING
the *first* school year

> *Getting the balance right*
>
> *from the start*

2 A balanced literacy program: Theory and practice

Theory

This chapter explains why teachers of beginning reading need to include strategies at both the meaning and word level in order to provide a balanced early literacy program.

The responsibility of primary/ elementary teachers to develop a love of reading in their young students can be overwhelming. Consequently, it is not surprising that many people feel the salaries of early childhood teachers should be commensurate with those of university/college lecturers. Most primary/elementary teachers, never-theless, do have at least one advantage over university lecturers: they have all undergone professional teacher training. This experience will have instilled in them the principles of effective classroom management, indispensable for teaching young children. Unfortunately, not all primary/elementary teachers are provided with expertise in every area of the primary curriculum during their pre-service years, and I suspect that this applies particularly to early literacy instruction.

The late Candace Bos from the University of Texas-Austin and her associates (Bos et al., 2001, p. 18) found that pre-service and in-service educators, themselves, considered they were only somewhat prepared to teach early reading to low-progress readers. They appeared not to under-stand the salient differences and similarities between spoken and written language discussed in the previous section. In addition, many teachers were confused about the differences between phonological awareness and phonics (to be discussed in this and subsequent sections), limiting their ability to teach reading explicitly to children who struggle in regular class-rooms. The authors concluded that advances in knowledge about reading instruction have not yet had a substantial impact upon educator knowledge, despite increased emphasis in the literature, as well as national and state initiatives (Bos et al., 2001, p. 18).

This finding has been reinforced by Cunningham and her colleagues in their study of how teachers spend their time in teaching language arts (Cunningham et al., 2002). Their data suggest that there is a continuing mismatch between what educators believe and know and what convergent research supports as effective early reading instruction for children at-risk of reading difficulties. This book, therefore, concentrates on the curriculum area of literacy in an attempt to correct this mismatch.

As stated in chapter 1, reading essentially involves two basic processes (Gough & Tunmer, 1986; Hoover & Gough, 1990). One is learning how to decipher print and the other is understanding what the print means. Thus, in the early years of reading, spelling and writing instruction, teachers must teach the somewhat unnatural process of deciphering print (often called word recognition) and develop, at the same time, the more natural process of listening comprehension. These two processes must be taught in balance because, while both are necessary, neither is sufficient on its own to ensure children will derive meaning (and therefore pleasure) from text reading.

There can be no argument about the need to decipher print. A text of Chinese logographs would present a real challenge to the average English reader. Indeed, a page of English text can easily be as indecipherable to the beginning reader as a page of Chinese logographs is to the mature English reader. However, deciphering print on its own will not necessarily produce text understanding (think of Milton's daughters or your own efforts with an advanced statistics text of which you can decipher every word but not understand a single concept). Take the following example:

> As noted previously, the primary analysis was a multi-variate analysis of covariance (MANCOVA), with total correct scores for each subject on each of the four post-tests entered as dependent variables. The total correct pretest score was the covariate.

Decipherable? Yes! Meaningful to non-statisticians? No!

While the ability to decipher print and not understand what it means occurs only in a small percentage of young readers, teachers in inclusive classrooms must still attend to the development of listening comprehension strategies. This will be necessary for this small minority and of great benefit to the rest of the class.

Most reading problems, however, appear to arise when children do not decipher print fluently enough to be able to understand what it means. When school children experience this type of difficulty, they will often develop a level of frustration that may lead to concomitant behaviour problems, particularly in boys (Waring et al., 1996). That is why effective reading instruction, from the point of school entry, becomes such a priority for the primary/elementary classroom teacher.

If we review the students entering a typical classroom on their first day of school, we will always find a few children who come to school already familiar with deciphering print. These children have absorbed the alphabetic code and automatic sight word recognition on their own through a happy confluence of heredity and environment. Unless they have a distinct personality clash with their classroom teacher, they will become mature readers irrespective of the class literacy program.

Some students (and they often prove to be the same ones) will also come to school with such well-developed language skills that listening comprehension strategy instruction will be redundant for them. But, for most children, the two basic processes of word recognition and listening comprehension should form a non-negotiable core of the early literacy program. So let's examine some practical teaching ideas for teaching beginning reading in inclusive classrooms.

Practice

Let's assume that a young teacher encounters a new kindergarten class in an average suburb of an average city. Despite the wide disparity in the pre-school environments of these young children, the aim of the early literacy program remains the same for them all: to engender in each child a love of literacy which transcends, but must include, teaching the child to decipher print and to gain meaning from print.

Most children, upon arrival at school, do not even realise that speech is made up of sequences of words and that words are composed of sequences of phonemes or sounds. It is the rare child, at school entry, who knows, for example, that 'sun' and 'sail' begin with the same sound. Children's pre-school experiences revolve around getting meaning from speech (semantics) in order to communicate with their parents and friends, not around consciously analysing speech in order to determine its structure. They may not even understand that print is a form of speech which is written down, particularly if connections between speech and print have not been explicitly detailed in story-telling sessions. To attempt to teach children to decipher print will be difficult, if not downright impossible, if these prerequisites are missing and are not addressed when a child arrives at school. Thus the phonemic structure of language needs to be explained very early in a child's school career.

It is also possible that teachers will find that some of their young pupils will not have been exposed to lively verbal interchanges with their parents or caregivers. They may not have been fortunate enough to have engaged in storybook reading and discussion, or to have watched appropriate television programs—the typical ways that good language and comprehension skills develop in the pre-school child. After all, there is an increasing number of pre-school children whose parents work, and busy staff in child-minding facilities do not always have time to foster one-on-one linguistic play. In addition, there has been recent evidence of the negative academic impact on young children who spend extended time in poor quality family day-care facilities that are not centre-based (NICHD, 2002).

In our multicultural society, there are also many children whose pre-school experiences are not necessarily aligned with Anglo-Saxon middle-class school expectations. While their home experiences are equally rich, they are not necessarily geared towards literacy acquisition (see Nicholson, 2000). Thus it will also be incumbent upon teachers to help a large number of their new pupils develop listening comprehension strategies, so that all students beginning school, and particularly those at-risk, are able to extract meaning from the diverse types of texts encountered in primary and secondary schools.

Some teachers with whom I have spoken worry that, by starting with activities to develop skills both at the meaning and word level, they may be needlessly boring those children who enter school with these prerequisites in place. I really believe this is an unnecessary anxiety. Eagerness to learn is not usually diminished by reinforcing pre-existing knowledge. In my experience, teaching a concept that has already been mastered by young children at home will only increase their confidence and make them even more receptive to classroom instruction. If, however, teachers identify a child who starts school as a fluent reader, it is their responsibility to place that child in a classroom where the teaching of reading, rather than its prerequisites, is already taking place. It is extremely rare to encounter more than one or two of these precocious pupils in a school year.

The balance between teaching skills and strategies that foster listening comprehension and those that foster word recognition must be carefully maintained in the early years of school in order to prevent as many children as possible from developing meaning or word level difficulties. The following list of instructional strategies for children in their first year of school has been adapted from Snow et al. (1998, p. 189).

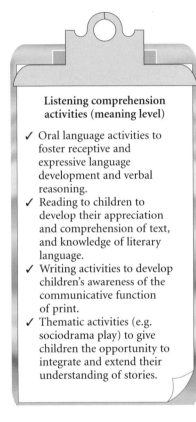

Listening comprehension activities (meaning level)

✓ Oral language activities to foster receptive and expressive language development and verbal reasoning.
✓ Reading to children to develop their appreciation and comprehension of text, and knowledge of literary language.
✓ Writing activities to develop children's awareness of the communicative function of print.
✓ Thematic activities (e.g. sociodrama play) to give children the opportunity to integrate and extend their understanding of stories.

Word recognition activities (word level)

✓ Shared reading to develop concepts about print and basic reading processes.
✓ writing activities to develop children's printing and spelling abilities.
✓ Print-directed activities to enable children to recognise and print the letters of the alphabet.
✓ Phonological/phonemic analysis activities to develop children's phonological and phonemic awareness.
✓ Word-directed activities to assist children to acquire a basic sight vocabulary and to understand the alphabetic principle.

You can see how each of these instructional strategies is either geared to develop the prerequisites for word recognition or to foster listening comprehension. Let's now see how these recommendations can be translated into a whole-class program.

First, despite their diverse home backgrounds, most kindergarten children come to school with well-developed speech skills (even if not necessarily in English). Thus they will all probably enjoy the familiar oral language, shared reading and thematic activities suggested by Snow et al. (1998), designed to foster listening comprehension. This is an excellent way to link home and school activities for children beginning kindergarten. However, not all of them will have a detailed knowledge of print, so teachers will also need to instruct children in print-directed activities during book exploration sessions, as a precursor to developing word recognition in beginning readers. Furthermore, an even smaller number of children entering kindergarten is likely to be competent in the processes of phonemic analysis necessary to decipher print. Consequently, phonological processing activities, designed to foster word recognition, will also be vital for most children entering school for the first time, and particularly so for all at-risk pupils.

It thus makes organisational sense, at least at the beginning of the first school year, to teach these activities in a whole-class group. You will then become aware of the children who need additional assistance in any or all of these areas and arrange individual or small-group intervention for those displaying difficulties in either language (meaning level) or print/phonological awareness (word level) activities. You will also be able to identify those exceptional children for whom these activities are unnecessary and who need reading rather than pre-reading opportunities.

Summary

In this chapter, I have shown that there still appears to be a mismatch between what educators believe and know and what appears to be best literacy practice for children at-risk of reading difficulties. After providing a rationale for reading as the product of decoding and listening comprehension, I made the case for a balanced early literacy program. Activities designed to promote skills and strategies at the meaning and word level were presented and their incorporation into a whole-class program was briefly outlined.

A detailed description of a possible whole-class program at the beginning of the first school year is presented in the next chapter.

3 Listening comprehension

Developing skills and strategies at the meaning level

This chapter outlines a series of strategies to facilitate the development of meaning level skills in all children at the start of the first school year. First, a suggested interactive text reading program to foster listening comprehension ability is presented. Ideas to develop syntactic awareness, oral language and early writing are then discussed.

Given that one and a half hours per day has been recommended as optimal for language arts instruction in the early school years (Kemp, 2000), what is the most effective way to maximise this time to develop skills and strategies at both the meaning and word level in a balanced teaching program at the start of the first school year?

Probably the most appealing initial activity for both teacher and pupils is one that involves story telling, as it provides the best way of connecting home (and known) activities with school (and unknown) activities. That's why I would begin by teaching strategies at the meaning level.

Research indicates that reading books to children with appropriate coaching and support from adults is linked to later reading success (Mason, 1992, p. 237). Story reading to children is a most engaging way to introduce literacy, since hearing and discussing texts with literate persons can help young children establish connections between speech (with which they are familiar) and print (with which they will need to become familiar).

Structured book reading, where explanations, interpretations and clarifications are provided, develops listening comprehension ability, one of the key ingredients in obtaining meaning from written text. Meaningful discussion of unknown vocabulary, opportunities to learn about text structure, extension of thinking and reasoning skills (Torgesen, 2000, p. 257), as well as directed exposure to the language of text, also provide children with the prerequisites for reading comprehension and for writing. There appears to be little doubt that a print-rich environment, where children are immersed in good literature, helps to increase their understanding of the nature of reading and writing (Pressley, 1998).

Another prerequisite skill for reading comprehension, which is facilitated by structured book reading, is the development of a strategic way of thinking about texts. When relevant strategies before, during, and after reading have been systematically activated during shared reading, it is much easier for the child to internalise these meta-comprehension (*see* glossary) strategies and apply them to the task of reading comprehension, once word recognition has been established. It thus appears that through the 'user-friendly' medium of interactive book reading, children, and particularly those at-risk, can learn a great deal about the skills and strategies needed to derive meaning from print.

It is also important that texts read to children at this stage should be challenging, to enable children in their first year at school to grapple with ideas and take an active stance toward constructing meaning (Beck & McKeown, 2001). You will remember, from the earlier sections, that while young children are still unable to read texts because of limited word recognition, the listening comprehension skills of five-year olds are quite sophisticated and should be fully engaged when adults read to them.

I was recently listening to a factual text being read to a group of children (aged from two to three years) in a long day-care centre which I was visiting. In a section dealing with vegetables, the children were shown a drawing of a radish. One little boy asked what it was and on being told its name, he said he had tasted it at home and didn't like it. The teacher remarked that he would probably develop a taste for it as he grew older, upon which he replied brightly, 'I suppose I will like it, once I'm five.' What a number of challenging concepts can be derived from one interchange about a humble radish, even at a pre-kindergarten level!

Another consideration when choosing texts, particularly Big Books (*see* chapter 4), for reading to young children for interactive discussion, concerns the pictures that accompany a text (Beck & McKeown, 2001). These authors suggest that pictures can be of two types: either complementing the text or conflicting with it. In the first instance, it is much easier for children to answer a question about the text by referring to the picture, rather than by responding to the linguistic content. There is, therefore, an argument for not showing the picture until after the question has been asked. In the second instance, the picture may confuse the child and could also be shown after the discussion of text events.

While I'm sure that most teachers in the early school years are quite familiar with interactive text reading, I would like to go over the essential characteristics of an effective interactive text reading program, because it is possible that some of these elements could be overlooked in the usual busy schedule of a regular classroom. Furthermore, if teachers understand the rationale behind each element, they will be more inclined to incorporate them into their story telling programming.

The interactive text reading program I have chosen is derived from the work of Karweit (1989b) but it also contains ideas from Text Talk, based on the work of Beck & McKeown (2001). Karweit's program contains four activities, which I shall cover in some detail, together with Beck & McKeown's observations on read-alouds.

These four activities are taught in order to develop listening comprehension and oral language skills. They relate specifically to literary texts of the narrative type, which are more accessible for interactive study at this early stage. However, this in no way precludes teachers from accessing different text types for interactive study (*see* chapter 12). Using the procedures outlined below, two texts per school week can be studied intensively, although teachers would be typically reading many other books to children during the week in a less structured manner.

Interactive text reading program

✓ Story introduction
✓ Story reading
✓ Story review
✓ Story retelling: group
✓ Story retelling: individual

Story introduction

Activating background knowledge

We, as adults, choose books to read for any number of compelling reasons. Kindergarten children, on the other hand, tend to have books chosen for them, so teachers need to make children as motivated as we are ourselves when we open a new book. To do this, spend a little time introducing the book you have selected for them.

It makes sense to first activate children's background knowledge so that they are able to link their own experiences to the book that is about to be read to them. For example, if the book is about a rural area, you can ask children to discuss any country experiences they may have had in order to make the story more meaningful and relevant. Listening to their comments and extending their remarks serve the double purpose of motivating them as listeners and enriching their verbal skills.

From their classroom observations on teachers reading aloud to their students, Beck and McKeown (2001, p. 12) issue a number of caveats about the inappropriate use of background knowledge, specifically in response to text questioning. Teachers should realise that the point of invoking background knowledge is to integrate it with text content to assist comprehension. They should be wary of its use at other times during interactive text study, particularly when questions about the text are being answered. For example, children could respond to text questions by using their background knowledge rather than by using the story information, since this is much easier than processing decontextualised language.

If children persist with this procedure, insisting, for instance, that monkeys eat bananas when asked a question about monkeys in a text that specifically eschewed their banana-eating habits, they will not be establishing the major story concepts of the book under discussion. Teachers should be aware of this, once background knowledge has been activated. They could then gently discourage a 'hodgepodge' of personal anecdotes from children in favour of integration, rather than domination, of background knowledge into the processing of the linguistic context of the text.

Discussing new vocabulary

Having just finished a novel by John Banville (2000), where I needed the *Shorter Oxford Dictionary* as a constant companion, I cannot overstate the importance of discussing new vocabulary with children when appropriate. While Banville's novel contained at least two unknown words per page (and it is to his credit as a novelist that I persisted to the end), I think this is rather exaggerating the goal of vocabulary training. At this stage I would recommend discussion of no more than two or three key words per story.

Remember also that word meanings are most readily assimilated when they are not only defined, but their use is also illustrated in natural sounding contexts (Nagy, 1994, p. 9). How many times have you looked up the meaning of a word you have encountered in text, but have been totally frustrated by your inability to insinuate it successfully into your conversation?

When you come across a word that seems a likely candidate for instruction (Beck & McKeown's definition for such a word is that it should be unfamiliar but likely to be used in normal conversation), take it out of the text and explain its meaning. Children should repeat the word, so they can develop an appropriate phonological representation of it, and they should be involved in using and responding to the word.

Another important issue the authors raise is the need for maintenance of the target word after initial instruction, which, of course, applies to adult learning as well. I wince at the number of times a delicious new word I encountered two months ago escaped my personal lexicon just when I was trying to impress an audience. Beck and McKeown's strategy is to create a chart of words from each story, and to get teachers to tally each citing or use of the word (p. 18). As with adults, it is amazing how often a newly learnt word appears in other stories or discussions, so take each opportunity as it arises. I will say more about vocabulary instruction when I start tackling listening comprehension strategies more intensively in the third school year (*see* Section 5).

Encouraging students to predict the story

Another familiarisation technique involves some prediction on the part of the students to develop engagement with the text. Confirmation or denial of anticipated events should help maintain students' interest in the book under discussion. This constant dynamic of prediction/confirmation and prediction/negation involves the student in what Allington (2001) calls text-to-world connections, where students link what they've read to what they already know in the world. The modification of original predictions by text revelations is a means of keeping the reader in thrall as the text is processed.

A typical strategy for prediction is to get students to look at the picture at the front of the book and guess what the story may be about and what characters may be involved in it. (I admit that in this post-modern age not all story covers lend themselves easily to the aims of story prediction.) At this early stage, prediction will probably be oral for most students and can be another vehicle for extending their verbal skills. In the second school year, however, students can be encouraged to write down their predictions. Prediction/confirmation or negation can be encouraged only when teachers stop at critical sections of the text and discuss the original predictions of their students in the light of text development. This, of course, should be an integral part of the interactive reading procedure during story reading.

Giving a purpose for listening

The last part of the story introduction establishes a purpose for listening to the story. Since this is usually a text selected by a teacher rather than by a child, teachers must try to 'sell' the book by outlining its most exciting and interesting features (if it is a literary text), in much the same way as a movie preview. A key question relating to the focal point of a narrative text may be appropriate here. The excitement of gaining new information readily provides a purpose for listening to a factual or procedural text.

Story reading

It must be remembered that in the first months of school, when many children are unable to read themselves, appropriate interactive text reading by an adult provides a model for children to learn how to derive meaning from print as they move from listening comprehension to reading comprehension. When reading books to children, teachers intuitively read aloud with enthusiasm and expression. It is thus interesting to note that recent research data indicates that reader behaviour which includes appropriate pitch or intonation, stress and/or emphasis, tempo and the rhythmic patterns of language (defined as prosody) may be a cause of good comprehension and is thought likely to contribute to children's development of fluent reading (Kuhn & Stahl, 2000).

A useful strategy during story reading designed to consolidate students' story recall is to stop frequently and ask summative questions about events that have occurred in the story. However, as the eventual aim of questioning is not simply a quickly retrieved answer, remember that predictions must also be confirmed or denied and elaborative questions need to be judiciously added. Finally, teachers could end the reading by asking the question which relates to the original purpose of the story discussed in the story introduction. For example, using *Who Sank the Boat?* (Allen, 1990) as an example, you might say, 'Well, we read the book to find out who sank the boat and the answer is . . . ?'

Needless to say, Beck and McKeown (2001) have a number of important points to make about story questioning as a result of their classroom observations. First, they suggest that books which present an event structure, rather than a series of situations, are more likely to provide the extended, connected content for building meaning that is the focus of interactive text reading. Second, questions asked by teachers should be open-ended, rather than constrain children into making limited responses. In answering such questions, teachers should be aware of the difficulties children face in gaining meaning from decontextualised language. (Remember, 'Where have you been?'/'Out.' 'What have you been doing?'/'Nothing.') Consequently, teachers have to design questions that encourage children to talk about and connect ideas and then develop follow-up questions that scaffold (*see* Glossary) the children's original responses.

A similar procedure, known as dialogic reading, has been advocated by Whitehurst et al. (1994), and it involves a shift of roles. In dialogic reading, the child becomes the story teller, while the adult assumes the role of an active listener, asking open-ended questions, adding information and prompting the child to increase the sophistication of descriptions from the material in the story (Whitehurst et al., 1994, p. 680). While educationally and statistically significant effects of dialogic reading have been found on measures of expressive vocabulary and grammatical complexity, the intervention was small-group rather than whole-class and involved pre-school rather than school-age children.

Whenever I have discussed with teachers the procedure of stopping text reading to ask meaningful questions, a few have voiced their apprehension about questions interrupting story flow. This is a genuine concern, but from observation and practice, it does not appear that interactive story telling dampens students' interest and certainly does appear to enhance verbal abilities and comprehension strategies (Senechal et al., 1995; Allington, 2001). After all, interactive reading represents a dialogue between teacher and student, rather than a monologue, and simply externalises the processes which skilful comprehenders have already internalised.

However, it is still a useful technique to re-read the story targeted for instruction right through without a break at some other time in the day, because repeated text reading is certainly beneficial to young listeners in terms of both their lexical growth and their conceptual development (Kerr & Mason, 1994). Moreover, other books are also being read to the children, during the day, without such exhaustive examination, so that students are still reaping the benefits of continuous text presentation.

Story review

When the story reading is finished, teachers could carry out a brief review of the main events and characters with students to consolidate the story in their memory. Then, in order to set the scene for a second day of related story-book activities, the session could begin with a quick review of the previous day's text.

Story retelling: Group

The purpose of group retelling is to give students an opportunity to be actively involved in the story. This type of involvement gives students some ownership of the story, enhances understanding of the nature of literature and develops oral language skills.

On the day after the story reading, group story retelling can take place using a number of activities. Two which have proved appealing to young students are those involving sequence cards or those employing socio-drama. Obviously, a combination of both activities or any creative games devised by teachers which activate students' retelling skills can be used.

Sequence cards, depicting the main events in the story, can be used in many imaginative and varied ways to help children review the events in the story read the previous day. (The least laborious way, if not the most accept-able, of making sequence cards is to buy a second copy of the book being studied and to cut it up.) This technique does need a caveat, however, and is useful for narrative texts only. While supervising an overenthusiastic student, I noticed that she was using sequence cards for a factual text that dealt with the variety of animals that inhabit a zoo. As the book presented no event structure, her young pupils were having inordinate difficulty placing a group of animals and their habitats into a temporal sequence.

Socio-dramatic play, on the other hand, is not restricted to narrative text. For teachers who wish to incorporate factual and procedural texts into early story retelling experiences, socio-dramatic play is a wonderful opportunity for children to revisit and extend their new knowledge (*see* Burns et al., 1999, for more details).

Story retelling: Individual

While the group retell is an important classroom technique for developing oral skills and comprehension strategies, it is also necessary for teachers to discover whether each individual pupil is benefiting from the interactive text reading instruction. This can be done with the help of an additional teacher, or more realistically, by a volunteer, either while the group retelling session is in progress, or at any other suitable time of the day.

Using a simple format of several literal, elaborative and, if appropriate, inferential questions about the text read, the teacher can quickly ascertain if any students need additional help. Questions about the story should relate to the characters, the setting, the main problem, the resolution and the coda or moral (if any), which represent the structural features of a narrative text. Questions about a factual text should include the topic(s), main event and supporting details. As the individual retell usually takes about five minutes, the whole class can generally be assessed within a week.

If the individual retell indicates that the regular classroom lesson in interactive text reading is insufficient for some students to have mastered details about the structure of a text, then appropriate action must be taken to provide more intensive (individual or small-group) intervention (*see* Section 6 for details of assessment and intervention for meaning level skills at the start of the school year).

I suggest that this pattern of teaching, specific assessment and individual/small-group intervention be applied to all literacy concepts that are covered in this text. While I am supporting the re-teaching of the same principles taught in the classroom program, I am not necessarily supporting the use of the same re-teaching methods. This is, of course, left to the skill and ingenuity of the classroom teacher. If, however, the assessments indicate that a large proportion of the class is having difficulty with developing listening comprehension strategies, then the pace of the whole-class lesson may need to be adjusted.

A suggested plan for structured interactive text reading of about 20–25 minutes duration appears below:

Interactive text reading program for the first school year

Day 1
✓ Story introduction
   – Activating background knowledge
   – Discussing new vocabulary
   – Encouraging students to predict the story
   – Giving a purpose for listening
✓ Story reading
✓ Summative, predictive and elaborative questions

Day 2
✓ Story review
✓ Story retelling: Group
✓ Story retelling: Individual

If teachers wish to introduce different text types, once the word program commences, the above procedures can be adapted to fit the structure of a factual text (topic, main idea and supporting details), and the absence of a defined temporal sequence.

Syntactic awareness

As students listen to and develop oral language skills during interactive text reading, teachers can begin to introduce the concept of syntactic or grammatical awareness to their students.

Syntactic awareness can be defined as a meta-linguistic skill, which is the ability to reflect on and manipulate aspects of the internal grammatical structures of sentences (Tunmer & Hoover, 1992). Thus meta-linguistic performance differs from language comprehension and production in that it requires the language system (rather than the meaning) to be treated as the object of thought (Bowey, 1994, p. 124).

While it is generally not until middle childhood that children develop syntactic awareness, there is evidence that it is causally related to learning to read (although not as strongly as phonological awareness). It is possible that syntactic awareness enables readers to monitor their ongoing comprehension processes more effectively (Bowey, 1986, cited in Tunmer & Hoover, 1992), by checking that their responses to the words of the text conform to the surrounding grammatical context.

Interactive text reading could thus present a 'no tears' opportunity to begin early syntactic awareness training. Teachers at the end of story-telling activities could easily take a sentence from a familiar story and present it orally to their pupils, with the word order jumbled. Students could then be asked if the sentence sounded right and if not, to correct it. However, there is a caveat to be issued here.

It has been argued by Gombert (1992, cited by Nunes et al., 1997, p. 155), and subsequently by Bowey (1994), that in order to unjumble sentences, semantic as well as syntactic processes are implicated, so that this procedure is therefore not a pure test of syntactic awareness. Furthermore, Bowey (1994) has also suggested that working memory, too, may be associated with a word-order correction task. Thus, while I would not over-emphasise this activity, it can still be inserted very easily at the end of story-telling sessions, and children seem to really enjoy correcting their teacher and one another.

It appears that teaching syntactic awareness is of benefit to children not only at the meaning level but at the word level also. There are some indications (Steinberg, 1985, cited by Tunmer & Hoover, 1992) that children can make use of their syntactic awareness to assist in the decoding of unfamiliar words, provided they have some graphophonic knowledge (letter–sound correspondence). It is a procedure that Share (1995) refers to as a self-teaching mechanism, and will be discussed later.

As there appear to be no negative side-effects associated with encouraging some syntactic awareness at this early stage, it seems reasonable to include a few relevant activities at the end of story-telling sessions.

Teaching oral language and early writing

Apart from interactive text reading incorporating early syntactic awareness, another device for stimulating oral language is the use of a daily, well-designed oral language program that emphasises expression, reception and conceptualisation of language. While I have seen the Peabody Language Program (Dunn et al., 1981), the Class Listening and Speaking Program (CLAS) (Plourde, 1995) and Language for Listening (Engelman & Osborn, 1999) working very effectively in many schools, obviously any effective language program will enhance the language skills that are being developed during the story-telling program.

Whole-class oral language programs are particularly appropriate in schools that contain a large number of children from non-English-speaking backgrounds (NESB), because such children can participate in the classroom program instead of in the more common withdrawal system practised in many schools. Some recent research (Chiappe et al., 2002) suggests that children from NESB fail to catch up with their native-speaking peers between kindergarten and first grade with respect to syntactic processing. The authors comment that NESB children did not exhibit deficits in skills which received the most instructional attention (i.e. literacy and phonological awareness), and advocate greater instruction in oral English communication from the point of school entry. (Also *see* Section 6 on individualised intervention for the non-English-speaking child.)

Early writing refers to the writing behaviours of young children that precede and develop into conventional literacy. Writing, in this context, refers to written communication, and not just to the mechanics of letter formation and word copying.

While there are many places to timetable writing activities, a good start could be after a Group Retell session. After teachers have read a story to their students, and it has been discussed, children could be given an opportunity themselves to write in response to the story. At this stage, any form of written communication could be accepted freely and reinforced by the teacher. This written communication might be a drawing, a scribble, a letter or a series of non-phonetic letters, invented or as conventional spelling.

Most children will have had little experience with writing. (Remember neither print awareness nor alphabet activities has yet been covered.) The whole aim of the informal literacy segment, at school entry, is for children to begin to understand the purposes of writing. Children can be encouraged to use writing in response to literature they hear and it will complement other writing activities that are regularly programmed by teachers. More refinement in the writing program can be expected after the introduction of Big Books and alphabet activities, when children will be eager to incorporate their new knowledge of letters and print conventions into their work.

Once phonological awareness activities are part of the daily program, children will start to use invented spelling in writing (e.g. 'katz' for 'cats') to demonstrate their developing knowledge of sounds in words. As Snow et al. (1998, p. 323) explain, 'The use of invented spelling is not in conflict with teaching correct spelling. Beginning writing with invented spelling can be helpful for developing understanding of phoneme identity, phoneme segmentation, and sound-spelling relationships.'

While still keeping to the simple view that reading consists of decoding and listening comprehension, it probably makes sense to look back at the principles on p. 23 of this text to see how many of them we've covered in the section on establishing skills and strategies at the meaning level. It seems to me that the activities outlined in this chapter satisfy all four of the principles at the meaning level outlined by Snow et al. (1998), and kindergarten teachers could continue with variations on these activities throughout the year. If teachers wish to introduce different text types during the kindergarten year, the format that could be employed for their study is discussed in chapter 12.

What we need to do now, to complement meaning level skills and strategies, is to introduce some activities to develop children's skills at the word level, as suggested by Snow and her colleagues; and this may be a more contentious issue.

In chapter 1, I suggested that speaking was a natural activity, while learning to read was not a biological imperative. While children still need practice and directed experiences in the development of listening comprehension and oral language skills, they are relatively natural processes, which most reading theorists and practitioners would always include in a beginning reading text. However, listening comprehension, while being a necessary component of learning to read, is not a sufficient one. The other critical component of reading is deciphering the printed word or word recognition. As this is the less natural and more difficult component of the reading equation, because it involves analysis at the individual phoneme level, some whole language theorists are more opposed to the inclusion of word level skills instruction in a beginning reading text. Those who support the case for balanced teaching, though, would agree upon the necessity of teaching word level skills in an early reading program.

Authors of beginning reading texts cannot ignore the existence of voluminous evidence that emphasises the importance of word recognition in the reading process, in addition to the critical role of comprehension. There is no longer any doubt that children (particularly reluctant readers) given training in phonological sensitivity and/or alphabetic code show superior outcomes on measures of comprehension and text reading as well as on measures of word recognition (Stanovich & Stanovich, 1999; Ehri, Nunes, Stahl & Willows, 2001; Rayner et al., 2002). By not including word level skills in a beginning reading program, teachers will be excluding a large minority of children from literacy competence and its attendant privileges. Consequently, the teaching of skills and strategies at the word level, at the start of the school year, will be addressed in the next chapter.

Summary

This chapter outlined a systematic text reading program designed to develop skills and strategies at the meaning level in all children, particularly those from impoverished English language backgrounds. The focus was on interactive text reading and retelling, but the program can be readily adapted for different text types. A brief section was also devoted to teaching syntactic awareness as well as the inclusion of an oral language and early writing program, in order to enhance both spoken and written communicative skills.

4 Phonological awareness

Developing skills and strategies at the word level

Learning about print

This chapter deals with procedures to assist children to develop skills at the word level at the start of the first school year. First, connections between speech and print are examined. Then activities designed to promote phonological awareness are introduced. Finally, the concept of generalisation to enhance effective classroom instruction is discussed.

Interactive text reading, discussed in the previous chapter, relied, to a great extent, on oral language discussion, because the picture books used were generally too small for a group of children to become aware of print. However, activities in this chapter involve children interacting with Big Books, where, of course, the print is much easier to see.

During interactive text reading, the focus for teacher and students was on language acquisition and development, as well as on deriving meaning from print through the use of spoken and written language. We began with this activity because children just starting school are already familiar with deriving meaning from the spoken word, or the semantics of language. However, during story telling, the focus on print, logistically, was minimal, and activities now need to be introduced which will direct children's attention to the printed word.

The importance of young children's awareness of print is becoming increasingly well recognised (Clay, 1985) and is found to predict future reading achievement (Tunmer et al., 1988). However, while the majority of children growing up in a print-rich environment develop quite sophisticated print awareness, even at the pre-school level, a large number of children come to school with no knowledge of the conventions of print (Adams, 1990, p. 337).

In her text on beginning reading, Adams also explains that many children do not know what a letter or word is, much less how to read one. In addition, children do not necessarily know the front from the back of a book, or that the print, rather than the picture is meant to convey meaning. For these children, initiation into print awareness is critical since 'global awareness of the forms, functions and uses of print provides not just the motivation, but the basic conceptual backdrop against which reading and writing may best be learned' (Adams, 1990, p. 337).

It is up to the kindergarten teacher to make children aware, very early in their school career, that print is categorically different from other kinds of visual patterns in their environment, and that adults in their world can extract meaning from it. Certainly, many parents are delighted when their two-year olds gleefully yell 'ABC' at the sight of the letters seen in their environment but not, for instance, when they see car number plates. Having isolated letters as an entity distinct from other visual patterns, the passage of these pre-school children into the world of reading may well be expedited through their early acquisition of print awareness.

Big Books

The use of Big Books, which are nothing more than large-sized books, offers print-learning opportunities to children that are not visually available when they are listening to stories from regular-sized books in a large classroom. Teachers, in the context of simple story telling from Big Books, can initiate students into print awareness by first showing them how to handle a book, and then how to recognise the front from the back. All too often kindergarten students have had no experience at all with books up until school entry.

After showing students the cover page and the title, predictions about the story can be made in the same way as was discussed in interactive text reading. However, the purpose of Big Books differs from that of interactive text reading, because the function of the former is, primarily, to make students aware of the nature of print.

When reading a Big Book aloud to children, teachers can point to each word as it is read (Holdaway, 1979, quoted in Adams, 1990, p. 369). Such finger-pointing illustrates that the text proceeds from top to bottom and left to right. Moreover, it indicates that it is the print, rather than the picture, that carries the story message, and that spoken language corresponds with written language (Ehri & Sweet, 1991).

Finger-pointing

Finger-pointing by adults can also highlight the conventions of print, such as punctuation (e.g. full stop, comma and question mark, at this early stage) which can be reinforced by pauses and changes in voice intonation during the passage reading. Capital letters after a full stop can also be pointed out, which would complement the alphabet activities that are also recommended for instruction in an early kindergarten classroom.

At this stage, however, I do want to issue one caveat about the use of finger-pointing by children. While this is a practice employed in many beginning reading classrooms as a method of encouraging children to read on their own, teachers should be aware of the underlying processes associated with finger-pointing reading by children (Uhry, 2002). In the absence of proficiency over these critical processes, finger-pointing, on its own, is unlikely to lead directly to word recognition. Uhry points out that teachers in balanced literacy classrooms who wish to incorporate finger-point reading by children into activities such as shared reading, must be aware that there needs to be a good match between direct instruction and proficiency in the skills associated with children's finger-pointing reading (Uhry, 2002, p. 340). To benefit from finger-pointing activities, children who are not yet proficient at word-level one-to-one correspondence need instruction in cutting and reassembling sentences, and in segmenting spoken sentences. For these latter procedures, the use of chips or tokens could be useful to early finger-pointing readers. For children who can finger-point using a 'counting words' strategy, the transition from word-level to phoneme-level one-to-one correspondence could be facilitated through direct instruction in phonemic segmentation and letter-sound association. Automaticity in letter-naming and letter-response is also an underlying process of finger-pointing and needs systematic practice to achieve mastery and complement finger-pointing reading.

All these critical underlying processes will be systematically covered in this and later sections. However, I chose print awareness activities in Big Books, using adult finger-pointing in the first instance, to introduce children to skills and strategies at the word level because such activities are appealing and encourage children to pay attention to the printed word as well as to the meaning of text.

To direct more attention to the printed word, letter recognition could also be taught as a complementary procedure to Big Book activities.

Alphabet activities

It seems timely to make a case for the systematic introduction of alphabet activities into the beginning reading syllabus at this juncture. There is no doubt that knowledge of letter names provides a substantial headstart for children at the point of school entry (Burns et al., 1999). Furthermore, evidence for the importance of letter knowledge and phonemic segmentation skill in building a sight vocabulary can be found in many studies following the seminal work of Share et al. in 1984. However, letter naming can be difficult for young children as it is a skill reliant completely on memory. Ehri and McCormick (1998, p. 144) suggest that when teaching letters, teachers should incorporate meaning into the learning process, provide mnemonic devices for enhancing memory, and involve the child in extended practice in order to accelerate the course of letter learning.

When is the best time to introduce alphabet activities into a beginning reading program? I believe that they should accompany procedures that are designed to teach children about print, that is, very early in the kindergarten year. In the first place, upper and lower case letters are being encountered in every Big Book session, so linkages are constantly being established between the two activities. Second, it is helpful for students to master all their letters before formal reading instruction commences (Ehri & McCormick, 1998, p. 144), so that any confusion between letter names and letter sounds may be minimised.

In practical terms, I have found that trying to discover or learn about two letter names a week seems to be a manageable goal, but the pace of letter introduction is, of course, up to the individual teacher. As a whole-class activity, where the assumption is made that many children enter school knowing only a few letters, Ehri & McCormack (1998) suggest programs such as Letterland (Wendon, 1993), which uses mnemonics to help children form memorable links between letters and their sounds. Bowey (2000) recommends a program called Jolly Phonics (Lloyd, 1998), in which children are first taught activities including the sounds and letters corresponding to the letters s, a, t, i, p.

While phonics programs like Jolly Phonics have proven highly successful when taught by classroom teachers to children in low-income areas (Morgan & Willows, 1996, quoted in Bowey, 2000), I feel that programs that concentrate on letter names and leave letter sounds alone are less confusing at this early stage. However, when letter names and their sounds are introduced in the phonics program (*see* chapter 7), it is extremely likely that Letterland and Jolly Phonics-type mnemonics help children learn sound/symbol correspondences better than mnemonics that do not link letter shapes to sounds (Ehri et al., 1984). Indeed, a modified Year 1 program developed by Tunmer et al. (in press) which introduced Jolly Phonics only after students had first experienced a phonemic awareness program (Byrne & Fielding-Barnsley, 1991) and a rhyme and analogy program (Goswami, 1995) showed impressive results with both European and Maori children in New Zealand (*see* chapter 18 for a more detailed description of this study).

Singing alphabet songs and introducing letters in alphabetical order, while playing detective games to isolate a mystery letter (Center & Freeman, 2000a) are a very accessible way of developing letter name learning in young children. In such games, various clues are given about the letter to be learnt and children use inductive processes to guess the letter under investigation.

Linking letter names to the first names of children in the class and printing them in lower and upper case have also proved a popular activity for kindergarten children. Getting children to write the letters has also been found to be a useful way to reinforce their acquisition. Finally, using letter names for invented spelling (by getting children to write down the spelling of 'ice' when they have learnt the letters I and S), not only helps children acquire letter knowledge, but also phonemic awareness.

Remember that the focus of alphabet activities is to enable children to develop letter name knowledge since accurate, immediate letter name recognition (automaticity) is one of the best predictors of learning to read (Share et al., 1984; Wolf, Bowers & Biddle, 2000; Uhry, 2002). Scott & Ehri (1989) found that having novice readers name letters in words helped them remember how to read the words. This is because many of the letter names contain relevant sounds such as /s/ in ess and /t/ in tee. Thus students who are already familiar with letter names can discover relationships between letters that they see in the spelling of words and sounds they detect in word pronunciations (Ehri, 1987).

You can now see why letter name knowledge reinforces the goal of this chapter, which is to help children in the first weeks of school develop skills at the word level as well as at the meaning level. The next critical procedure is concerned with developing children's phonological awareness.

Phonological/phonemic awareness: Theory

Children may come to school with some print awareness and some letter knowledge (which is why I commenced with these activities), but it is not so usual for them to start kindergarten with established phonological/phonemic awareness skills. While these skills are critical pre- and co-requisites for reading, writing and spelling, parents tend to be less familiar with these activities and thus less likely to have encouraged their development in pre-schoolers.

I think it is important to first present a definition of both phonological awareness and phonemic awareness, and to show how they differ from auditory discrimination, phonetics and phonics (also *see* Glossary). Then I'll discuss the relationship of phonological awareness and phonemic awareness to reading and spelling. Teaching phonological awareness using Big Books will be covered next, while teaching phonemic awareness activities, together with letter sound correspondences, will be addressed later in Section 3.

What is the difference between phonological and phonemic awareness?

Phonological awareness has been defined as sensitivity to the sound structure rather than to the meaning of speech (Foorman et al., 1998). Thus a child who is phonologically aware not only understands the meaning of the words 'cat' and 'hat', but also recognises that they rhyme. However, while they are aware of the correspondence between the last two sound units, ('at' in 'cat' and 'hat'), they cannot subdivide the words any further.

Foorman and her colleagues (1998) have defined phonemic awareness as the ability to deal explicitly and segmentally with the smallest unit in the spoken word, the phoneme (*see* Glossary). Thus a phonemically aware child will not only tell you that the words 'cat' and 'hat' rhyme but also that the word 'cat' consists of three phonemes, 'c'-'a'-'t', and that it differs from 'hat' only in its initial phoneme. It appears that developmentally, the ability to be phonologically aware precedes the ability to be phonemically aware.

Although many texts do not differentiate between phonological awareness and phonemic awareness, I have accepted the definition of Foorman and her associates in order to present the easier phonological activities and their prerequisites in this pre-reading section and leave phonemic awareness activities in the context of teaching phonics to the following section on formal reading instruction. I suspect that when children first enter kindergarten, they do not necessarily know that the word 'cat' represents anything other than a small, furry animal. They do not realise that a word exists as a separate entity, differing from other words in a sentence on the basis of its length and sound structure. Only when this concept (defined as lexical awareness) has been acquired, can teachers proceed to activities designed to teach phonological awareness in sub-lexical units (dividing 'cat' into its onset 'c' and its rime 'at').

Once children are secure in their phonological awareness knowledge, the concept of phonemic awareness (dividing 'cat' into its three phonemes, c/ a/ t) can be introduced. It makes sense to me, therefore, to teach phonemic awareness in the context of reading/spelling instruction.

How does phonological/phonemic awareness differ from other auditory and literacy skills?

It is essential to distinguish phonological/phonemic awareness from auditory discrimination. Even before the age of two, children have acquired auditory discrimination and distinguish between words which differ only by a single phoneme. A parent wouldn't get much response from two-year-old Pam, if he called 'Sam!' However, the same child who would come running once her name was called correctly, would be unlikely to realise that her name rhymed with that of Sam, and even less likely realise that the difference between the names consisted of only one phoneme. The ability to explicitly identify, isolate and manipulate large and small sub-lexical units —the hallmark of the phonemically aware—is beyond most two-year-old children, and without explicit teaching, may not be present even in normal four or five-year olds.

Another confusing concept for students of literacy is the difference between phonological/phonemic awareness and phonics. The former is purely an oral activity, while the latter is defined as sound/symbol instruction (e.g. teaching children that the written symbol 'b' corresponds to the oral sound /buh/) and, as an instructional device, has been the subject of much heated debate in the so-called 'reading wars' (explicit phonics training in isolation versus more implicit phonics instruction in context). Unless beginning readers know that words consist of sequences of sounds, which can be manipulated and juxtaposed (phonemic awareness), they are unlikely to benefit from phonics instruction or to acquire sound/symbol relationships by themselves (Juel, 1994).

Why should we teach phonological/phonemic awareness?

Phonological/phonemic awareness is one of a number of phonological abilities which is a stronger predictor of success in reading and spelling acquisition than other important correlates of literacy such as intelligence, vocabulary and listening comprehension.

In fact, the discovery of the core phonological problems associated with specific reading disability has scuttled the long-held theory that the word-reading difficulties of children with low intelligence are qualitatively different from those of children with average or above-average intelligence (Share & Stanovich, 1995; Torgesen, 2000) and that different forms of remediation are needed for the two groups. Converging research data from literally hundreds of experimental and training studies has demonstrated a strong association between phonological/phonemic awareness knowledge and reading and spelling achievement.

For example, in a meta-analysis undertaken by Ehri and her colleagues (Ehri, Nunes & Willows, 2001), the authors found that phonemic awareness training exerted a moderate, statistically significant impact on reading and spelling. The impact was not only on word reading, but also on reading comprehension. Moreover, phonemic awareness training helped normally developing readers, at-risk and disabled readers, pre-schoolers, kindergarten-ers, first graders, and children of both low and mid–high socio-economic status. Most importantly, classroom teachers were effective instructors of phonemic awareness, although the results indicated that small-group instruction was more efficient than whole class teaching.

The reason for this, as has been discussed before in chapter 1, is that while children come to school with well-developed spoken language, they will only develop reading, spelling and writing skills if written language or print also gains entry to the central equipment that people use to process speech (Ehri, 1998; Liberman, 1997). As we are biologically programmed to under-stand and produce speech, we require no formal instruction for the development of language. However, reading and writing an alphabetic script are not biologically programmed in the same way, do not occur in every culture and may not develop without explicit tuition. Thus one of the primary tasks of teachers in beginning reading classrooms is to transfer the wonders of phonology from speech to script (Liberman & Liberman, 1992). This is a difficult process, because sensitivity to the phonemes of one's native language is not a conscious process for speakers. Readers, however, need to analyse speech consciously in order to turn it into the signals that will permeate the central processor.

For children to gain access to the alphabetic script (in order to read and spell novel words), they must first recognise that spoken words can be subdivided into smaller sub-lexical units such as the syllable or the onset/rime (phonological awareness) and ultimately into phonemes (phonemic awareness). They must then learn how these phonemic units are mapped by the written script (phonics). Children who fail to make these connections are forced to rely on a visual or logographic (whole word) strategy, which prevents them from becoming independent readers and spellers since their access to new words is restricted (Andrews, 1990). These are the children who tend to develop into students with reading difficulties.

An interesting study, reported by Rayner and colleagues (2002) in the *Scientific American*, illustrates this point quite dramatically. English-speaking university students were trained to read unfamiliar symbols such as Arabic letters. One group learned the sounds associated with each symbol (phonics group) and the other group learned the whole word associated with certain strings of Arabic letters. When asked to read new words constructed from the original symbols, the phonics group significantly outperformed the whole-word trained students, because whole-word learning is, unfortunately, non-generative.

Just a word of caution before we embark on phonological awareness instruction. While early reading programs now stress the importance of including phonological/phonemic awareness training, we must be aware that other phonological processes are also associated with beginning reading acquisition. For example, children who experience problems with the retrieval, perception and temporary retention of phonological structures, in which orthographic processes may also be implicated (Bowers & Wolf, 1993; Wolf, Bowers & Biddle, 2000), are also at-risk of reading problems. This difficulty in the retrieval of phonological processes is generally detected by word finding errors and slowness on rapid naming tasks, using colours, and particularly letters or numbers as stimuli (Blachman, 2000; Cardoso-Martins & Pennington, 2004). Naming speed difficulties, sometimes called rapid automatic naming (RAN), interfere with accurate and fluent word recognition, and children with both phonological awareness and RAN problems are considered to have a double deficit with respect to reading acquisition.

While some researchers have conceptualised RAN as a subset of phonological processing (Torgesen Wagner, Rashotte, Burgess & Hecht, 1997), others (Wolf, Bowers & Biddle, 2000) believe that it represents a second major core deficit of reading acquisition. Indeed, in a recent article on models of reading acquisition, Bowers and Newby-Clark (2002) hypothesised that the major impact of phonemic awareness is on the ability to sound out novel words, whereas the major impact of rapid naming is on the ease of building up orthographic knowledge leading to fluency. More recently, a study conducted by Cardoso-Martins and Pennington (2004, p. 47) supported the view that both phoneme awareness and rapid naming ability are strongly implicated in reading acquisition, but suggested that RAN seems to play a more modest role than does phonemic awareness.

Another phonological processing difficulty which besets some children is poor verbal short-term memory (usually measured by recall of a series of digits or words), which causes them to form less accurate and less stable phonological representations in working memory. The consequence is that it is more difficult for children with these problems to hold on to information in working memory, creating processing limitations that contribute to both poor decoding and poor sentence comprehension (Blachman, 2000).

The reason I have chosen to concentrate on phonological and phonemic awareness training at the expense of RAN and poor verbal short-term memory is partly theoretical but also pragmatic. There has been dramatic progress in both our theoretical understanding of the concept of phonological awareness and in our ability to improve children's reading acquisition through successful phonological awareness training programs. I must, however, draw attention to the work of Wolf, Miller and Donnelly (2000) in the United States, whose RAVE-O program is currently attempting to address the issue of poor naming speed and associated fluency difficulties of children in their third and fourth years at school.

Phonological awareness: Practice

➡ The prerequisites: Lexical awareness, identical words, long and short words
➡ Onset and rime
➡ Blending, segmenting and manipulating

The prerequisites: Lexical awareness

As has already been mentioned, phonological awareness refers to conscious awareness of the internal structure of a word, for example, a child recognising that 'cat' and 'hat' rhyme, without of course being able to articulate that both words possess the common rime unit 'at'. This is a very big step, since many children starting school may even be unaware that sentences can be subdivided into words and that words themselves can be subdivided into smaller units. So, in order to ensure children develop phonological awareness, we have to take a step backward and teach them the necessary prerequisites. We need to develop lexical awareness in children before they can be brought to conscious awareness of the internal structure of a word.

The meta-linguistic skill of word or lexical awareness (the understanding that a word has structural properties as well as semantic ones) appears to be strongly related to learning to read (Tunmer & Hoover, 1992). This aware-ness is, of course, unnecessary in speech, where only the meaning of a word is relevant, but it is critical to learning to read and must be mastered before phonological awareness can be achieved. Examples of early word or lexical awareness include segmentation of phrases and sentences into words, separation of words from their referents and judgement of word lengths (Tunmer & Hoover, 1992).

Teachers can initiate lexical awareness activities by starting from the concept of a sentence, since sentences are the linguistic packages through which we convey our separate thoughts (Adams et al., 1998, p. 39). A few lessons could be devoted to simple explanations and demonstrations of sentences (and also non-sentences to reinforce the concept). Then short sentences can be generated, covering different attributes of students or objects in the classroom. A brief description of easy-to-see pictures can also provide a pleasant introduction to sentences.

When children are able to produce simple sentences independently, either spontaneously or in response to different stimuli, teachers can write these sentences down on the board. Writing sentences as children present them orally, and highlighting the words, can reinforce the concept of words as a distinct entity in a sentence. This is a much harder concept to learn from speech alone since words in sentences are seamless with no indication of word boundaries. After all, 'Gladly, my cross-eyed bear' (Gladly, my cross I'd bear) would never have emerged if children from a Christian culture had been able to read their prayers before reciting them.

Using the titles of stories that teachers are reading to the class as target sentences is a useful way of linking activities that are taking place in an early reading classroom. For example, after reading the story of *The Very Hungry Caterpillar* (Carle, 1989) as a Big Book activity, teachers could draw their students' attention to the title in the book and point to each word. Then the sentence could be written on the board, with a box around each word, and teachers could point to each word again as they read the sentence aloud to the class. Picture-grams could be drawn under each word to reinforce the concept of the word. Teachers could also give pupils sentence strips with two or three words corresponding to a book title that has already been discussed and let them cut up the sentence strip into its constituent words. Games, like lining up all the children and getting one child to step forward each time a word in a sentence is being read out, can also be played.

There are many other activities that teachers can use to teach the concept of a word as a discrete unit (for instance, cutting up sentences into indi-vidual words and re-assembling them, getting two (or more) students to hold up two (or more) words, or clapping out the number of words in a sentence). The important thing is not to lose sight of the concept being taught in a flurry of creativity. Testing the concept on all students after sufficient time has been devoted to its instruction should alert teachers to the extent of their teaching effectiveness.

The prerequisites: Identical words

Once you have ensured the children in your class have acquired the concept of a word as a discrete unit, teachers can move on to more sophisticated concepts of lexical awareness. At this point, you might show students two identical words in a text, e.g. the book title *One fish, two fish, red fish, blue fish* (Seuss, 2003). By showing children that the same printed word is *usually* represented by the same spoken word, teachers are reinforcing the concept of a word and also making useful connections between the familiar notion of speech and the unfamiliar notion of print. I stress *usually* because homophones sound the same when read out and yet do not look the same when written down, e.g. fare/fair, blew/blue.

You can test whether your students have acquired this notion by writing down two identical words and one dissimilar word and getting them to identify the identical words and the odd one out, despite the fact that they cannot yet read. For example, getting them to 'read' 'Hip' in Hip! Hip! Hooray! should identify those children who still need help with this concept.

The prerequisites: Long and short words

You are now ready to move on to teaching long and short words, since research (Rozin, Bressman & Taft, 1974, cited by Adams, 1990) has shown that an awareness of the relation between the spoken and printed lengths of words is a strong indicator of reading readiness.

It appears that many children are unaware of the acoustic properties of their own language. Rozin, Bressman and Taft (1974), cited by Perfetti (1999) found that many pre-school children could not perform the 'mow-motorcycle' test. This involves asking children which of two printed words corresponds to each of the two spoken words, 'mow' and 'motorcycle'. (In fact, a recent unpublished study suggested that fewer than twenty per cent of children aged four to seven years were successful on this test.) Successful performance on this task requires not awareness of phonemes, but merely the idea that acoustic length might correspond to visual length or numbers of letters (Perfetti, 1999).

Using any exceptionally long or short words encountered during Big Book reading is a reasonable starting point for teaching this activity, and continues our theme of making connections between print and speech. For instance, teachers could write two words, greatly dissimilar in length, on the board, one directly under the other in the same size print, and show the children that the word that looks long (relative to the other) sounds long (relative to the other).

Clapping out the syllables as you say the words can reinforce the concept of word length. It is probably a good idea to practise first with children's names in the classroom.

Another activity which lends itself to mastery of long and short words is the direct comparison of compound words. For example, you could write down the words '**rain**' and '**raindrop**', one directly under the other. Children can now see easily that one of the words is longer than the other and that one of the words sounds longer than the other. (You can get children to clap out the syllables here as well.) At the same time, this game reinforces the concept of identical words. Children can immediately see that the word 'rain' occurs in both the simple and the compound word.

Teachers can even introduce the idea of addition and deletion of words by starting with '**rain**' as a written word, then adding '**drop**' to it, and showing how this addition lengthens both the written and the spoken word. You can then show the children the process in reverse. I would suggest that if compound words are being used to illustrate the principle of word length, you should restrict each part of the compound syllable to one syllable ('**toothbrush**' rather than '**basketball**', so that weaker students in the class are not confused by syllabification).

You can also provide extension activities by writing a short word, such as '**pen**' on the board and telling your students what the word is (remember, they still can't read!). Ask students to think of longer words using the base word '**pen**' (such as '**pencil**', '**penknife**'), which you can write underneath to reinforce the concept of long and short words and, incidentally, the concept of identical words at the same time. This exercise could even have long-term benefits for reading multi-syllabic words (see Section 5). By clapping out '**pen**' and '**pencil**', the children will also be introduced (albeit implicitly) to the idea of syllables.

When teaching student teachers about the concept of long and short words, I thought that I had done a rather reasonable job of getting the idea across to them. Unfortunately, that type of assumption should never be made by a teacher. In one classroom I visited, the student teacher had written the targetted long word in tiny print and the small word in large print, and was at a loss to understand why her students were taking so long to get the idea. In another classroom, a teacher had chosen two words from his Big Book that were not greatly dissimilar in length and had written them across the board, rather than one under the other. His students, too, were having inordinate difficulty with the concept of long and short words.

Another teacher, very keen to instil the concept of long and short words, had done everything correctly, by writing the two words under examination in the same-sized print, one directly under the other. Unfortunately, she had chosen the word '**ant**' as an example of a short word and the word '**elephant**' as an example of a long word. It's so easy for children to regress to semantics with the example just mentioned. They can think (and often do) that '**ant**' is a small word because ant is a small insect and that '**elephant**', of course, is a big word because an elephant is a big animal. '**Caterpillar**' and '**lion**' would have been better choices. Teachers need to be aware of the misconceptions to which children can be prone to ensure their teaching strategies do not encourage their pupils to make conceptual mistakes at the early stages of reading instruction.

And now, with the prerequisites taught, assessed and re-taught if necessary, either at the class or small-group level, let's move onto an examination of the sub-lexical units of onset and rime.

Onset and rime

Phonological awareness or phonological sensitivity can be viewed along a continuum, ranging from '**deep**' to '**shallow**' sensitivity (Stanovich, 1992; see also the definition by Foorman et al., 1998).[3]

Shallow phonological sensitivity generally requires children to manipulate larger phonological units, such as deciding whether '**pin**' and '**thin**' rhyme (defined by Foorman et al., 1998, as phonological awareness). Tasks that require children to manipulate the smallest units of sounds—phonemes (dividing '**thin**' into its three constituent phonemes, /th/, /i/, /n/) may be regarded as assessing deep phonological sensitivity (defined by Foorman as phonemic awareness).

When we look at the words in the first example ('**thin**' and '**pin**') we can most easily subdivide each of them into the sub-lexical units known as the onset and the rime. The onset is the optional consonant or consonants preceding the vowel within a syllable (/**p**/ in pin and /**th**/ in thin). I say

---

3 Phonological awareness has been defined as sensitivity to the sound structure rather than to the meaning of speech.

'optional' because in the word 'in' there is no onset at all. The rime is the obligatory vowel and any consonants following the vowel (/in/ in 'pin' and 'thin' and 'in'). Note that in the word 'ma', /m/ is the onset and /a/ is the rime.

Onset and rime awareness corresponds to children's sensitivity to the sound/s at the beginning of words (sometimes called alliteration) and to the rhyming sounds at the end of words. You may now see why it was necessary to develop lexical awareness in children before you could expect them to develop onset and rime awareness.

Children's knowledge of rhyming and initial sounds (rime and onset) are phonological awareness skills, which are considered to be critical to literacy (Maclean et al., 1987; Bryant & Cavendish, 2001). Of course, nothing is entirely straightforward in beginning reading research, and there is currently some debate among literacy researchers suggesting that children's sensitivity to phonemes is a better predictor of literacy success than sensitivity to onsets and rimes (Muter, 2000; Castles & Coltheart, 2004). However, most researchers agree that teaching rhyme sensitivity facilitates the development of phonemic awareness and hence literacy success, particularly in children at-risk of reading failure (Bowey, 2000). Furthermore, there is additional evidence (Goswami and Bryant, 1992) that teaching rhyme sensitivity to children encourages them to read and spell by analogy (if Mary can read and spell **'right'**, she can also read and spell **'might'**), an important step towards automaticity in word reading and efficient spelling. Thus, it seems to me that there is a cogent case for including training in rime and onset in a beginning reading program, particularly if we are to prevent reading failure in our most difficult-to-teach children.

Teaching rhyme (rime sensitivity training)

Before children can be expected to recognise that a pair of words rhyme, they must be provided with opportunities to hear rhyming words, particularly in context. Most children, of course, have had many opportunities to become familiar with rhyme before starting school but, in inclusive classrooms, there will still be a sizeable minority for whom the concept is entirely new.

When teachers are seeking to establish familiarity with rhyme, attention needs to be focused explicitly on pairs of words which rhyme so that students at-risk understand the message. Teachers can always start simply by using students' names to rhyme with real or nonsense words (such as Bob/job/dob/tob; Ella/fella/bella) to particularise the concept. Additional games proposed by Adams and her colleagues (1998) in *Phonemic Awareness in Young Children* offer plenty of creative activities to facilitate rhyme awareness.

Once you feel that familiarity has been established, it is important that children have group and individual opportunities to recognise rhyme. The easiest form of recognition is for children to decide whether a pair of words rhyme or not; e.g. 'do cat and bat rhyme?', 'do dog and cat rhyme?' This could be followed by activities sometimes called 'odd one out'. In this type of activity, children are presented with two words that rhyme and one that does not. They are then asked to either select the two rhyming words or the odd one out. It's advisable to vary the order of word presentation so that students are not guessing the rhyming words simply on the basis of position.

To increase connections between speech and print, in the same way as in lexical awareness, it is a good idea to write down the rhyming words, one below the other, and highlight the rhyming part. Now children can see the portion of **'cat'** and **'bat'** that is identical (the rime) and that which is different (the single onset, **'c'** and **'b'**). This is also good preparation for the onset or initial sound activities that could follow recognition of rhyme. Connections between speech and print can also be made with an 'odd one out activity', so children can see that the rime which sounds different in speech, **'cat'**, **'dog'**, **'bat'**, also looks different in print. Alternatively, teachers can write two rhyming words on the board and ask children to put a box around the identical rime in both words.

As it appears important that children achieve mastery over rime detection (Bowey, 2000), ensure you assess all the children and provide additional assistance to those who are still unsure of the concept. The case for mastery over production of rhyme before proceeding further is more problematic. My feeling is that teachers should introduce children to rhyme production, and model the activities for them in as many interesting ways as possible (see Adams et al., 1998, if you're lacking in inspiration). A favourite group activity is asking, for example, for the name of an animal that rhymes with **'house'**, and then writing both words on the board to highlight the rime.

Many children will grasp the concept immediately and practise this new found skill zealously. For those not so precocious, teachers can always provide the onset (in this case, **'m'**) which will also cue children in to the next activity to be mastered in the phonological activity program. While production of rhyme activities will be found in most early phonemic awareness programs, it's probably not worth waiting until all children have mastered the concept before you move to single onset training, or you may never move on at all. A recent unpublished study that I undertook together with colleagues indicated that most students would be able to produce rhyme at the end of the year, even if it is not explicitly taught.

Teaching alliteration (single onset training)

Before children can be expected to recognise the single onset at the beginning of a spoken word ('s' in 'seed', but avoid 'st' in 'steed')) and
understand its *invariance*, they must be given opportunities, once again, to
hear initial sounds in context. Many Big Books make use of alliteration,
and this gives children the chance to both hear and see the initial sound of
a word. Grouping children whose first names start with the same sound
is another pleasurable activity designed to focus on the concept of onset
sensitivity.

While this is a slightly more difficult activity than rhyme awareness
because a single onset, unlike the rime, is a phoneme, it has been shown that
even pre-school children can cope with the concept (Byrne & Fielding-
Barnsley, 1989). There is also evidence that if letters are introduced at the
same time, this can facilitate the identification of the singleton onset
(Bowey, 2000). Thus linking some of the more common letters already
learnt in the alphabet program, such as 'b' or 'm' with single onset familiarity activities, could be useful both for this task and for discovering the
alphabetic principle.

Once teachers feel that familiarity with initial sounds has been established, they could implement recognition and selection of single onset
activities similar to the ones detailed for recognition and selection of rhyme.
'I spy' games are always popular but see Adams et al. (1998) for additional
activities.

The important point to remember is that connections between speech
and print could also be incorporated into single onset tasks, in the same way
as they were done for rhyme. This will reinforce the concept of the alphabetic code. Once again, emphasis on *production* of single onsets (give me the
name of a small furry animal that catches mice and has the same first sound
as 'corn') is not stressed for the whole group of students, but could be used
as an extension activity for more advanced students.

Teaching phoneme identity

I would also include another activity into single onset training, which is
commonly called developing phoneme identity. The idea behind identity-
based teaching is concept formation (Stahl & Murray, 1998), and the
identities of a small number of phonemes are taught in a variety of words.

Byrne & Fielding-Barnsley (1989, 1993) used this approach with a sample
of pre-schoolers, who were taught to recognise only the phonemes /s/ and

/m/ in words by isolating and stretching these phonemes. They then received guided practice in reliably selecting words which began with these phonemes. (Byrne and Fielding-Barnsley actually also taught phoneme identity for words that ended with these two sounds as well but because of task difficulty, I have sequenced this activity a little later.)

The children in this sample also learned letter–sound correspondences for the letters 's', 'm', 'b' and 'f', and were then asked whether the written word /mow/ said the spoken word 'mow' or 'sow'. This is a task of phonetic cue reading (Ehri, 1991), because participants need only focus on the first letter sound as a cue in order to respond (Stahl & Murray, 1998). Children who had experienced this training fared better than untrained children in being able to 'read' words starting with letters whose phoneme identities had not been explicitly taught.

These results suggest that children with identity training had acquired a larger sense of phonological awareness that permitted them to use simple correspondence information to quickly get a handle on the identities of these phonemes and succeed in phonetic cue reading (Stahl & Murray, 1998, p. 71). As success in phonetic cue reading means that children have emerged from the pre-alphabetic phase of reading that characterises most kindergarteners, it appears useful to include phoneme identity training in any program of phonological awareness.

In conclusion, it seems that in inclusive classrooms, which may contain a number of students with possible literacy difficulties, an onset/rime approach, such as the one outlined, tends to make children more responsive to subsequent phonemic awareness training. While formal phonemic awareness training only has been emphasised in most texts dealing with beginning reading, there is enough evidence to suggest that the less ambitious onset/rime sensitivity and phoneme identity training, as a precursor, can succeed in orienting children to focus on the sound structure of language (Bowey, 2000, p. 238; *see* also Goswami, 2000; Bryant & Cavendish, 2001). As Bowey (2000, p. 238) also states, 'This focus on the sound structure of language is the hallmark of meta-linguistics functioning, and thus represents a critical skill to be mastered prior to the development of deep phonological tasks like blending and segmentation.'

Blending, segmenting and manipulating

Are you concerned that 'real' reading tuition has still not begun? Don't be. The year is still young, probably only six weeks or so have gone by, and the students will have had an excellent start. This text is not designed for league tables that have some kindergarteners reading by the end of first term. It is designed to ensure that as many children as possible will have automatic word recognition and good listening/reading comprehension skills by the end of their third year in school.

To arrive at this goal, I will end the phonological awareness instruction in this chapter by explaining how to teach children to blend and segment words and the larger sub-lexical units (syllables and onset/rimes), as well as to manipulate words and onset/rimes. Then in Section 3, I will be able to start the formal program of teaching phonemic awareness involving the blending, segmenting and manipulation of individual phonemes (the smallest units in spoken words). Individual phoneme training will be accompanied by the introduction of letter/sound correspondences (phonics) so that children will be able to translate the written word back into speech (that is, of course, learning to read!).

Blending (synthesis)

Students need to learn blending because it is a necessary skill in order to transform graphemes into recognisable words (Ehri, Nunes, Willow et al., 2001). I strongly believe that when you are attempting to teach a new and difficult principle, you must make it as easy and as appealing as possible to minimise frustration and failure. Even if you don't subscribe to the principles of precision teaching, just remember what you thought of the patronising technocrat on the computer help-line whose technical jargon in no way resembled the English language. That's why this blending program starts with the blending of compound words (large units), and only slowly works up to the blending of phonemes (the smallest units) in the following section.

Blending compound words

You could start by getting together some pictures of objects that make up compound words, preferably of one syllable, for example, tooth/brush, foot/ball, ice/block. I've suggested one syllable words to reduce confusion, as blending syllables will also be discussed in this section, but I certainly don't think you need to be too rigid on this issue. Then by pushing the pictures of tooth and brush together and labelling each verbally, you can show your students how these two parts fit together to represent a toothbrush, illustrated by the appropriate third picture with its verbal label. As this type of exercise can be repeated endlessly, I can only invoke teachers' creativity with this concept.

Blending syllables

While there appears to be some evidence that rime awareness precedes awareness of syllables (Gipstein et al., 2000), I have sequenced blending of syllables before that of onset/rime because children will be handling larger chunks of words in syllable blending. In addition, many games involving syllable blending can be devised using children's names and clapping out the syllables—a pleasant introduction to a decontextualised activity which children may feel is rather meaningless.

You could start with children who have a two-syllable name, such as Stephen or Gazal. Get the children to clap out the two syllables in these names. You could pick one child to represent 'Ste'/'Ga' and another to be 'phen'/'zal' and then move them together to stand in front of the child with the actual name, making sure you verbalise the names at the same time. Children with three syllables in their name could then be used, reinforcing both blending and syllabification through this game. Those children with one-syllable names could be encouraged to blend syllables in their parents' or siblings' names, if you feel a revolt coming on.

Blending onsets and rimes

You can see that we are moving progressively closer to teaching blending of individual phonemes, since in onset/rime blending children need to concentrate on the initial phoneme of the target word. Teachers can begin onset/rime blending training by explaining to students that they are going to speak like a computer and it is the children's job to translate this awkward speech into a proper word. For example, if /man/ is to be the target word, first emphasise the initial phoneme /m/, pause, then add the rime /an/. Hold up a picture of a man to emphasise the word in question. Get the children to use the word in a sentence to reinforce the meaning of the word.

If you provide plenty of practice with this concept, initially keeping to the same onset and varying the rime, children should have little trouble with this blending task. At the beginning, you could use single continuous sounds like /m/, /s/, /l/, etc. for the onset. It is relatively easy to enunciate these sounds correctly but you should be careful with non-continuous (stop) sounds like /b/, where an unwanted /buh/ sound may creep in involuntarily. Eventually, however, it would be sensible to use the onset that corresponds to the alphabetic letter you are currently studying if enough real words involving that letter can be found. At this stage, however, I would avoid consonant blends, which will be treated later in this text.

Continuing with connections between print and speech, teachers could write on the board or on flashcards the list of onsets and rimes that you have used orally, in order to show your students how the same initial spoken sound corresponds to the same initial written sound (boxed or highlighted). For instance, you could write **d-og, d-am, d-ot**, one under the other, so that your students can see that the spoken sound '**d**' (the onset) on each occasion corresponds to the written sound /d/, while there is variability with the spoken and written rime. In this way, you are reinforcing the alphabetic code, and introducing your pupils to letter/sound translations. In addition, you can vary the onset and keep the rime constant (orally at first), and when this exercise is written down, for example, **d-og, f-og, l-og**, you will also be showing the children that the spoken sounds '**og**' (the rime) correspond with the written sounds /og/, while there is variability with the spoken and written onset. In this exercise, teachers will also have introduced students to the concept of word families and early analogy teaching. For additional examples, consult Adams et al., 1998, or any other reputable text on teaching phonemic awareness to vary the activities you can use for each onset/rime blending.

Segmenting (analysis)

There appears to be some doubt about the correct sequencing of phonemic awareness tasks, and some authors feel that manipulating phonemes could be easier than segmenting (Schatschneider et al., 1999). I have sequenced segmenting ahead of manipulating because it is such an important skill for the acquisition of spelling and because, being the inverse of blending, it seems to be a logical follow-on. I'm sure that this is not a critical issue, provided you approach it through carefully graded tasks as was suggested for blending activities.

Segmenting compound words

This, of course, is the reverse procedure from that of blending compound words. Once again, you could begin with single-syllable compound words to minimise task difficulty. If the word you have selected is, for example, /cowboy/ and you have shown your students the relevant picture, ask them what two words they can hear in the compound word. Ask them to find pictures that represent the two simple words in the compound word 'cowboy' from worksheets that you have previously prepared. Using these worksheets, children can colour in the relevant two pictures that constitute compound word segmentation for any number of examples, once each compound word has been named for the children. Teachers can then increase the difficulty level by giving pupils a forced choice. For example, after segmenting the word **'toothbrush'** orally, give them a choice of selecting two correct pictures, **'tooth/brush'** and one incorrect picture **'hair'**, varying the order of the incorrect choice to make up the compound word. You could also intersperse simple one-syllable words into your oral examples and ask students to hold up two counters for compound words containing two simple words and one counter for simple words that cannot be segmented.

Segmenting syllables

For this activity, which represents a slightly higher level of difficulty than segmenting compound words, teachers could begin by telling students they are going to learn how to break up a word into its parts. Just for fun, bring into your classroom a large cage, containing a number of toy animals, the names of which contain a varying number of syllables, such as a kangaroo, an ant, a camel and a hippopotamus. As you bring each animal out of its cage and name it, exaggerate the syllables in each word and place a sticker on the board to represent each syllable enunciated. In order to reinforce the concept of long and short words discussed previously, you could also write each word on the board next to its relevant sticker. Revisiting earlier concepts is generally a sound teaching technique.

Teachers can repeat the process, getting the children, either as individuals or in a group, to place stickers on the board or to clap out the syllables. Of course, segmenting syllables, like the previous exercise of blending syllables, also works well when you devise games using students' names.

Segmenting onsets and rimes

Once again, it is probably wise to begin this activity using a continuous sound like /m/, which has already been taught in phoneme identity training. Taking the word /mat/ as an example, you could show your pupils how to break up or stretch the word into its two onset/rime parts by pulling away the initial sound /m/, pausing and then saying the rime /at/. Write the word on the board and highlight the onset and rime.

Repeat this procedure using other one-syllable words which begin with the sound /m/ and write those down on the board. This will reinforce both segmentation of onset/rime and phoneme identity training. As was the case for blending, you can switch to other onsets, beginning with continuous ones, and keeping the rime constant. Write the segmented words down on the board, one under the other, as before. This will reinforce segmentation of onset/rime and reintroduce the concept of word families/ analogies.

Manipulation

As mentioned before, this activity could well precede segmentation and, when working with compound words and onset/rimes, is not too dissimilar from segmentation activities. You and your students, however, may find it a little more exciting.

Manipulation of compound words: Deletion/addition

Using similar materials to the ones for blending and segmenting, show your students two pictures that make up a compound word, such as **tooth** and **brush**. Ask them what compound word they make when pushed together. Now remove the picture of either the **tooth** or the **brush** and ask your students what word remains. Repeat the activity, deleting the other half of the compound word, and use a number of examples to reinforce the concept. When you feel the children have mastered the concept, you could proceed with deletion of compound words orally without using pictures as a model.

For the teaching of the concept of addition with compound words, you would simply start with the first part of the compound word and add the second simple word, asking your students to name the new word created: **foot + ball = football**.

There is no section here dealing with the manipulation (deletion and addition) of syllables, because this activity is not a logical precursor to manipulation of phonemes. Furthermore, no real words or natural word boundaries are created when such an activity is conducted with syllables.

Manipulation of onsets and rimes: Deletion/addition

Once again, you could take your overworked word /mat/, and ask your pupils to repeat it. Now tell them that you are going to remove the 'm' sound and ask them to articulate the remaining sounds. (You may need to help them here.) This oral activity can be repeated, using the same onset with a number of different rimes, written on the board and then continued using different onsets and the same rimes. Once children see this latter procedure written on the board, they will again have the rime/analogy/word family reinforced. Obviously, the opposite procedure will need to be employed for addition of onset and rime.

A suggested phonological awareness program for the first part of the school year follows:

Phonological awareness program

Weeks 1–3
✓ Teaching lexical awareness
- – The concept of a sentence
- – The concept of a word
- – Identical words
- – Long and short words

✓ Assessment

Weeks 4–7
✓ Teaching onset and rime (rhyme)
- – Establishing familiarity with rhyme
- – Rhyme recognition and selection
- – Exposure to rhyme production
- – Establishing familiarity with alliteration (single onset)
- – Recognition and selection of single onset
- – Exposure to single onset production
- – Phoneme identity

✓ Assessment

Weeks 8–10
✓ Teaching blending, segmenting and manipulation
- – Blending compound words
- – Blending syllables
- – Blending onsets and rimes
- – Segmenting compound words
- – Segmenting syllables
- – Segmenting onsets and rimes
- – Manipulation of compound words: deletion/addition
- – Manipulation of onsets and rimes: deletion/addition

✓ Assessment

Most children should now be ready for phonemic awareness training using individual phonemes in conjunction with instruction in letter/sound correspondences (phonics). It makes sense to teach these two processes together, because phonemic awareness, unlike phonological awareness, is a co-requisite for reading and develops reciprocally with literacy instruction.

Keeping in mind the simple view of reading—decoding x listening comprehension—the prerequisites for the first critical component have been completed and it is now time to address word recognition together with spelling, grammar and written expression. Listening (and reading) comprehension instruction continues in a balanced teaching program, as we move through the first and most of the second school year in the following sections.

Generalisation

Before embarking on the formal literacy program, I would like to discuss the concept of generalisation. This is one of the most important elements of effective teaching that may be often overlooked in the busy classroom. Generalisation simply means that a concept (let's say understanding rhyme) has become part of a child's cognitive repertoire and will occur outside of the immediate training setting (the classroom) and beyond the example trained ('cat' and 'hat').

Generalisation has sometimes been called the ultimate test of intelligence, since the ease of acquiring a new concept appears to vary directly with the intelligence of the person involved. Obviously, those who are the most intelligent need very little exposure to assimilate a new concept into their repertoire. Those less gifted will need more exposures, and children at-risk of learning difficulties will probably need multiple instances of the concept distributed throughout the day.

In most instances, Mark, my small grandson, has found learning new ideas challenging and easy. However, he had tremendous difficulty learning to recognise and name colours, although he had no difficulty at all with shapes or letters—possibly harder concepts to acquire. For a long time, he avoided answering any colour questions that his overanxious relatives kept putting to him. Avoidance is a useful strategy to employ whenever things are too difficult. So we tried to help Mark, not by constant questioning, but by exposing him to colour experiences in different situations to allow generalisation opportunities to kick in and finally permit assimilation of the concept.

Mark's inexplicable difficulties with colour learning are going to be echoed by a small number of keen learners in the beginning reading classroom, as students with potential literacy problems struggle to acquire new concepts at both the meaning and word level. To help such students in the regular classroom, teachers should make use of generalisation techniques to provide children with more opportunities to learn. For example, if you are teaching rime (rhyme) acquisition in the phonological awareness segment, make sure you use rhymes throughout the day in other activities and draw attention to them. This gives children who are slower to learn a concept on the first exposure, a second and third chance. It won't obviate the need for individual remediation for all children, but such effective classroom teaching practices may dramatically reduce the numbers who will need it.

On the topic of effective instruction, I need to stress that I have tried to outline the concepts needed for beginning reading instruction, not the creative teaching activities that children need to learn the concept. That is a skill that teachers possess, and which not all academics can emulate. My only word of caution is not to lose sight of the concept to be taught in the excitement of creative teaching. Always test the children on the skills to be mastered, move on if the majority of them have learnt them and provide assistance for the few who need additional support. If the majority of the class has not grasped the concept after your teaching program, the chances are you have been too creative, and you may need to re-teach the concept a little more explicitly.

To test the phonological awareness skills described in this section, teachers could use a standardised test such as the Phonological Abilities Test (Muter et al., 1997), a criterion-referenced test such as the Phonological Awareness Assessment Instrument (Adams et al., 1998) or easily devise an assessment of their own, using different examples from the ones used in the phonological awareness procedures outlined in this section (*see* also chapter 17).

Summary

This chapter described a number of activities that assist students to develop skills at the word level, to complement the previous chapter dealing with teaching skills and strategies at the meaning level. Children are first taught to focus on print as well as on the meaning of stories through the judicious use of Big Books, and alphabet activities, in order to prepare them for the introduction of sound/symbol translations.

Next, graded oral phonological awareness activities were introduced to help students concentrate on the structure of language as distinct from its meaning, and to prime them for the phonemic awareness and phonics instruction covered in the next section. Finally, a brief overview of the important concept of generalisation for effective classroom instruction was also presented.

THE *FIRST* YEAR
at school

Since literacy is not a virus,

it should be taught,

not caught

5 The formal literacy program: Theory

What is literacy?

This chapter discusses the formal literacy program in the first school year. First, literacy is defined, then a model of literacy acquisition is presented. Finally, ways in which a formal beginning reading program can be set up in a classroom are described.

It is important to understand that not all educationalists and researchers can agree on just what literacy is. For example, in a recent Australian review of the research literature relating to the acquisition of literacy (de Lemos, 2002), two different definitions of literacy are presented. The first, says de Lemos (p. 3), is usually adopted by those who view literacy primarily as a social process that develops through exposure to literacy practices within a particular environment, and is inseparable from its social and cultural context. This view rejects the notion that literacy can be defined in terms of a set of narrow psychological skills, and places emphasis on literacy as a process of deriving meaning from text. This definition of literacy usually covers additional language skills such as listening and speaking, as well as a range of other abilities including the interpretation of visual material, the use and understanding of mathematical concepts and notation, computer literacy and critical thinking.

A second view, usually referred to as the conventional, commonsense or cognitive/psychological approach, defines literacy as the ability to read and write; that is, to be able to convert the written text to the spoken word, and the spoken word to the appropriate written text. Perfetti (2003, p. 16) has argued that the basic formulation of what it means to read is a child's learning how his or her writing system encodes his or her language.

The goal, however, of learning to read is the ability to both comprehend and produce written text.

Inevitably, concludes de Lemos, these two opposing views of literacy will have different implications for both reading researchers and reading teachers.

The socio-cultural view, generally espoused by proponents of a whole-language approach to reading instruction, has led to ethnographic research studies (a case-study approach) that tend to document the interactions between the literacy learner and the environment in a range of different contexts. The teaching implications of this approach are not explicit but have been subsumed under the following headings suggested by Adams (1991).

- teacher empowerment
- child-centred instruction
- integration of reading and writing
- disavowal of the value of teaching and learning phonics
- natural predisposition of children towards written language acquisition.

Furthermore, as the social/cultural approach rejects the concept of a single literacy, subscribers to this model tend to be wary of assessment procedures. They argue that as literacy is socially defined, there are (presumably) as many literacies as there are social groups to define them. Consequently, since literacy is not an objective reality, it cannot be a skill that is amenable to assessment (Gough, 1999, p. 3).

The cognitive/psychological approach, on the other hand, has led to experimental studies designed to identify the specific processes that underlie the acquisition of reading and writing and the ways in which these processes can be enhanced by specific teaching. As a result of these studies, reading researchers who subscribe to the cognitive/ psychological approach have been more explicit about the implications of their results for teachers of beginning reading. While they would raise no objection to the first three teaching precepts of social/cultural theorists, summarised by Adams (1991) as:

- teacher empowerment
- child-centred instruction
- integration of reading and writing;

they would be strongly opposed to the last two:

- disavowal of the value of teaching and learning phonics
- natural predisposition of children towards written language acquisition.

They would also say that without assessment, we would never be able to determine who reads well, and who is in need of assistance. Surely that should be a cardinal aim of teachers who teach reading? To espouse the view that texts have no independent meaning, thus making assessment irrelevant, is to prevent the early identification of children at-risk of failing literacy acquisition.

If I were to adopt the social/cultural approach in its most extreme form, I confess I would feel a little nervous in a beginning reading classroom because I would lack a teaching direction. I'd have no problems putting the first three teaching precepts of this approach into practice. Like everyone else, I'd be keen to promote my empowerment as a teacher (and would hope my principal would feel the same way). I'd like to think that my classroom would be child-centred, and I would continue to encourage writing in the context of interactive text reading. But if I were to comply with the last two teaching suggestions attributed to the socio-culturalists and their position on assessment, what would be my role as a teacher in the classroom? Should I just be a facilitator of all children's natural literacy processes and expect them to induce word recognition on their own?

From the current research evidence, I do not believe that that is a viable option for all children. Over the past twenty years, reading researchers have proved conclusively that some phonics instruction is necessary for children to develop word recognition. I also believe that reading research has shown, beyond any reasonable doubt, that reading is a less natural process for children than is speaking. And, finally, if literacy is defined as translating print into speech and its goal is reading words to derive meaning from print, then children's literacy progress can be objectively determined through appropriate assessment so that assistance can be provided if necessary.

We have already discussed that:

> ... the brain is specialised for processing spoken language, but it has no special central equipment for processing written language. In order to read and write, or to decipher and produce print, written symbols need also to be processed by the central equipment that biologically accommodates itself to speech. For this to happen, written language must penetrate and gain a foothold in the central equipment used to process speech. Letters or combinations of letters (known as graphemes) must become attached to deep phonemes (sounds), not simply to 'surface' sounds within words (Ehri, 1998, p. 5), before the central processor can do its work.

> It is this phonemic analysis of spoken language which is difficult and unnatural, because speech is seamless on the surface, with no breaks signalling phonemic units. Furthermore, there is no need to analyse speech sounds

consciously as a listener, because, as is true of all biological modules, their processes are not available to conscious inspection. (Liberman, 1997, p. 12)

This is precisely why a growing child learns speech effortlessly on mere exposure, but why many children need directed teaching experiences to learn to read and write. It is also the reason why the last precept of the socio-cultural approach—that children are naturally predisposed to literacy acquisition—must be regarded as specious.

I also want to make a point about the teaching of phonics, which is central to the teaching ideas that follow in this section and that conflict with the fourth precept of the socio-cultural view. Many years of converging reading research data indicate that for children to gain meaning from print, they must attain mastery over the alphabetic principle, the system of graph-emephoneme correspondences (Gough & Wren, 1999). Only when word recognition is efficient and effortless can a child or adult invoke the comprehension skills necessary to derive meaning from text, which is the goal of all reading teachers. In order to do so, phonemic awareness together with some explicit phonics instruction are essential, particularly for children who are at-risk in the literacy acquisition process. While advocates of the cultural/social approach insist the real world of reading is making sense of print, rather than recognising words (Goodman, 1993), reading researchers from the cognitive/psychological perspective have shown conclusively that a reader must first recognise words in order to make sense of print.

While semantics and syntax (context) are helpful in comprehension (for example, determining which 'bow' is intended by the author), they are not particularly helpful in the decoding of the word 'bow'. If you can't read it, it is very unlikely contextual cues will help you work out its pronunciation and its consequent meaning. It appears that only about ten per cent of the most important content words in a sentence can be actually guessed correctly (Gough, 1993). At the initial stage of reading instruction, grapho-phonic cues (translations of graphemes into phonemes) must take precedence over contextual ones.

You may notice I also said 'explicit phonics' instruction. Recent research has indicated that systematic instruction in letter–sound correspondences (Ehri, Nunes, Stahl, et al., 2001), practised in decodable text (Foorman et al., 1998; Center et al., 2001; Foorman et al., 2004), resulted in faster and higher word recognition skills than less direct instruction or implicit phonics instruction for at-risk children. Indeed, a recent large-scale early childhood longitudinal study (Xue & Meisels, 2004, p. 220) found that phonics instruction was effective for all children, regardless of their initial ability.

Nevertheless, I must draw attention to a recently published study (Jenkins et al., 2004), which suggested that, in the short-term, texts which were 85 per cent decodable were no more effective than texts which were 11 per cent decodable for at-risk children, when used in a 25-week intervention program. Since these more and less decodable texts were used in supplementary tutorial or remedial groups only, these results cannot be generalised to the use of decodable texts in a regular whole-class program. Indeed, see Menon and Hiebert (2005) for an opposing opinion. In view, however, of non-converging research evidence on this issue, the use of decodable texts remains an important curriculum area which needs further investigation.

I believe that Marilyn Adams (1999, p. 224) sums up the problematic issue of systematic phonics instruction most cogently:

> Scientific research objectively, meticulously, repeatedly, and incontrovertibly documents, first, that to read with fluency and reflective comprehension, students must acquire deep and ready working knowledge of the spelling of words and their mappings to speech, and second, that poorly developed knowledge of spelling and spelling-sound correspondences is the most pervasive cause of reading delay and disability.

Obviously, the cognitive/psychological approach does not mean that the teaching of comprehension should be abandoned, since gaining meaning from print is the ultimate goal of reading; there is no disagreement with the socio-cultural view in this regard. The cognitive/psychological view is, essentially, that the graphophonic skills underlying the acquisition of fluent, effortless word recognition must also be taught in a beginning reading classroom, to ensure students with poor phonological skills are given the tools to derive meaning from print. That, I feel, is what Michael Pressley (1998) means when he puts the case for a balanced approach to teaching beginning reading.

Interestingly, a recent article (Cunningham et al., 2002) indicated that teachers who chose to emphasise literature when teaching reading did so by reducing the time devoted to phonics teaching. On the other hand, teachers who chose to emphasise phonics when teaching reading, took time incrementally away from every domain across the board, and not from any single category. Thus their pupils received a balanced collection of literature and skill-based instructional experiences.

Perhaps an analogy from tennis may be of practical help here. Martina Hingis is an intelligent tennis player because, lacking the power of some of her opponents, she needs to rely on guile and strategy to win an event. Her analysis of her rival's game can be compared with an analysis of a written text or a critical comprehension: her mastery over every basic stroke through painstaking practice both in isolation and in context (compare with word recognition) means she is able, during the course of the match, to analyse an opponent's game and plan her own.

If I were playing against Jennifer Capriatti, I would be so busy getting my grip right, my swing right, my feet right and deciding on the right shot, that I would be totally unable to analyse Jennifer's game, let alone plan a strategy that would grant me victory. If I have to concentrate on the basic stroke production (word recognition) during the game, I wouldn't have enough cognitive space left to concentrate on an analysis of my opponent's play (comprehension).

We accept this in sport, but find it much harder to accept with reading. This is odd, since efficient reading processes are of more use to most of us than is efficient tennis playing.

Theoretical model for teaching literacy

Perhaps the easiest way to understand the scope and sequence of this book is to examine the model of literacy acquisition (*see* opposite page) proposed by Juel et al. (1986).

You can see that the authors include ethnicity and IQ as determinants of literacy acquisition. This is true, but as these are beyond the remit of all classroom teachers, they are not addressed specifically in this book. However, in the previous section, considerable time was devoted to oral language development (interactive text reading, an oral language program and early writing) and phonological awareness. Exposure to print was also covered in the context of Big Books, together with alphabet activities as prerequisites to both decoding and lexical (sight word) knowledge.

In this section, I will be looking at phonemic awareness, cipher knowledge (decoding) and lexical knowledge as one of the ways to establish word recognition. Instruction in reading comprehension as well as listening comprehension will also take place, once decodable texts (to practise phonics) and levelled readers (to develop lexical or sight word knowledge) are introduced into the word recognition program. However, these books will be at a lower cognitive level than those used in listening comprehension instruction, since children at this stage will only be able to read fairly rudimentary texts independently.

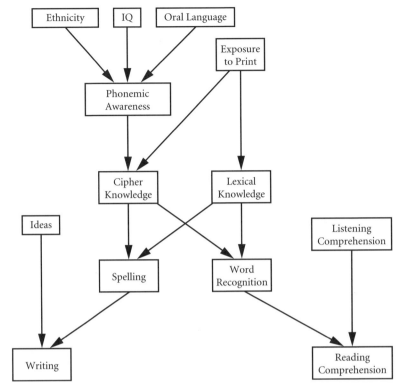

Figure 5.1 Proposed model of literacy acquisition. 'Acquisition of Literacy: A Longitudinal Study of Children in First and Second Grade' by Juel, Griffith & Gough, *Journal of Educational Psychology*, 78, 1986, p. 246. Reprinted by permission.

Listening comprehension relevant to different text types will also commence in this section and will be expanded in Sections 4 and 5. While spelling and early grammar will be addressed together with word recognition in this section, morphological awareness, more complex written expression (ideation) and listening/reading comprehension, will be covered later on.

Classroom organisation for teaching literacy

Now that the first few months of kindergarten have been safely negotiated, teachers face perhaps the most important job in the business of education: teaching their pupils to be literate (to decipher and understand print), rather than assuming they will acquire it by osmosis.

While most of the students will have responded well to early listening comprehension instruction and the prerequisites to word recognition, not everyone will have attained satisfactory levels in some or all of these activities. This is, of course, inevitable, since not all at-risk children will have benefited from whole-class instruction, or even from small-group intervention. Nevertheless, as suggested assessment procedures have been implemented (also *see* Section 6 for details), teachers can identify those children ready to proceed with formal literacy instruction and those who will need additional and maybe ongoing assistance.

The difficult part, for most teachers in primary/elementary classrooms, still remains. How can the classroom be organised in the best possible way to accommodate the disparity of beginning reading levels that appropriate assessment procedures have revealed? There are, of course, some solutions for this problem, but they are not always popular with administrators, and teachers will need a certain amount of determination to implement the class restructuring I am about to propose.

With respect to class restructuring, I would like to acknowledge my debt to Slavin et al. (1992), since the organisational and curriculum procedures described in this section have been adapted from their program, Success for All (SFA). It is particularly gratifying that a recent meta-analysis on comprehensive school reform (CSR) and achievement found the Success for All program was among the three CSR models showing the strongest evidence of effectiveness for schools and students across the United States (Borman et al., 2003).

My first solution would be to beg, borrow or simply steal an extra teacher to form an additional class for teaching word recognition. This proposition may bring instant transfer to another school, unless your particular school is committed to whole school literacy acquisition in the early years. Fortunately, most governments, both in Australia and overseas, have taken up this commitment, with an emphasis on the prevention rather than on the remediation of reading difficulties (Snow et al., 1998; van Kraayenoord et al., 2000). Furthermore, the notion of creating an extra teacher is less difficult than it sounds. Most primary/elementary schools already have additional teachers, such as support/resource/remedial teachers, English as second language teachers, or integration teachers, even if not employed full-time. Perhaps they can be persuaded to teach the additional class formed, as there is research evidence to suggest that doing so will contribute to the literacy health of the school more effectively than being tied to the specialist resource room (*see* Slavin & Madden, 2001, for international examples of creative classroom organisation procedures for literacy teaching).

I am not advocating the abandonment of additional one-on-one assistance. This must be provided, but I am taking one challenging step at a time. While we know that one-on-one assistance by a professional is, generally, better than small group help (Wasik & Slavin, 1993; *see* also Section 6 of this text), there is resistance to providing individualised assistance in kindergarten classes. This probably stems from inadequate school resources and the precepts of Reading Recovery (one of the most popular forms of individualised assistance in the USA, the UK, Canada, Australia and New Zealand), which only starts 'recovering' children in their second year of school. Teachers may not have an outright win on this issue, but don't abandon the fight.

Let's assume you have won the first battle, and you have about 75 children in your kindergarten class. For the hour or so per day typically allotted to formal reading tuition, you can divide them into three classes of about 20 students, homogeneously grouped with respect to reading proficiency, plus an additional smaller class of at-risk children. It is also highly advisable that the at-risk class teacher should be a competent and experienced reading teacher, not the new recruit who forgot to take a step backward at the first class assignment meeting.

In practice, this class restructuring will probably commence only after the first assessment results of the formal reading program, toward the middle of the kindergarten year. However, once the kindergarten classes are grouped in this manner, each class can move at its own pace. This does not mean that the at-risk class should move at a snail's pace. It just ensures that children who still cannot manipulate large sub-lexical units, such as syllables or onsets/rimes, are not expected to identify first and last sounds in words (phonemes) and learn their appropriate graphemes. In the words of Juel (1994), if a child believes that the first sound in the word 'cat' is 'miaow', because she still perceives 'cat' as a whole word (unable to disassociate from word semantics to word structure), she is not ready to learn the grapheme for the sound /k/.

Conversely, children who already demonstrate good decoding and vocabulary skills at this early stage of their school life may need fewer teacher-managed explicit instructional activities than their classmates with weaker literacy abilities at school entry. Recent research (*see* Connor et al., 2004, for a full coverage of this issue) suggests that the decoding skills of the former group of students may benefit slightly more from child-managed implicit instructional activities, such as independent reading or writing. However, it is important to point out that by erring on the side of teacher-managed explicit instructional activities for all students in the first part of the school year, children with weak literacy entry skills will be maximally advantaged in terms of their decoding skills, while the negative effect on their more advanced counterparts will be educationally insignificant.

These observations notwithstanding, regular assessment procedures should be instituted (perhaps every four to five weeks), so that class members can be reassigned on the basis of their performance (*see* Section 6, where reading words in isolation, reading words in context and phonemic awareness assessment are discussed). It must be noted, however, that Venezky (1998), in a qualitative review of the implementation of Success for All, reported dissatisfaction on the part of many teachers with such regular assessment, particularly for low-ability students. At several schools, these assessments were done 'only as necessary', and not everyone beyond year 1 was regularly assessed. I can understand teachers' irritation with assessment's possible interference with teaching; however, failure to use regular testing and to move students in accordance with assessment results could be the reason why Venezky found that SFA worked better in year 1 than in subsequent grades (but *see* the more recent and more positive meta-analysis of Borman et al., 2003). If children remain in reading groups that are inappropriately paced, it could affect their motivation and their performance. Class placement for reading should not be a terminal arrangement, so that those children making progress can be gradually weaned from teacher-managed explicit instructional activities to child-managed ones.

If you didn't win the battle for an extra teacher, then borrow one for 20 minutes a day. This time can be spent providing individual assistance to the identified at-risk children to prepare them more quickly for the phonemic awareness and explicit phonics instruction which may prove difficult for them in a class ready for formal reading instruction.

While this grouping works well for teaching phonemic awareness, phonics and spelling, I believe that listening comprehension instruction, early writing activities and the oral language program can proceed, without restructuring, in children's original classrooms. It probably makes sense to maintain a wide diversity of linguistic abilities when developing more natural skills like comprehension and oral language, so that weaker students get exposure to stronger linguistic role models. In this way, restructuring using an additional class is only necessary for about one hour of the school day.

Format of literacy program

As previously mentioned, the formal reading program, in restructured groups (after the first assessment), will probably take about one hour daily. It is also suggested that interactive text reading takes place, as before, in the whole-class group, to extend children's listening comprehension strategies using literary and other text types at the level of the children's oral language skills. Suggestions for the comprehension of factual and procedural text will be provided in this section, but will be discussed in more detail in Section 4.

I would also recommend the continued use of an appropriate oral language program at least until the end of kindergarten, particularly if there are a number of children in the grade from non-English-speaking backgrounds. In practice, I know that this is the first component of any formal reading program to be discontinued whenever there are time constraints; however, I find it particularly valuable in multicultural classrooms in view of the positive effects of good oral language skills on listening comprehension.

You would thus be spending about one and a half hours per day on a structured language arts program for the remainder of the first school year, with an extra class operating just for the formal reading lesson. Additional time would probably be spent on writing, re-reading stories (from the interactive story-telling program) and other texts, together with less structured language activities organised during the course of the day.

While all this sounds like a lot of hard work, teaching beginning reading was never meant to be easy! If it were, reading difficulties and possible related behaviour problems would be non-existent. Moreover, if all primary/elementary teachers had received comprehensive instruction in beginning reading processes, the following actual classroom scenario could have been avoided.

A friend of mine has a son who is a capable and efficient teacher, with about five years' experience in upper primary/elementary classes. This year, he was transferred to a lower middle-class school region and allotted a second grade (the third year of compulsory schooling in NSW, Australia). When he discovered at the beginning of the school year that eighty per cent of his class were non-readers, he literally did not know what to do. His preservice training had not equipped him for such a challenge, and there did not seem to be anyone at his school who could give him the assistance he needed. This clearly illustrates that it is definitely better to get it right from the start.

Summary

This chapter presented two definitions of literacy. The model of literacy acquisition proposed by Jual et al. was used to provide the rationale for the early literacy instructional program described in this text. Different ways of organising the classroom to facilitate this instruction were then presented and the chapter concluded with a few details on the organisation of the formal reading program.

Let's now move on to the formal literacy program.

6 The formal literacy program: Rationale and outline

This chapter provides a rationale for moving the focus of instruction from meaning to word level skills at this stage of the first school year. First, the development of skills and strategies at the meaning level is briefly explored. Then word level strategies are presented in some detail.

As we move into the first school year, the focus of instruction is on word recognition, rather than on comprehension. This is not because teaching skills and strategies at the meaning level is considered less important, but because the emphasis at this stage of our reading instruction has shifted from a top-down (meaning-driven) to a bottom-up (word-driven) approach (Stanovich,1980; 1984). While the acquisition of word recognition—the less natural part of reading—is the predominant goal in this section, it is vital that children's listening comprehension skills continue to be developed. I will return to a more comprehensive investigation of teaching skills and strategies at the meaning level in the sections that follow.

Developing skills and strategies at the meaning level

In order to keep developing skills and strategies at the meaning level, I am advocating the continuation of the interactive text reading program that was outlined in Section 2 at the start of the school year, and the same assessment procedures (*see* Section 6). If necessary, small intervention groups could be set up in the same way, and could operate until the end of the kindergarten year. Most school curricula suggest the use of other text types in shared reading sessions, in addition to the literary texts discussed extensively in chapter 3. If teachers wish to introduce their students to different text types in the first school year, they could easily replace the second literary text in interactive text reading with a factual or procedural text of their choice.

If you refer back to chapter 3, you will see that many of the procedures outlined for interactive narrative text study would be equally applicable to other text types. Activating background knowledge, discussing new vocabulary, linking the story to the students' knowledge (with all the caveats observed) and providing a purpose for listening would work just as well for factual texts. However, the structural features of a factual text differ from those of a narrative, so teachers would have to recast the group retell activities. For a factual/information text, the structural features consist of the title, the topic(s), the main idea and the supporting details, rather than the characters, setting, problem, resolution and coda that characterise a narrative. Remember the inappropriate use of a temporal sequence, using sequence cards, when students were recounting the animals who lived in a zoo (*see* chapter 3)?

On the other hand, a temporal sequence, in retelling, works very well for a procedural text if, for instance, students are recounting the procedure for making a cake. It may be less important if your children are just recalling a list of ingredients. I will be going into much more detail on text structure when I look at an extended listening and reading comprehension program in the second year of school, so more ideas for different text types will also be provided in the next section.

In this component on developing skills and strategies at the meaning level, however, the early writing program that typically accompanies the interactive text reading program, as well as syntactic awareness activities where appropriate, could also be included. Persist, if you can, with the oral language program as well, at least until the end of the kindergarten year. It will pay dividends, particularly with children from non-English-speaking backgrounds.

Now is the time to address the issue of word recognition, the focus of this section, to ensure that all children, including those at-risk, become competent readers as well as competent listeners.

Developing skills and strategies at the word level

Theoretical considerations

In the simple view of reading enunciated by Gough and Tunmer (1986) and Hoover and Gough (1990), reading is the product of decoding and comprehension, where decoding is a proxy for word recognition. Furthermore, word recognition needs to be both accurate and fluent in order to achieve the ultimate goal—comprehending the meaning of print. However, it is important to understand that decoding and word recognition are not synonymous. Decoding is only one means, albeit a critical one, of achieving word recognition. According to Ehri and McCormick (1998, p. 137) readers can achieve word recognition in at least four different ways:

➡ by assembling letters into a blend of sounds, referred to as decoding (**c-a-t** = **cat**)

➡ by analogy, that is recognising that the spelling of an unfamiliar word is similar to that of a familiar word (knowing how to read the word 'light' and the sound /f/, and thereby being able to read the unfamiliar word 'fight')

➡ by prediction, that is guessing the unfamiliar word from the context or from picture cues, when knowing the first sound, for example the sound /s/. This is not a very useful strategy because most content words cannot be guessed very accurately (as discussed previously) and if encouraged too often, may prevent children from developing an accurate, phonological representation of each new word they encounter (*see* chapter 13 for further discussion of this issue)

➡ by sight, that is when the sight of the word immediately activates its spelling, pronunciation and meaning in memory, because it has been read sufficiently often before. This form of word recognition exemplifies that used by mature readers.

Sight word acquisition is the automatic stage of word recognition and the ultimate aim, because it is effortless and allows the reader to expend energy only on the meaning of the print.

Ehri and McCormick (1998, p. 138) have suggested that:

> . . . readers learn sight words by forming connections between graphemes in the spellings and phonemes underlying the pronunciations of individual words. Readers look at the spelling of a particular word, pronounce the word, and apply their graphophonic knowledge to analyse how letters symbolise individual phonemes detectable in the word's pronunciation. This secures the sight word in memory.

Furthermore, they explain (p. 140) that:

> Spellings of words are like maps that visually lay out their phonological forms. Skilled readers are able to compute these mapping relations very quickly when

they read words. Knowledge of letter/sound relations provides a powerful mnemonic system that bonds the written forms of specific words to their pronunciations in memory.

When readers acquire working knowledge of the alphabetic spelling system, they can build a lexicon of sight words easily as they encounter new words in their reading.

This process is illustrated in the following diagram adapted from Ehri and McCormick, 1998, p. 139.

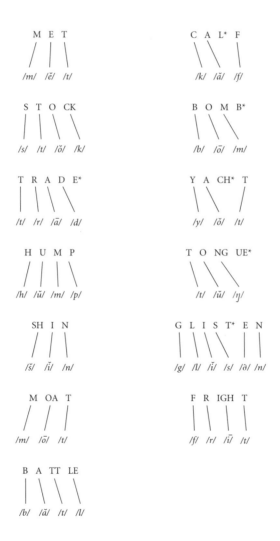

Our job as teachers is to lead children from the pre-alphabetic phase of reading (Ehri & McCormick, 1998, p. 140), when they have very little knowledge of the alphabetic system at the start of their literacy journey, to the partial-alphabetic phase, where they should arrive by the end of kindergarten. At this point, students should be using letter/sound associations to some extent, but their decoding and analogising will still be weak.

By the end of the second school year, most children should have almost reached the full-alphabetic and consolidated-alphabetic phase of reading development. They will then have mastery over the major grapheme/phoneme correspondences, will be able to read unfamiliar words by analogy to familiar ones, and will know chunks of letters that recur in different words (syntactic inflections such as 'look', 'looks', 'looking', 'looked', and prefixes and suffixes as in 'dark', 'darker', 'darkest').

They will then be ready, roughly at the beginning of the third school year, to enter the automatic phase of word identification, when the focus is on speedy and fluent word retrieval. Why is this stage so terribly important to reach? Precisely because fluent word recognition frees the reader's attention to focus on text meaning (reading comprehension), where the emphasis will be placed in the third and subsequent school years.

Outline of formal reading program at the word level

The program suggested for formal reading instruction in the first school year is directed at kindergarten students at the pre-alphabetic phase of word learning (Ehri & McCormick, 1998). Obviously, children at the partial-alphabetic phase would not be placed at the beginning of this program, but would be slotted in at a more advanced level.

The word-level instructional program, loosely adapted from Madden and her colleagues (1996), has the following components:

➻   instruction in sound/symbol correspondences (phonics/decoding)
➻   phonemic awareness activities
➻   guided reading with decodable texts
➻   word family introduction and fluency practice
➻   text features (early grammar)
➻   spelling activities; orthographic constraints.

This program typically takes just under an hour per day to deliver, with the recommendation that about a week be devoted to the introduction of each consonant (and possibly two weeks for vowels) in the context of the activities listed above. Each component of the word level program is discussed in detail in the following chapters.

The program format throughout the first year remains reasonably uniform, although not all the listed components are introduced at once. For example, decodable readers, to facilitate the practice of new letter/sound correspondences in connected text, are only introduced after children have mastered the first four sounds. They then become a regular feature of the program. Spelling, word family instruction and fluency activities, text features and orthographic constraints also do not commence in the first few weeks, but once introduced, remain a set part of the format. As each component is discussed in detail, its entry into the program will be outlined.

Teachers have occasionally said that they dislike keeping to such a routine, as they assume it bores the children. Generally, however, we have found that children thrive on structure and explicit teaching. It seems to enable them to cope more easily, both with the novel school environment and with all the new cognitive skills they are so rapidly acquiring at this stage. In any case, this program is presented essentially as a guide for teachers. Provided the instructional goals are agreed upon, individual teachers may wish to modify the program as they feel necessary.

In the second and third year of school, while the basic format of the program remains the same, the components increase in complexity, and are covered in detail in the appropriate chapters of Sections 4 and 5. The program is designed with the aim that students, including those most at-risk of literacy difficulties, should have reached the automatic phase of word identification by the end of their third year at school.

On the topic of automatic word identification, I heard a cautionary tale recently on a local health report program (Swan, 2002). A journalist, specialising in critical health issues, was interviewing a well-known United States reading researcher and clinician about children's reading problems. The latter was explaining the difficulties many children faced, especially those in low socio-economic areas, when teachers felt that the direct instruction of word recognition was detrimental to children's eagerness to learn to read. She cited the instance of a very gifted elementary teacher in Germany, where the orthography (writing system of a language) is more transparent than in English (Lyster, 2002), since it exhibits less irregularity in grapheme/phoneme correspondence. This particular teacher had become aware of the movement away from direct phonics instruction in the (mistaken) belief that reading was as natural a process as speaking. She was determined not to subject her pupils to repetitive drill, and so she exposed them, instead, to real literature through which sound/symbol translations could be implicitly induced.

At the end of the year, when her reading results (both at the word and at the meaning level) were compared with those of other teachers not possessing her pedagogical skills, she was horrified. The reading results of a significant group of her children were well below those of the pupils taught by traditional German methods. A certain number of children, she now realised, could not induce word recognition on their own and, without explicit phonics teaching, would be cut off from the wonderful literary world she was so eager for her pupils to enter.

Summary

This chapter introduced the skills and strategies at both the meaning and word level, which will be developed throughout the first year of school. While meaning level strategies continue to be taught in a balanced literacy program, the emphasis has now shifted to the systematic instruction of word level skills. First, some theory on word recognition, based on the work of Ehri and McCormick (1998) was described, followed by an outline of the activities and materials used in the formal reading program in the first school year.

We are now ready to examine the first component of the word-level program—teaching sound/symbol correspondence (phonics/decoding/cipher knowledge).

7 Sound/symbol correspondence

Developing skills and strategies at the word level

This chapter outlines the first component of the word recognition program, teaching sound/symbol correspondence. This is followed by a suggested sequence of sound/symbol introduction in the first school year.

Instruction in sound/symbol correspondence (phonics, decoding, cracking the alphabetic code, cipher knowledge) is the first component of a suggested word recognition program in the first school year to be outlined. This component typically consists of the four activities listed below:

➤ the reason for learning sounds and letters
➤ introducing the sound
➤ introducing the letter
➤ writing the letter.

The reason for learning sounds and letters

As each new sound and letter combination is introduced, students could be reminded that they learn sounds and letters to help them read. This procedure can prevent sound/symbol correspondence instruction appearing irrelevant or totally decontextualised. This is particularly important with the introduction of the first four sounds in the proposed word recognition program, as connected texts in which to practise the sounds are not yet a feature of the word program. However, text reading (shared story reading with small and big books) by the teacher is continuing and should provide ample opportunities in context for teachers and students to hear, see and discuss the sounds under study.

Let's suppose that the first sound/letter correspondence introduced is /m/ and 'm', where slashes denote the letter sound (phoneme) and quotation marks denote the letter name (grapheme). I'm suggesting starting with /m/ because it is a continuous sound and is used in the first little decodable readers to be introduced shortly. However, any logical order of single sound introduction can, of course, be adopted. By concentrating on single sounds, you can see we are entering the domain of phonemes and phonemic awareness. That's why it makes sense to teach sound/letter translations and phonemic awareness together (*see* the following chapter on phonemic awareness instruction).

Introducing the sound

Once children have been told that teaching them sounds and letters enables them to read the wonderful books that are all around the classroom, teachers could take out a special box filled with objects beginning with /m/. While it is relatively easy to enunciate the /m/ sound correctly (and that is why it is a good starting point), teachers should be careful with non-continuous (stop) sounds like /t/, where an involuntary /tuh/ sound may creep in. Try to keep the sound as pure as possible to avoid teaching children that non-continuous sounds like /t/, /b/, etc. contain an additional vowel. As you say the sound /m/, focus on the shape of your mouth while you enunciate it, and show the children that your lips are closed in order to pronounce it. Describe the humming sound that is coming through the nose and the breath that is expelled. Get the children to copy you and monitor the position of their own lips as they say the sound that corresponds to the letter 'm'. They can also observe their neighbour making the sound or use a mirror to check their own lip position and breath exhalation.

As they learn to feel the changes in the shape of their mouths when new sounds are introduced, they will understand more clearly the concept that words are made up of groups of sounds. This understanding is crucial to decoding. Furthermore, as they begin to write words after the introduction of several letter/sound correspondences (spelling), the children will be able to use the feeling of change between sounds as an important way of recognising separate sounds.

Castiglioni-Spalten and Ehri (2003) have suggested making blocks with mouth shapes pasted on them to reinforce the articulatory pattern for each sound, and using them in the associated phonemic activities. The authors explain that according to the motoric theory of speech perception

(Liberman & Mattingly, 1985), phonemes are not actually sounds, but abstract motoric structures that govern the articulatory gestures that produce sounds in speech.

If articulatory gestures are closer to the heart of phonological representations than sounds, this suggests that teaching children to monitor these gestures when they pronounce sounds in words may be an effective way of enhancing phonemic awareness and its impact on reading and spelling (Castiglioni-Spalten & Ehri, 2003, p. 27). Thus, the physical exercise of articulation may help children to appreciate the distinctiveness of each sound—a vital component in learning to read and spell (Calfee, 1998).

Introducing the letter

Once you have discussed the sound /m/, ask the children to name the letter that corresponds to the sound by pulling out the letter 'm' from a special box containing letter cards. Be as inventive as you can when retrieving this letter card (using puppets etc.) but try to keep the emphasis for all the children on the letter under investigation. Singing a familiar alphabet song is usually most effective at this point.

Letter introduction should be relatively easy following the alphabet activities discussed in chapter 4, but some children may not be familiar with the appearance of the small letter 'm'. Write the capital letter and the small letter on the board together to reinforce the concept, although the word program will focus on the small letters rather than the capital ones. This could be an appropriate place to use Letterland (Wendon, 1993) or Jolly Phonics (Lloyd, 1998) type mnemonics as mentioned in chapter 4.

This is really the first time that the connection is being explicitly made between the letter name and the letter sound, apart from early initial phoneme identity activities, discussed in the section on phonological awareness. To reinforce the connection, you could display four objects that start with the sound /m/. As the children name each one, write the relevant word on the board, highlighting the first sound /m/ so the students can see that when we say the sound /m/ in a word, we represent it with its letter name 'm'. If the four words are written vertically, one underneath the other, the connection is clarified.

To vary the sound/letter translation routine, teachers can switch from real objects to pictures. From your box, pick out two pictures, one of which begins with /m/ and one which does not. Get the children to name each picture. Then, either using the whole class or individuals, encourage the children to point to the picture beginning with /m/. Write the pair of words vertically, perhaps using green chalk to highlight the initial /m/ sound and red chalk to highlight the initial sound which is not /m/.

Teachers can be as inventive as possible with the two-picture game, remembering, of course, to vary the presentation of the pictures. It always seems to me, as I have mentioned before, that children most resistant to learning letter/sound translations are the quickest to detect invariant presentation patterns and learn incorrect rules.

This could also be an appropriate time to introduce a segment called 'sounds in sentences' (Madden et al., 1996), in which teachers write a sentence on the board containing the sound being currently taught, and get children to point out the words which start (or end) with the relevant sound. Such an activity can also reinforce the concept of a sentence.

More practice is provided for children to produce rather than select words beginning with 'm' in the 'I'm thinking' game, which is introduced and described in the phonemic awareness activities in the next chapter. As sound introduction and phonemic awareness activities are complementary and mutually reinforcing, phonemic awareness activities typically accompany the presentation of each novel sound.

You could now take out your 'm' letter card or your mouth position 'm' block and encourage your students to make the sound again, remembering the articulation components practised before. As you write the capital 'm' and the small 'm' on the board, explain again that there are two ways to make 'm'. Encourage your students to compare the two forms visually and comment on their similarities and differences.

Writing the letter

Teachers could introduce the actual writing of 'm' by telling the children they are going to practise making the letter 'm' so they can write 'm' whenever they hear the sound /m/ (the first spelling lesson?). Soon they will be able to read and write words containing /m/ when a few more sounds are learnt. Explain that you are going to concentrate on the small 'm' as it is the more common form used in reading and writing.

A very appealing and helpful way of teaching letter shapes is to introduce a verbal cue phrase (*see* Appendix for suggestions) as you write the letter on the board (Slavin et al., 1992). These authors characterised the writing of 'm' by describing it as 'one stroke down, back up, a bump and a bump'. No doubt teachers can discover an equally sophisticated mnemonic to assist with letter formation!

Students could be encouraged to make the letter shape in the air, modelling the one drawn on the board, and repeating the cue phrase as they make the gestures. Teachers could also let pupils draw the letter on their desks with their fingers, and on the back of the child sitting in front of them. Using a handwriting booklet in which the letter 'm' is already drawn, let students trace over the letter with their finger, as they say the cue phrase with you in unison. The first part of sound/symbol correspondence introduction could be concluded by asking children to bring objects and pictures starting with /m/ to school the next day, both to enhance home/school connections, and to prepare them for the review of the sound /m/.

When reviewing the sound and letter just introduced, teachers could present the 'm' letter card and/or 'm' mouth position block and revise the name and sound of the letter. Make a large letter 'm' on the board as you say the cue phrase and let the students make a large 'm' in the air as you model it (reversed, as you are facing them), saying the cue phrase in unison.

Briefly present the key objects or pictures once again, but allow students to guess the objects before you pull them out of their box. This could be a good time to let pupils show their classmates the pictures or objects that they have brought from home. As the children bring out their objects or pictures, write the names of each one vertically, on the board, highlighting the onset 'm'.

As a first exercise in fluency training with lexical units, line up a series of objects or pictures and get the children to call them out as quickly as possible. I have already discussed that Wolf and her colleagues (Wolf, Bowers & Biddle, 2000) believe that an additional source of failure in reading acquisition, apart from phonological awareness difficulties, is associated with slower access to lexical and sub-lexical information. This is because naming speed problems may impede the development of fluency in reading which, in turn, impedes comprehension. Thus fluency training, even at this early level, could possibly obviate later naming speed difficulties.

Teachers could also play some more games to reinforce the initial phoneme /m/. One that is very easy was devised by Madden and her colleagues (1996) and is called the 'Yes–No game'. Try it in its visual form first by posting a sign with the word 'Yes' (maybe in green) on one side of the room and a sign with 'No' (maybe in red) on the other. After explaining the signs, pull out a number of previously prepared pictures, some of which begin with the initial phoneme /m/, and some which do not. As each picture is randomly drawn from the box, get pupils to name the object and think about its initial phoneme. Give them about five seconds thinking time, and then get them, as a group, to point to the correct sign. Of course, the game can be played by teams of students or by individuals. A variant of this game is its auditory version, where the students do not get a picture clue. Teachers call out a series of objects, one at a time, ask if the word begins with /**m**/ and then get their pupils to assign each one to its correct category of 'yes' or 'no'.

As the emphasis in the first part of the week was on the consonant in its initial position, the concept of /**m**/ as a final phoneme, using some of the games employed previously, can be dealt with in the latter part. Thus teachers could also have a box containing objects and pictures of words where the final sound is /**m**/. However, a caveat should be issued here: as long as the final phoneme /**m**/ is introduced orally and the connections between sounds and letters are not being made, words like 'lamb' or 'home', as well as words like 'foam' or 'ham' can be freely used but, any time the word is written on the board, teachers should avoid the ones that do not actually end with '**m**' as the final letter, even though the final phoneme is /**m**/ (as in '**lamb**' or '**home**').

For example, teachers could start by putting out a series of objects or pictures that end with /**m**/, a task which is a little harder than one involving initial phonemes. How about '**plum**', '**drum**', '**pram**', '**film**'? These can all be written down vertically, to emphasise the connections between the final letter '**m**' (highlighted) and the final sound /**m**/. Then pupils can be encouraged to provide their own words that end with /**m**/, although this is quite a difficult enterprise. Perhaps asking children to call out nonsense words ending in /**m**/ would provide a welcome diversion.

When the two-picture game (both visual and auditory) is reintroduced, teachers could use objects and pictures where the final phoneme is /**m**/, rather than the initial phoneme. As these words are not going to be written on the board at this stage, you can use words like '**lamb**', as well as words like '**foam**', because the focus is on the children's ability to detect the final /**m**/ sound.

Review the sound/symbol relationship by showing the '**m**' letter card or articulation block, and letting the children make the /**m**/ sound while tracing the letter in the air. At this point, you could distribute a previously prepared handwriting booklet, where the children can trace the '**m**', as they all recite the cue phrase in unison. Give them a number of tracing examples and then encourage them to make the letter for themselves. Make sure that children having difficulties practise the tracing '**m**' activities for a longer period of time. There will be more opportunity to practise letter writing during the early writing segment which accompanies interactive text reading, and during other writing activities scheduled throughout the day.

This suggested weekly format is merely a guide for sound and letter introduction in the word recognition program. Obviously, teachers do not need to rigidly follow the format in their own classroom, provided children have the opportunity to hear, feel, see and practise the sounds and letters in both the initial and final position (where appropriate) when dealing with consonants. The rationale of introducing only one sound per week seems to fit in with most teachers' programs, as they struggle to teach literacy in the face of increasing curriculum demands. However, if you have a class with above-average students, you may need to accelerate the pace of letter/sound introduction.

A possible sequence following 'm' and /m/ could be the sounds and letters, /s/, 's' and /t/, 't' in both initial and final positions, remembering that /t/ is a stop sound and needs to be pronounced crisply. Cue phrases for new letter formations are included in the Appendix, but these may be improved upon by the ones teachers invent themselves.

At this early stage of sound and letter introduction, only word fluency practice and phonological/phonemic awareness activities, using onset/rime units, are taught concurrently and included in the program. The sequence of phonemic awareness activities used in the word level program will be fully detailed in the following chapter.

With the introduction of the next suggested sound in the sequence—the short vowel /a/, 'a'—the word level program takes on an extended format as instruction in word families or sub-lexical units commences. In addition, guided reading using decodable texts also begins in order to put sound/symbol instruction into immediate practice and relevance (*see* chapter 9).

I have suggested spending two school weeks when introducing vowels into the word level program, because one week could easily be spent on a vowel in the initial position and one on the vowel in its medial position, together with the four associated activities listed at the beginning of chapter 7. In practice, however, time spent on vowel instruction should vary directly with its difficulty level. For example, less time could be devoted to /a/ as in 'at' than to /e/ as in 'e', because children find the latter vowel sound more difficult to acquire (Treiman, 1993, p. 125).

Interestingly, Calfee (1998, p. 322) in his Word Work program suggests that when vowels are introduced in the medial position in a monosyllabic word, they should be taught as the glue in a CVC (consonant/vowel/consonant) sandwich, since they 'glue' two consonants together. His quote marks are intentional, since he considers that 'vivid language around familiar terms helps students understand abstract concepts'. In any event, to facilitate learning short vowel sounds, I have also included in the Appendix five visual vowel cues adapted from Madden et al. (1996), which can be phased out as soon as teachers feel they are no longer helpful.

A possible sequence following the four sounds just discussed could be the introduction of /p/, /n/, hard 'c' (k), and /d/. This sequence is justified on the grounds that it avoids the juxtaposition of two confusing sounds. Furthermore, decodable texts to facilitate the practice of these sounds in context are available (Center & Freeman, 2000b; 2000c). If teachers are using other readers or are writing their own to accompany a sound/letter introduction program, the sequence will differ, but the activities could easily parallel the ones outlined here.

With this group of new letter/sound correspondences, a number of novel activities are added to the word level program. The first is a matching game (Madden et al., 1996), which is a variation on the Yes–No game, but involves the use of letter cards to provide practice in letter/sound matching. Two levels of the game are used in teaching each letter. At the first level, picture cards are matched with letter cards; at the second level, spoken words (without the picture prompt) are matched with the letter cards.

Let me give you an example. Suppose teachers introduce this game when they start teaching the sixth sound, which in the suggested sequence would be /n/. Take the letter card 'n' and the letter cards of two previously taught sounds, for example 'p' and 'a', and place them on the board—one letter on the left side, one in the middle and one on the right. Using pictures you have previously prepared, hold up one at a time. As the students name the picture in unison, let them point to the left, middle or right side of the board to identify the letter with which the word starts. Alternatively, you can hand out a picture to individual students, get them to show it to the class, name it and place it under the appropriate letter card, although the order of presentation will need to be randomised.

For the matching game (auditory), teachers can use spoken words that start with the relevant letters, such as 'nuts', 'pebble', 'apple'. At this level of the game, the picture cue has been removed and children must concentrate on the initial sound of the target word and isolate it, before they are able to point to the correct letter card. Although this game is added to the schedule only at this juncture, it can be utilised to revise all sounds that have already been learnt or, alternatively, the review week can be employed for this purpose. The two versions of this game can also be practised with all appropriate consonants in the final position.

If teachers are following the suggested sequence for sound/symbol correspondence instruction, the next sound to be introduced is the second vowel, the short /i/ in both initial and medial positions. A possible sequence of new sounds to teach after the introduction of the short /i/ are the consonants /r/, /h/ (both in the initial position only at this stage) and /l/ since there are appropriate decodable texts written to accompany them (Center & Freeman, 2000b; 2000c).

If you are using these decodable texts (which I have called 'little readers'), you would also be teaching new exception words that appear in the text before you start the text reading, while letting students decode new regular words as they read the text. Obviously if you are using other texts, your sequence of sounds, your exception words and your regular decoding words would be completely different, but could still follow the same format used here.

The next suggested group of sounds to be introduced are /b/, /f/, hard /g/ and /k/, although students should be made aware that the letter 'k' rarely or never occurs in the final position without an accompanying letter. While no changes are made to the word recognition activities that accompany the introduction of these new sounds, the students' repertoire of new decodable words will be constantly expanding with the addition of each new letter/sound.

I must also stress the importance of a review week, typically instituted every four or five weeks after the introduction of four or five new sounds. This review also permits individual student assessments to be undertaken (*see* Section 6 for assessment suggestions for reading words both in context and in isolation). A word of caution needs to be issued here. I have occasionally seen teachers dutifully assess their students regularly, put the assessments into a folder and then ignore the results! This is of no use to either the students or the teacher. A little more effort is required so the reviews are not a waste of time but a basis for learning.

Following this proposed letter/sound instructional sequence, regular review and assessment, teachers should have almost reached the end of the first school year. Thus the sounds and letters **m, s, t, p, n, d**, hard '**c**' (/k/), **r, h, l, b, f**, hard **g, k, a** and **i** should be in their students' repertoire, and regular words containing these sounds should now be readily decoded.

Obviously, the pace of letter/sound introduction will vary with class ability, and the sequence of letter/sound introduction will depend both on teachers' preferences and on available readers. It is quite possible, of course, that teachers would prefer to cover all the single consonant sounds and short vowels in the first year, reserving the more complex consonant clusters, consonant doublets, long vowels and vowel digraphs for the following year. A suggested sequence follows.

Sequence of sound-symbol correspondences

Year 1

m, s, t, a

p, n, hard c, d

i, r, h, l

b, f, hard g, k

Year 2

inflectional morpheme s

o, final double consonants, vcc (for example, and)

w, initial consonant cluster, ccv (for example, sli)

u, initial and final consonant digraphs (for example, sh),
    j, y

e, initial and final digraph (for example ch)

v, z, consonant digraphs th, wh

rimes ank, ink, onk, unk

rimes ang, ing, ong, ung

a/e (for example, ate), i/e, o/e, u/e

oo, ee, ea, ai, ay, soft c

y, er, ir, or, ur, ar, q, x

ight, oa, ow

inflectional morpheme ed

Year 3

still outstanding grapheme/phoneme correspondences and
analogies that occur in text reading

Summary

This chapter on teaching skills and strategies at the word level presented a suggested plan for a word recognition program. The first component of the plan, teaching sound/symbol correspondence in the first school year, was outlined and a number of single consonant and short vowel phoneme/grapheme translations were then introduced.

It is now time to look at the second component of the word level program—teaching phonemic awareness activities, in conjunction with sound/symbol correspondences.

8 Phonemic awareness

Developing skills and strategies at the word level

This chapter on phonemic awareness instruction in the first year of school builds on the phonological awareness activities introduced at school entry. It presents a phonemic awareness program, using both untaught and taught phonemes, to accompany the sound/symbol correspondence instruction covered in the previous chapter.

Phonemic awareness and knowledge of sound/symbol correspondence (phonics) are the means by which children can gain access to an alphabetic script in order to read and spell novel words. However, before phonemic awareness instruction can commence, children must recognise that spoken words can be subdivided into smaller sub-lexical units such as the syllable or the onset/rime (phonological awareness).

This procedure has already been taught at the beginning of the school year. Now students need to learn how words can be divided into phonemes (phonemic awareness) and how these phonemic units are mapped by the written script (phonics). That is why I have introduced phonemic awareness instruction in conjunction with instruction in sound/symbol relationships.

The phonemic awareness activities covered in this chapter consist of:

➡ phoneme identity training (initial and final phonemes)
➡ onset/rime blending and segmenting (review)
➡ phoneme identity training (medial phonemes)
➡ phoneme blending and segmenting: untaught sounds
➡ phoneme blending and segmenting: taught sounds
➡ initial and final phoneme manipulation: deletion, addition, substitution.

Phoneme identity training: Initial phoneme

When children are being taught to isolate the initial sound or phoneme in a word, as was required of them when learning phoneme/grapheme translations, they are beginning to deal with the concept of phonemic awareness. This activity is not entirely novel, as it occurred earlier when teaching alliteration (single onset) skills (*see* chapter 4). Now, however, by writing the letter on the board, we are combining the phonemic awareness activity with letter/sound correspondence. This was not systematically taught in phonological awareness activities at school entry, apart from phoneme identity training, since phonological/phonemic awareness training, unlike phonics, is an oral process.

As an introduction to phonemic awareness instruction, it would be appropriate to review the phoneme identity training that we did earlier, since it is good teaching practice to move from the familiar to the unknown. At that stage, I concentrated on initial phonemes only, because I thought final phoneme identity training could be too difficult. Now, however, I feel it could be introduced, as the children are being taught to concentrate on single phonemes both at the beginning and end of words as soon as novel sounds are introduced.

Since all children seem to enjoy phonological awareness activities, it makes good sense to start with the familiar initial phoneme identity training first. Teachers could use a game entitled 'I'm thinking' for this activity, as it reinforces initial phoneme identity, resurrects rhyming skills and reinforces sound/symbol translations. For example, teachers could say, 'I'm thinking of a magic word. It starts with /m/ and rhymes with "house". As you have given the children both the onset /m/ and the rime /ouse/, this could be a little easier than just asking children to call out any word they know that begins with the /m/ sound. It also turns them into word detectives just before they enter the stage of initial phoneme production. Highlight the /m/ sound as you write the words on the board and use the block with mouth positions as an articulation reinforcer. Repeat the game as often as you feel it is necessary.

Now write 'sow' and 'mow' on the board, vertically, and choose one student to tell you which one says 'mow'. Ask the child to explain how she was able to pick the right word. Give your class plenty of examples in this type of phoneme identity training and share your children's pleasure as they realise they are beginning to read. The task they are engaged in, as has been mentioned before, is phonetic cue reading (Ehri, 1991) because children need focus only on the first letter sound to read the word (Stahl & Murray, 1998).

As a final task on initial phoneme learning, ask the children to call out objects that they can think of starting with /**m**/. Nonsense words as well as real ones should be encouraged in this exercise. This concept will also be reinforced when children look for things beginning with /**m**/ in the playground and discuss them with their friends. A child who is able to generate words beginning with a given sound and who has also acquired a basic knowledge of letter/sound correspondences will be in a position to generate a plausible candidate for a novel word when reading connected text at an independent level (Share, 1995; 1999; and *see* chapter 13 of this text). That's the goal towards which we are aiming in this early word level program.

Phoneme identity training: Final phoneme

Once the concept of initial phoneme identity training has been revised, teachers can introduce final phoneme identity with the focus on /**m**/ as the final phoneme rather than as the initial one. You can see how this activity is inextricably bound to the introduction of the final /**m**/ sound in the sound/symbol correspondence component.

Write '**rum**' and '**rug**' and ask a student to come to the board and tell you which one says '**rum**'. Encourage her to explain her choice to the other students. Remember that the task children are engaged in is harder than phonetic cue reading using the first sound, because the children must inspect all sounds serially in order to 'read' the word. Teachers can always facilitate the activity by highlighting the final sound, an example of task complexity analysis (*see* Glossary).

Repeat this activity using a number of examples, ensuring the cue words you choose end in '**m**' (not '**home**'). It is not necessary for the onset in each pair of words to be identical (e.g. '**bed**' and '**gum**'), but it is probably easier for children to detect the targetted final sound when all the other letters are identical.

Review of onset/rime blending and segmenting activities

Now let's introduce some blending and segmenting activities, which are similar to the ones already practised in onset/rime blending and segmenting (*see* chapter 4), but which will also use the sounds and letters learnt in the sound/symbol correspondence lessons. Blending and segmenting is introduced as part of the phonemic awareness activities to reinforce the concept that reading is (roughly speaking, of course) 'speech written down', and that letters represent sounds and sounds make words. However, I think it's good practice to start by reviewing onset/rime blending activities in the first few lessons, before plunging into phoneme blending and segmenting.

To refresh the students' memories, teachers could tell them that they are going to speak like a computer which cannot put the sounds together in a word. For example, you could say /l/ —og. Show the children a picture of a log and then ask them to say the word quickly. Get them to use the word in a sentence, so that you are relating sounds to words and to sentences. Repeat this exercise orally, using other monosyllabic words that the children know well.

This time, you can use the learnt sound /m/ (the first sound in the suggested sequence) in blending and segmenting exercises which will be both oral and written. Tell your pupils that they are going to put some sounds together to make words. Start, for example, with the word 'mat', and show the children a picture of a mat. Retrieve the letter card 'm' (and the mouth position block for articulation practice), and another card with 'at' written on it. Ask students what sound the letter 'm' makes. Tell them that 'at' says 'at'—very shortly, they will know this themselves. Get them to repeat the rime several times. Push 'm' towards 'at', saying **mmmm at**, in unison with the students. Then say it quickly, 'mmat', 'mat'. Ask several pupils to make up a sentence containing the word 'mat'.

Now introduce the opposite process, segmenting, where you will be stretching out the word 'mat' to reinforce the sounds contained within the word. As you pull 'm' away from 'at', say 'm at'. Push the onset and rime together on the board and ask some of the children to pull them apart in the same way as you did and segment 'mat'. Then ask some others to push 'm' towards 'at' to reinforce blending and thus reading. Repeat the blending and segmenting routine using other monosyllabic words where /m/ is the onset, but the rimes vary (the rime will need to be read to your students at this early stage). After segmenting, it is a good idea to blend the word again and ask several children to use the blended word in a sentence.

In the latter part of the week, when teachers are reviewing the suggested first sound /m/, I would still advise practising onset/rime blending and segmenting activities, particularly for children at-risk of literacy difficulties as they may need a considerable amount of time devoted to this concept. You could practise some examples orally first, which do not necessarily involve the /m/ sound ('cup' for example with a picture cue), giving the explanation, as before, that you are going to speak like a computer which cannot put together the sounds in a word (c_p). When the children are comfortable with the oral blending of onset and rime, repeat the activities using the sound /m/, the block with the 'm' mouth position and the letter 'm' (oral and written examples).

Have a number of pictures prepared where 'm' is both the initial phoneme and the final phoneme. Start with an example like 'mouse', using an appropriate picture cue. After telling the children they are going to put some sounds together to make the word 'mouse', take out the letter card 'm' and another with 'ouse' written on it. Ask the students to make the sound /m/. Tell them the rime 'ouse' and get them to repeat it several times. As you push 'm' towards 'ouse' get the children to say **mmmm ouse**. Then get them to say it quickly—'mouse'. Pull away the 'm' and get the children to segment 'mouse' into its onset 'm' and its rime 'ouse'. Complete the activity by asking a pupil to come to the front and blend the word by pushing 'm' towards 'ouse' and making the word 'mouse'. Ask another child to use the word in a sentence. See if any children know another meaning for 'mouse' (always use opportunities to develop multiple word meanings where appropriate). Teachers can always have a few more examples prepared where /m/ is the onset and a different rime is used.

Let's now consider blending and segmenting activities where /m/ is the final phoneme, using pictures such as **ham**, **ram** and **jam**. With this sequence, however, teachers will have to model the activities themselves, as the children are still unfamiliar with either the onsets or the rime 'am'. Still, it is teaching them to see and hear the sound /m/ and letter 'm' in the final position and reinforcing the concept of sounds making words. Soon, they will be able to do it for themselves.

One thing they can already do independently, however, is put the blended word into a sentence and discuss its meaning, an activity to be encouraged whenever a word has multiple meanings. As I recently heard an articulate three-year-old at a pre-school centre volunteering two meanings for 'jam', an exercise like this should not prove too onerous for children in kindergarten.

I would suggest that these onset/rime blending and segmenting activities accompany the introduction of the first three single consonant sounds /m/, /s/ and /t/ in the proposed sequence of sound and letter introduction in the word recognition program.

It is important, before proceeding further, to assess all children in order to determine whether they have grasped the insight that words can share an initial or final phoneme. Standardised tests such as the Phonological Awareness Test (Roberts & Salter, 1995), the Comprehensive Test of Phonological Processing (Wagner et al., 1997), or the Test of Phonological Awareness (Torgesen & Bryant, 1994) could be used for this purpose.

Alternatively, teachers could create their own criterion-referenced assessments by using different objects and pictures from the ones presented in the word program. As this is such a critical concept, children having difficulty should be immediately provided with individual or small-group assistance.

Phoneme identity training: Medial phonemes

Once the first short vowel sound (/a/) is introduced, a wonderful opportunity arises to introduce phonemic awareness activities (using phonemes now instead of onsets and rimes) to facilitate decoding. However, this will be a little different to phoneme identity training activities. It could be inadvisable to use phoneme identity training with /a/ in the initial position as we did with single consonants, because the examples are too restricted. (How many commercial children's books teach /a/ for 'aeroplane'?) You could wait until you have introduced /a/ in the medial position and then children can be asked to 'read' 'ham', when presented with the examples 'ham' and 'hum'. Quite a few forced choices like this can be generated from single consonants already in the students' repertoire, for instance, 'mit' and 'mat', 'dim' and 'dam'. Don't forget to institute assessment procedures again for phonemes in the medial position.

Phoneme blending and segmenting: Untaught sounds

With the introduction of the first vowel sound, phonemic awareness instruction can start in earnest. Blending and segmenting routines using onsets and rimes are now replaced with those employing phonemes, and as these are purely oral in the beginning, untaught sounds can be employed in the activities. For example, teachers could use monosyllabic words like 'lip' (lll—iii—p) to show that the word can be broken up into three constituent sounds, always remembering the need for the children to monitor their articulation. Stretch out the individual sounds, blend them together, say them fast, and then say the word. Get the students to use the word in a sentence.

The next step is to put out a counter or chip to match each sound as it is made. At this stage you could also use counters with mouth positions drawn on them to reinforce the concept of different articulatory gestures for each phoneme (*see* Castiglioni-Spalten & Ehri, 2003). Help the children to count the chips so they can see how many sounds exist in the word made.

Repeat the game for different monosyllabic words, using the blending and segmenting sequence, and ending with blending the word and using it in a sentence. Do not, however, use phonemic awareness activities with letter cards at this stage, as you are still working with unfamiliar sounds. Remember, too, that low progress children will need a lot of practice with these activities.

Phoneme blending and segmenting: taught sounds

When teachers feel that their pupils have grasped the principle of blending/segmenting untaught sounds (oral), it's time to introduce blending and segmenting procedures using taught sound/letter correspondences. These procedures can now be performed together with letter cards and mouth position blocks, using words and pseudowords such as **mat, sat, tam, Sam**. As soon as these familiar letters and their corresponding sounds are blended together by the students during phonemic awareness activities, the reading process has begun (even if all the words do not make sense). We have finally arrived at our first destination!

Use the real words in a sentence, remembering to discuss multiple meanings if appropriate. Teachers could also paste the words around the room in green, thus indicating to the children that these are words they can read on their own by sounding them out and blending them. Wait a minute! Isn't there something else the children can do? If they segment the words into their constituent sounds and then see you write the sounds down, one by one, aren't they also learning about spelling? Very soon, they will be doing it for themselves. Despite all your possible worries with preliminary activities, it hasn't really taken long to start reading, has it? You're only about half way through the first school year.

Initial, final and medial phoneme manipulation: Deletion, addition, substitution

With the introduction of the next suggested group of four sounds, /p/, /n/, hard 'c' (/k/) and /d/ into the word level program, initial and final phoneme manipulation (or simply, the 'quick change' game) is added to the blending/segmenting activities when working with learnt sounds. The objective of this game is to challenge children to attend to the initial phoneme of a word and to help them separate the sounds of words from their meanings (Adams et al., 1998, p. 64).

Starting with initial phoneme manipulation, using familiar words like 'sat', 'mat', 'Sam' and 'Pam' (remember /p/ is a stop sound and harder to articulate cleanly), show the children how you can make a different word by removing the initial consonant. Using letter cards and mouth shape blocks, articulate the consonant that has been removed and discuss the difference in the number of phonemes. Then show your students the inverse process, by reinstating the initial phoneme and making the original word return. Talk about the two different words that have been formed and use them in sentences so you can indicate how the deletion/addition activity has created different parts of speech.

For phoneme substitution routines, the process can be repeated, but this time a new word is formed through initial sound substitution so, for example, 'Sam' becomes 'Pam' and, less contentiously, 'sat' becomes 'mat'. However, when teachers introduce final phoneme manipulation, using all taught sounds, substitution activities are obviously more appropriate than addition/deletion of final phonemes.

You could tell your students that you will write a word on the board and this time you will create a new word by changing the last letter. For example, teachers could write 'cap' on the board and read it aloud with their students. Then erase 'p' and replace it with 'n'. Your pupils will enjoy discovering the new word. After you have used the new word in a sentence, and discussed all its possible meanings, distribute individual letter cards so that the children can turn old words into new. Give them a number of examples: 'sap' to 'sad', 'cat' to 'can', 'pan' to 'pad'. There is a lot of scope for creative word discussion here.

The other new activities that accompany the introduction of this group of sounds are spelling, text features and fluency practice with sub-lexical units, all of which are fully discussed in subsequent chapters.

With the introduction of the second vowel /i/ in the medial position, you could start phoneme substitution of the medial sound. For example, using all taught sounds, you could change 'pat' to 'pit' and 'sit' to 'sat'.

As the new consonant sounds /r/, /h/, /l/, /b/, /t/, /f/, /g/ and /k/ are introduced into the first year word level program, they will provide additional practice for all the phonemic awareness activities discussed in this chapter. I must issue a caveat, however, when teaching final phoneme substitution activities with some of these new sounds: a few of them, such as 'f' (as in 'fan'), 'k' (without its companion 'c') and 'h' rarely occur at the end of a real word, while 'r' as a final consonant alters the pronunciation of the preceding vowel, and will be studied at a later stage.

Summary

This chapter stressed the need for phonemic awareness to be taught in conjunction with sound/symbol correspondence so that children can get access to the alphabetic code. First, phonological awareness activities were reviewed, and then a sequence of graded phonemic awareness procedures were presented, using both untaught and taught phonemes.

We now move to an examination of the next three components of the word level program in the first year of school: guided reading with decodable texts, word families and early text features.

9 Decodable texts, word families and text features
Developing skills and strategies at the word level

Decodable texts

This chapter presents a rationale for using decodable texts in the word level program in the first school year. This is followed by an outline of a guided reading session using 'little readers'. The need to include word families and early text features in a word level program is also discussed.

We now come to another critical component of the word level program, decodable texts. Decodable or phonically constrained texts, when aligned with a phonics program, enable students to practise their decoding in context, so that the process becomes meaningful for them (Beck & Juel, 1992; Foorman et al., 1998; Foorman et al., 2004).

Most early texts for children, designed for interest value, do not generally contain enough of the relevant sounds taught in a classroom program to allow children (particularly those at-risk) to induce the necessary grapheme/phoneme translations through practice. Consequently, some colleagues and I (Center & Freeman, 2000b; 2000c) produced a number of decodable texts called 'little readers' (*see* Appendix for *A big bad bug*, an example of a little reader). These were adapted from the shared stories designed by Slavin and his colleagues (Slavin et al., 1992), to accompany the sound/symbol correspondence component of the word level program. Teachers, naturally, can design their own decodable texts to complement the sequence of sounds they teach in the classroom, adapt appropriate texts, or access commercial phonic readers such as *The Book to Remember* series. The only constraint with this procedure is that the reader should contain some words with the sounds that students have already learnt in isolation.

Our little readers emphasise immediate application of learnt phonic skills to real reading since they can be accessed from the time children have learnt only about four phoneme/grapheme translations (Slavin et al., 1992). To reduce the unnatural quality of decodable texts and to add richness and background to the story, these little readers include text read by adults as well as by children. Furthermore, the inclusion of 'readles' (*see* Appendix for an example of a 'readle'), which are iconic representations of unknown words, increase the readability of these early little readers, as do the inclusion of exception, and as yet undecodable words.

The presence of levelled readers in the classroom (for which Reading Recovery tutors and teachers are gratefully acknowledged) to increase lexical knowledge as well as daily shared reading of imaginative texts should ensure that children are continually exposed to quality literature as well as to decodable texts. I hope that this counters the argument, often put forward by opponents of decodable texts, that children will miss out on 'real' literature, if such 'unnatural' texts are employed. Obviously, they must not miss out on 'real' literature but as I have said before, reading is not an inherently natural process, and children must definitely not miss out on instruction in word recognition either.

Remember, also, that for many children at this early stage, non-phonically constrained readers will not be advancing word recognition skills. This is because early and at-risk readers will not know sufficient sound/symbol correspondences to work out novel words in the self-teaching manner that we hope will become a feature of their reading, as they master more sound/symbol translations (*see* Section 4). However, reading decodable texts, exploring books from the class book box and developing listening comprehension skills through teacher-directed shared reading of good literature should ensure that most children will soon successfully negotiate the magical word of reading.

Before introducing a little reader that can be used in a word recognition program, I would first revise the concept of both a sentence and a word, using either familiar sentences and words from past activities, or encouraging children to produce their own oral sentences. At this point, I'm going to use some of the sentences and words that are featured in our little readers as examples, but teachers could easily use sentences and words from any phonically based reader of their choice.

The first little reader we introduce after four sounds have been taught is entitled *Two Friends*. It contains the sentence, 'I like' with a noun complement. Two flashcards, with the words 'I' and 'like' written on them, are shown to the children, who are told that they are ready to learn to read words which they cannot sound out by blending familiar sounds. When such words appear on flashcards, they are accompanied by a red dot, signalling that these words have to be remembered, rather than worked out.

Then the words 'I am' are written on the board with 'I' in red and 'am' in green, and teachers read the words together with their pupils, emphasising the children's ability to read the word in green. Finally, children are encouraged to call out sentences which use 'I like' and 'I am' with a noun complement (I like cheese, etc.) and teachers can write them on the board.

After this practice session with red and green words (or dots) in sentences, a picture of one of the characters, whom the class will be reading about in the little readers, is shown to students and introduced as 'Mark'. As the word 'Mark' goes on the board next to his picture, it should reinforce the first sound taught in the word program, the sound /m/.

The next suggested step in the procedure is to write the sentence 'I am Mark' on the board and read it in unison, with the teacher pointing to each word as it is read to indicate the correspondence between spoken and written words. As Liz is the next character in the first little reader, the same procedure is repeated, although no sounds in her name are familiar.

As the text would be very limited if only a few sight words and one decodable word are used, readles are included in the reader for words like 'school', 'cake', 'ice-cream', 'sandwiches'. All sentences, with and without readles, are read together from the board, and pasted up as sentence strips around the room for revision during the day.

We have thus reached our second destination, as children begin to read connected text in guided reading sessions! Teachers can now distribute a photocopied little reader to each child and use the familiar but modified interactive text reading procedure to introduce the story. First, teachers can read the title and adult text (in small print) at the top of the first page and ask children to predict the story (if appropriate). Then the children are encouraged to read the text (in large print) at the bottom of the page together with the teacher, and suitable questions about the text can be asked. Once the book has been read, the story is reviewed with all the children.

For homework, the students can take their little reader home and read it to their parents, or caregivers, indicating the section in small print that adults should read. It is also a good idea to send a record book home with each student to be signed by everyone who managed to hear her read. In this way, teachers can get some idea of whether the home/school connections are being maintained.

I suggest that two appropriate little readers should now be included with the introduction of each new sound/symbol correspondence, in order to practise both the novel phoneme/grapheme translation and revise the familiar ones in connected text.

Word families and fluency practice

At about the same time as little readers are introduced, when three consonants and a short vowel have been learnt, the teaching of word families can also become a feature of the word level program.

Once the words 'tam' and 'Sam' have been introduced, they could be written on the board (and then on a wall chart that stays in the room). Children could then be encouraged to call out different words that end in **am**, with your assistance if necessary. Point out the rime (rhyme). Write the words on the board and read them with the students, saying the first sound yourself and then letting the children provide the rime /am/. It is probably a little early to add these to the wall chart of the /am/ word family until the relevant initial consonant has been learnt later in the phonics program. Teachers could repeat the procedure for the word family 'at'.

Fluency training (Wolf, Bowers & Biddle, 2000) with word families (sub-lexical units) can commence when the wall chart becomes a bit more respectable, probably by the time about ten sounds have been introduced. There should now be about five words that have been learnt for each relevant word family and can be included on a word family wall chart ('am', 'at', 'an', 'ap', 'ad'). Invent a game to get the children to read the words as quickly as possible, on a regular basis, to develop fluency at the sub-lexical level, as this practice may also assist children to move from word recognition by decoding single sounds to word recognition using analogies.

Fluency practice with regular and exception words (lexical units) could commence even earlier, from the time that children start to read connected text. Although fluency training will be discussed in detail in Section 4, when children are accessing many more texts, I have considered it important to add this component already in the first year to attempt to circumvent possible future lexical retrieval difficulties (Wolf, Miller & Donnelly, 2000).

As teachers and students read the two new little readers that accompany the introduction of each novel sound, an increasing number of decodable (green dot) words will be encountered that can be added to the fluency list. Exception or as yet non-decodable (red dot) words which appear in each new text are introduced before story reading and can be practised for fluency from then on. Obviously, if you are reading texts of your own and have chosen a different order of sound presentation, your fluency list, at least of decodable words, will be quite different from the one that is suggested here.

With the addition of the second vowel sound in the medial position, you will also find that you have many new words (lexical units) and word families (sub-lexical units) with which to practise fluency. If teachers are using little readers to accompany their letter/sound program, the exception/irregular words or words that cannot yet be sounded out would include such words as 'like', 'here', 'sees', 'said', 'you', 'yes', 'he', 'to', 'not', 'has', 'his', 'as', 'there', 'a'. Similar exception words will probably also be covered if teachers are using other readers.

As soon as any non-decodable word can be decoded, when the relevant sound/symbol correspondences have been taught, it can be transferred to the green word list, while the exception words can remain in the red! Fluency practice with this expanded repertoire could continue, and so could the extension of students' vocabulary knowledge with each new regular word learnt, particularly if it has multiple meanings. All new regular words will also be targeted for spelling practice, which will be discussed in the next chapter.

Text features

After the introduction of about six sound/symbol correspondences, teachers can begin to draw children's attention in a more systematic way to text features (early grammatical concepts and punctuation conventions). With respect to the latter, full-stops and capitalisation have already been introduced during shared reading using Big Books and can easily be reviewed as sentence markers during the early guided reading sessions. In the little reader that accompanies the introduction of the sixth sound, quotation and question marks should appear. These can be highlighted and discussed when relevant sentences from the text are written on the board, before the story is read. Later in the guided reading program, novel punctuation conventions appear, such as the exclamation mark, which can also be brought to children's awareness. Teachers may wish to generalise these punctuation conventions to books in shared or independent reading, or in any creative writing that has already taken place.

Early grammar concepts are also introduced about this time, since research data (Nunes et al., 1997) indicate that grammatical awareness plays a crucial role in spelling. These authors state that, 'Our idea is that children's sensitivity to the distinction between different parts of speech is the basis for their eventual mastery of the conventional spelling of grammatical morphemes (p. 165).' Nevertheless, they also indicate that intervention studies are needed to clinch the causal argument and readily acknowledge that they have no ready answer to the question of what to teach children about grammar (p. 169).

Perhaps if we start with the functional use of words in sentences (since both concepts are already familiar to the students) and attempt to contextualise the process, grammatical analysis may seem more understandable and relevant to young readers.

The two parts of speech that I would introduce to students at this early stage are the noun and the verb. The term '**noun**' (participant) covers the people, ideas or things taking part in an activity. **Verbs** (processes) can be physical, mental or verbal activities, as well as states of being and having. Let's take a simple sentence as an example: *Sam sees the cat.* In traditional grammar, '**Sam**', a proper noun, would be considered the subject of the sentence, '**sees**' would be defined as a verb, and '**the cat**', a common noun (not having a capital letter) would be regarded as a noun object or predicate. (In functional grammar—a form of grammar used in some curricula— '**Sam**', a noun group (because it could include 'Sam, a little boy') would be a participant, '**sees**' (a verb group because it could be 'is seeing') would be a process (in this case, a mental process), and '**the cat**' would be another participant in the process.)

If this sentence had been more complex—*Sam sees a ginger cat under the house*—the sentence would have contained a descriptive adjective (ginger) and an adverbial phrase (under the house). (In functional grammar, '**ginger**' would be classified as a describer, and '**under the house**' would be called a circumstance of the prepositional phrase variety.) Thank goodness, at this early stage, we are just gently raising students' awareness level about the structure of a simple sentence and introducing the function of a noun within it.

Let's use 'Sam sees the cat', to show children how a sentence is constructed, so that they can both recognise it in their reading, and reproduce it in their writing. If you write this sentence on the board (with the relevant feature highlighted) and get the children to read it together, you can ask the following question, 'Who sees the cat?' This gives the children an opportunity to see the noun subject in the sentence. Make sure you give many more examples of a simple sentence, taken from a familiar story, so that children become proficient at isolating the noun subject. Students could also be asked to supply other suitable noun subjects for this simple sentence, and even produce new sentences of their own, which contain a noun subject.

Teachers could then start teaching students about nouns as objects. Using sentences such as 'Sam likes Liz', you could ask questions like: Who(m) does Sam like? With a sentence like 'Sam did not see the man', you could ask: Who(m) didn't Sam see? This time teachers could ask students to substitute appropriate but different words for nouns as objects in this simple sentence, and then make up new sentences, containing a noun object. You could also scramble sentences that the children must put in the right order to show the correct English sequence of noun as subject/verb/noun as object and the effect of transposing that order. Have fun with 'The mother punishes the child'.

As teachers and students progress through the word level program, pupils could be asked about nouns as subjects and objects whenever they occur in the same sentence, to make text features study a little more complex. At this stage, teachers could also ask students to produce novel sentences using different subjects and objects, while keeping the verb constant.

Teachers could continue text features study, reviewing nouns as objects and subjects, before focusing on verbs in a simple sentence. I suggest you first concentrate on action verbs (material processes), which are probably the easiest for the students. For example, if you pick a simple sentence, such as 'Penny throws the ball', you could spend some time discussing the role of 'throws' in the sentence. Ask your pupils to provide different action verbs that make sense when the subject and object remain constant. As an extension exercise, teachers could select an inappropriate verb (such as **thinks** or **knows**) for this sentence and discuss the reasons for its non-applicability.

While teachers can no doubt be much more creative than I with examples to enhance children's awareness of early grammar and punctuation conventions in context, the aim of this component is to prepare pupils for more formal grammatical analysis that is covered in later sections.

Summary

In this chapter, a rationale for using decodable texts in guided reading to accompany the phonics program was presented, and this was followed by a detailed outline of a typical guided reading session using little readers. The teaching of word families was then addressed, with fluency practice suggested at both the lexical and sub-lexical level. The chapter concluded with a section on teaching text features to young students in order to facilitate their reading and writing.

The rationale behind early spelling instruction will be addressed in the following chapter.

10 Spelling

Developing skills and strategies at the word level

Why include spelling in an early word recognition program?

This chapter presents a rationale for including spelling in an early word level program in the first school year. This is followed by an outline of a suggested spelling program, together with a description of an orthographic constraints component. The chapter concludes with an overview of the first school year program at the meaning and word level.

If we return to Juel's suggested plan for reading acquisition in chapter 5, which included accurate word recognition as a prerequisite of reading comprehension, you will also see the inclusion of spelling as a prerequisite of writing skills. As reading and spelling are symbiotic, it makes sense to teach them together.

Despite the presence of spell-checks on computers, the ability to spell words easily and accurately is an important part of being a good writer (Treiman, 1993, p. 3). In 1993, in her seminal book on spelling, based on a study of first-grade children, Treiman concluded that writing is actually more potent than reading in forcing children to come to grips with the alphabetic principle (p. 289), which is, of course, the aim of these early chapters at the word level. In a later article (1998b), Treiman presented further compelling evidence for incorporating spelling instruction into a beginning reading program rather than either delaying its introduction or treating it as a separate subject. Fortunately, this belief is now shared by proponents of both skill-based and whole language approaches and thus should not prove contentious.

In a research-based discussion of why spelling and reading instruction should be integrated as early as possible, Treiman (1998b) reviews the English writing system (orthography), the sound system of spoken English (phonology) and the normal course of spelling development. As I strongly believe that theoretical understanding underlies all good teaching practice, I shall briefly deal with these three issues in turn.

Despite its apparent and often annoying irregularity, the English writing system can be accessed quite easily, if the learner becomes aware of (or is taught) its rules and patterns. Let's begin with an example involving rule-governed orthographic constraints. A very young literacy learner may produce the spelling 'ficks' for 'fix', but will be unlikely to render it as 'fim' once phonemic awareness and some phoneme/grapheme sophistication are in place. At a more advanced level, most children will learn (and others can easily be taught) that words beginning with the initial sound /k/ can be written with a 'c' or 'k', but not with 'ck'. This latter letter combination occurs in the middle of words or at the end of words, but never at the beginning.

The morphological structure of a word (whether a word is made up of smaller meaningful parts) also influences its spelling (Treiman, 1998b, p. 291). When having difficulty with the spelling of 'stealth' ('stelth' is after all phonologically acceptable), knowledge of its morphology (the root word 'steal') makes its spelling logical rather than just haphazard (morphology instruction to help access the English writing system will be covered in chapter 13).

While it does sound a bit onerous, teaching children about the linguistic roots of words (e.g. Latin 'tion', Greek 'phon', Anglo-Celtic 'ful') can smooth their path into both the reading and spelling of multi-syllabic words. Indeed, Bryant and his colleagues (Bryant et al., 2004) demonstrated that children can quite easily be helped to learn simple but usually untaught rules about derivational morphemes and their spelling, for example that 'ian' endings are for people, as in 'magician', whereas 'ion' endings are not, as in the word 'emotion'. Even more interestingly, they found that such teaching actually works in a classroom situation as well as in a laboratory setting. Furthermore, knowing word histories and how spellings have mutated over the years helps explain the presence of silent letters in words like 'sword'. (For an excellent and accessible history of the English spelling system and its application to spelling instruction, *see* Invernizzi & Hayes, 2004.)

Finally, knowledge of morphological inflections in English words is extremely helpful to struggling readers and spellers. For example, if words that end with the sound /t/ or /d/ are regular verbs in the simple past tense, they will be spelt with 'ed', a spelling that actually flouts grapheme-phoneme rules (Bryant, 2002, p. 203). Children taught this rule as part of spelling instruction, are less likely to spell '**trapped**' as '**trapt**'. If, at the same time, they also learn that uninflected words like '**fist**' or '**bird**' are spelt phonetically, they may just realise that there is some method in English spelling's apparent madness. Indeed, if children are shown that English orthography obeys certain well-defined rules, this may remove the anxiety with which many students approach spelling tasks and their process writing. Thus, in a spelling lesson, the teacher must convey to children that spelling is not necessarily part of a diabolical plot, and should teach any rules that will demystify the orthographic system.

Some children will absorb these rules simply through sufficient exposure to print and corrected spelling attempts. A sizeable minority will not, and will thus benefit enormously by appropriate tuition. That is why it makes sense to delay the introduction of irregular word spelling until the principle of spelling regularity is instilled. It seems logical, therefore, to begin with the spelling of regular consonant/vowel/consonant (CVC) words that children have encountered in their reading books, since children can read back their spelling attempts in order to check their accuracy. Treiman (1998b, p. 309) provides research evidence for this practice by quoting the study of Mason, McDaniel and Callaway (1974). Their results suggested that children who are taught to spell words from their reading program progress more rapidly than children taught to spell words that are not in their texts.

Knowledge of the sound system of spoken English is also considered a sine qua non of teachers wanting to teach spelling effectively. Without such knowledge, teachers may fail to understand why a child spells '**drum**' with a soft '**g**' sound or the word '**spider**' with '**sb**' (say the words to yourself). When children spell words in this way, they are using their phonemic awareness skills to react to the word's phonology, because they are unaware of its orthography. The teacher, as a skilled reader, has had the phonological effect overridden by the word's known orthography. That's also why many children believe (correctly) that the word '**hatch**' has three phonemes and some adults do not. When I try this exercise on my undergraduate students, the majority are convinced the word has four phonemes.

It appears that teaching spelling gradually brings children's representations of sound in line with those assumed by the conventional writing system (Treiman, 1998b, p. 298), as grammatical awareness is superimposed upon earlier phonological representations.

Treiman's (1998b) third essential ingredient for effective spelling instruction is knowledge of spelling acquisition. After the stage of scribbles and unrelated conventional letters, children begin to relate letters in spelling to the sounds they hear in words as they master the alphabetic principle. They may begin with the initial letter of a word **b** for **bed**, progress to **bd** and only later start to represent the vowel sound. As their exposure to print, knowledge of the sound system and the morphology of the language increases, they learn the conventional spellings of English words.

It is important to have knowledge about children's spelling acquisition when assessing children's spelling attempts. Let's imagine the following two attempts at spelling 'kissed'—*kist*; *cs*—in a first grade classroom. While both attempts could technically be marked as incorrect, a teacher would gain valuable insights into the children's phonological knowledge by examining each protocol in more detail. The first attempt is phonologically mature, but lacks morphological knowledge. The second attempt reveals that the child is only at the partial alphabetic stage of reading and writing word development and needs assistance with medial vowel sounds. As Treiman (1998b, p. 300) has emphasised, children's spelling provides an excellent window onto their knowledge of phonology and orthography and thus can direct teaching procedures—a compelling reason for including spelling in a literacy program as early as possible.

Turning now to more practical issues concerned with spelling, we may well ask why does spelling need to be taught at all? If it is a natural by-product of reading, won't it simply be acquired by lots of exposure to print? The answer to this question is a resounding 'NO'. In the first place, research has shown (Ehri & Wilce, 1980a) that first graders learn to spell words when they are practised out of context, rather than in connected text. Second, research results provided by Bosman and van Orden (1997) suggest that children need to read a word at least nine times before their spelling performance begins to improve. Copying the word, spelling it out loud or forming the word using letter tiles (Treiman, 1998b, p. 294) are superior to connected text reading as a means of learning a word's spelling. Furthermore, their evidence (cited by Perfetti, 1997, p. 30) also suggests that reading by itself will not dramatically improve spelling because reading does not practise the full orthographic retrieval process demanded by spelling. It is spelling itself that is most effective at improving the quality of word representation. Practice at spelling should help reading more than practice at reading helps spelling.

A word about invented spelling would not be out of place here. Treiman (1998b, p. 305) suggests that children should be encouraged to invent spellings while they are engaged in creative writing, as it appears to help them appreciate the alphabetic principle. However, she goes on to say that

'Once children have grasped this principle, invented spelling is no longer superior to traditional spelling' (p. 305). Furthermore, invented spelling for a word should no longer be accepted once the spelling of that word has been systematically taught. Still, it can be very helpful to use children's invented spelling for assessment purposes, as it may prove more instructive than early reading attempts.

I feel that Treiman (1993; 1998b) has made a persuasive case for the symbiotic effects of integrated reading/spelling tuition and that the early inclusion of spelling in a word level program is eminently desirable. Without labouring the point, I'd also like to include her justification for teaching spelling in the age of computerised spell-check programs: 'the ability to spell words easily and accurately is an important part of being a good writer. That is why I suggested earlier that poor spelling may inhibit a child's process writing. A person who must stop and puzzle over the spelling of each word, even if aided by a computerised spell-check program, has little attention left to devote to other aspects of writing. Just as learning to read words is an important part of reading comprehension, so learning to spell is an important part of writing (Treiman, 1993, p. 3).

Teaching spelling

It seems sensible to begin to teach spelling soon after the introduction of the first vowel sound, to complement phonemic awareness instruction. Remember how we used blending to create a word (synthesis) in the first few phonemic awareness activities? Now we are going to use the opposite process—segmentation—to serially analyse the sounds in a word and learn how to spell.

Teachers could ask their students to call out the individual phonemes in a new word they have learnt during phoneme manipulation activities, for example 's-a-t', and help pupils realise that calling out sounds (or letters) to make a word is called spelling. Let the children know that now they are going to practise spelling words.

Target the word to be spelt, say 'mat'—this word will be familiar to children from their text reading, as it should have been encountered in the first few little readers. First, let a child use the word 'mat' in a sentence. (If a word to be spelt has multiple meanings or represents different parts of speech, like 'map', use different sentences to cover the different usages.) Teachers could then say the word 'mat' and get their students to segment it. Put out a square for each phoneme and count the number of sounds together. Now stretch out (segment) the word again and this time, ask your students which letter stands for each sound as you exaggerate each one (**mmm, aaa, t**). Write each letter beneath the relevant square so your students can see the match. Maybe you could get students with difficulties in fine motor coordination to use letter cards or mouth shape blocks to spell the word themselves, to obviate the need for fine motor coordination skills necessary for actually writing the letters. You could end the spelling activity by saying aloud, in unison, that '**m**' '**a**' '**t**' spells '**mat**'.

Using letter blocks, repeat the spelling sequence for all real word combinations of letters and sounds already learnt, and continue the procedure with all new letter/sound combinations. Thus, by the end of the first school year, students should be able to read and spell all the regular words that are formed from the single consonants and short vowels in their repertoire.

Orthographic constraints

One interesting addition to the word-level program, which may well facilitate spelling instruction, is a component called orthographic constraints, which has been adapted from Treiman's Orthographic Constraints Test (Treiman, 1993). The purpose of this component is to link students' reading and spelling with respect to permissible letter combinations.

It appears that children who are consistently exposed to print will induce permissible letter sequences even if not specifically taught. For example, it seems that very early in children's schooling, they will recognise that in English words do not begin with a 'ck' or that 'uu' is very rare in print (Treiman, 1993, p. 172), although it is most unlikely that their teachers have given them formal lessons in orthographic constraints. Consequently, while letter to sound translations (phonics) have generally tended to be part of formal reading/spelling programs, it has not been customary to include the teaching of orthographic constraints. Treiman (1993, p.174) argues, however, that children might learn these patterns more rapidly and more completely, if the regularities were pointed out to them. Moreover, there is some evidence that children actually enjoy these activities and can derive much pleasure from selecting admissible from inadmissible letter combinations.

As this book is aimed at children in inclusive classes, some of whom may have difficulty inducing admissible letter combinations simply from lack of exposure to print, it probably makes sense to teach orthographic constraints in an early word level program. Consequently, after the introduction of the tenth sound/letter combination (/l/ and 'l' in the sequence that I have suggested), teachers could include an orthographic constraints activity, perhaps following a spelling activity. Teachers could then insert a couple of orthographic constraints examples into each subsequent sound introduction in the word level program (*see* 'Orthographic constraints' panel on the following page). For instance, consonant doublets do not usually occur at the beginning of words (**mell** is permissible: **llem** is not. Children could be shown two **real** words, containing consonant doublets, that obviously must use permissible letter patterns. If teachers are following the sequence in this book, they could print the words 'sill' and 'dill' on the board (sounds already taught), explaining to students that the usual occurrence of the consonant doublet 'll' is at the end of the word. The word 'silly' could also be printed and read to the children, as it is unfamiliar, to show them that 'll' combination is permissible in the middle of a word, if teachers think their students are ready for this exposure.

Teachers could follow this by presenting two non-words with permissible letter combinations, such as 'sall' and 'dall', explaining that they look like real words even though they are not. Then students could be given examples of non-words with permissible and non-permissible letter combinations using the consonants and vowels that have been covered thus far. For example, teachers could use non-words like 'llum' and 'rull' and get the children to choose the word that could not be a real word. Reinforce the principle of consonant doublets not occurring at the beginning of a word.

With the next phoneme/grapheme combination (/b/, 'b' in the suggested sequence) teachers could print 'bill' and 'dabble' (reading them to pupils, since it is very difficult to find a monosyllabic real word that ends with the doublet 'bb') on the board as examples of real words that illustrate the principle of consonant doublets not occurring at the beginning of words. Follow this with an example of two non-words that obey the laws of permissible consonant doublets like 'sabb' and 'mibb'. Then you could use 'mabb'/ 'bbim' as a permissible/non-permissible orthographic combination, and 'bbit'/'tibb', as a non-permissible/permissible combination to reinforce the principle of orthographic constraints.

With the introduction of the letter 'k', teachers could emphasise how this letter on its own can occur at the beginning of a word to make the /k/ sound, but needs a companion, 'c' to make the /k/ sound at the end of a word. Give your students a number of examples of real words to read, using the sounds already studied and ending with the /ck/ sound. For example, let them read 'sick', 'kick', 'back', 'pick', 'pack', 'sack', etc. Then show them **bik/fick**, and let them choose the one that could be a real word. Teachers could follow this example, which fits well with the word recognition program on 'k' and /k/,

Orthographic constraints

✓ Consonant doublets do not usually occur at the beginning of words
  - bbem, mebb
  - gganed, ganned

✓ kk and yy do not occur in English orthography
  - tukk, rull
  - tayying, tabbing

✓ ck does not occur at the beginning of words
  - ckog, gock
  - ckimer, micker

✓ aa, ii, and uu usually do not occur
  - viib, vibb
  - laan, lant
  - uut, ust

✓ Digraphs ending with y and w do not usually occur before consonants; those ending with i and u do not usually occur at the end of morphemes
  - poyt, poit
  - awd, aud
  - nei, ney
  - fau, faw

✓ i does not usually occur at the end of morphemes; y does not usually occur at the beginning or in the middle of morphemes
  - bli, bly
  - yg, ig
  - shyd, shid

(Source: adapted from Treiman, 1993, p. 168)

with the observation that 'ck' at the beginning of a word does not occur in English orthography. Then let students choose the admissible sound combination from **ckog/gock**, for example.

The reason I have not suggested using real words, such as 'ckat', 'cat', in these orthographic constraints exercises to illustrate the preceding example of inadmissible letter combinations, is because of the risk that some children may retain the incorrect spelling of the real word rather than the correct one. Bosman and van Orden (1997, p. 188) comment on the problem of erosion of spelling knowledge after conducting a large number of experiments using pseudohomophones. 'Harrass', 'harass' or 'harras' are three examples cited by the authors. It seems that being visually exposed to incorrect but phonologically possible spellings may have an adverse effect on existing spelling knowledge.

Summary

This chapter started by presenting a rationale for including spelling in an early word recognition program. This was followed by an outline of a suggested early spelling segment that could be added to a word recognition program to assist children's reading and writing. Finally, an orthographic constraints component, to familiarise children with permissible and non-permissible letter combinations, was outlined.

Conclusion to the first year at school

Now, the first school year is almost at an end. Teachers who have been following the sound/symbol correspondence sequence suggested in this text will have introduced their students to about sixteen phoneme/grapheme translations, whereas other teachers may have covered all single consonant and short vowel sound/symbol correspondences. Those teachers who are working specifically with students exhibiting reading difficulties could consult *The Phonics Handbook* (Nicholson, 2005) for additional assistance.

Phonemic awareness, word family, spelling and orthographic constraints activities will have reinforced the phonics program, while the use of decodable readers will have given children the opportunity to practise familiar and novel sound/letter combinations in connected text, as well as to develop fluency at the lexical level.

Throughout the word program in the first year of school, I have stressed the phonological connection because this is the most important connection when children are first introduced to the alphabet (Nunes et al., 1997, p. 152). Nevertheless, as students move into their second school year, they also have to encounter the grammatical connection in written language in order to understand that the phonological connection does not always underlie the spelling of every word. This has already been previewed and will be addressed more fully when we look at teaching skills and strategies at the word level in the second school year.

A suggested program at the word level for the first school year follows.

Program at the word level for the first school year

Day 1 (once little readers are introduced)

✓ **Reading revision:** Reading of previously introduced little reader

✓ **Sound/letter revision:** Revision of previously learnt sounds and letters

✓ **New sound introduction:** for new little reader
  – The reason for learning sounds and letters
  – Introducing the sound
  – Phoneme identity activities (beginning, end and medial positions)
  – Introducing the letter
  – Writing the letter
  – Worksheets for practising letter writing

✓ Re-reading little readerDay 2

Day 2

✓ Re-reading little reader

✓ **Phonemic awareness activities** (phonemes only)
  – Blending, segmenting and counting unlearnt sounds (oral)
  – Blending, segmenting and counting learnt sounds (with letter cards)
  – The quick-change game with learnt sounds (initial and final phoneme deletion/addition, where appropriate, phoneme substitution)

✓ **Segmenting and spelling**

✓ **Fluency training with word families**

✓ **Fluency training with decodable and sight words**

✓ **Text features and orthographic constraints**

✓ **Reading practice for new little reader, sight and decodable words**

✓ **Introduction of new little reader**

Regular review week and assessment after the introduction of four or five new sounds

With respect to teaching skills at the meaning level, about 30 decodable texts ('little readers') will have been read by the end of the first year. These stories have been designed not only to consolidate, in connected text, the sounds that have been taught, but also to give children an opportunity to practise comprehension activities at their reading level. At the same time, interactive text reading, possibly with different text types, as well as less structured text reading by the teacher, should have facilitated the acquisition of listening comprehension skills at a higher cognitive level than that provided by guided reading. Skill and strategy instruction, at the meaning level, will be continued in greater detail in the second and third school years.

An early writing program that accompanied the interactive text reading program at the beginning of the school year (*see* chapter 3), has also been suggested for the latter part of the first school year and will be developed much more systematically in later sections. Syntactic awareness instruction, just touched on in the first year, will also be formalised.

While I believe that a structured language program should be part of a first year reading program, and be continued into the second school year, I realise that it often becomes the victim of time constraints, and is discarded. However, it is critical that children are competent in the language in which they are being taught to read (Snow et al., 1998, p. 237; *see* also Section 6). Thus there exists a strong argument for maintaining a structured language program for a little longer in schools with a large intake of children from non-English-speaking backgrounds.

Finally, regular assessments have been taking place for both meaning and word level skills (*see* Section 6), so that small group intervention and appropriate class restructuring can be continually maintained.

So now we should be ready to move on to the second year at school.

THE *SECOND YEAR* at school

Most readers/writers are

made, not born

11 Literary texts

Teaching skills and strategies at the meaning level

In this chapter, the importance of teaching listening comprehension strategies explicitly to young children in their second school year is emphasised first. Then a suggested program for exploring a literary text (narrative, literary recount) is presented.

In the previous section, I devoted a lot of time to word level skills, but also insisted that meaning level strategies should continue to be taught through interactive text reading procedures. I have not, after all, resiled from the simple view of reading that includes both decoding and listening comprehension as the non-negotiable core of the literacy instructional process. Fortunately, this view continues to be reinforced in longitudinal studies (Catts et al., 2003) although it is generally agreed that the instructional emphasis shifts from decoding to listening/reading comprehension in higher grades, as children generally become more competent decoders.

In the second year of school, therefore, as part of a balanced approach to teaching early literacy, word recognition instruction will continue (*see* chapter 12). However, the major objective of this section is to develop listening comprehension strategies in the context of shared reading experiences between teachers and students. Not only must balance be achieved between teaching skills at the word level and at the meaning level but balance must also be maintained in a good comprehension instructional program. Consequently, teachers are encouraged to provide explicit training in specific comprehension strategies as well as opportunities for actual reading, writing and discussion of texts (Duke and Pearson, 2002, p. 205).

I strongly believe that comprehension strategies that promote children's listening and reading comprehension ability can and should be taught to beginning readers and not left either to chance or to osmosis. I base this belief on two facts. The first is that research into comprehension instruction suggests that primary school children receive very little instruction in listening/reading comprehension strategies (Beck et al., 1982; Pearson & Gallagher, 1983; Durkin, 1988; Aarnoutse, 1994; Pressley, 2002). From these studies, it appears that teachers conceptualise reading comprehension instruction merely as asking questions and giving assignments (Aarnoutse, 1994) rather than as teaching comprehension strategies. (In practice, however, I have seen a number of teachers who do encourage their pupils to use monitoring for meaning strategies during students' independent reading.)

The second is that, despite the dearth of comprehension instruction research at the primary grade level, there is evidence that listening/reading comprehension strategies should not be neglected during the important period when young children are mastering phonics, word recognition and fluency (Williams, 2002, p. 256). Furthermore, Duke and Pearson (2002) document studies to show that teachers can improve their students' overall comprehension of text (at very early school levels) by teaching them the strategies and processes used by good readers (p. 206).

Rather than having children induce comprehension strategies, a procedure which strongly favours those students with good language comprehension skills, teachers should aim to teach comprehension skills effectively to all elementary students by explaining, demonstrating and modelling these strategies in the course of listening comprehension instruction during shared reading (Aarnoutse, 1994). These skills can then be practised by students during their guided and independent reading of decodable and levelled texts in the classroom.

Cognitive and meta-cognitive strategies

Listening/reading comprehension strategies can, for the sake of simplicity, be organised in the following two ways: cognitive strategies, which are essentially text-based and refer to the text and its structure, and meta-cognitive strategies, which are largely reader-based and involve students' control over their own thinking.

In teaching cognitive strategies, we can show students explicitly the strategies to use before, during and after listening/comprehension activities. For example we can teach them to:

➤➤ activate background knowledge
➤➤ integrate new vocabulary into existing schema

➥ use prediction both before and during reading
➥ use think-alouds and visualisation
➥ make inferences
➥ understand the structure of different text types
➥ review the text when it has been read.

In teaching meta-cognitive strategies, we can teach students to be active readers and to explicitly exercise self-knowledge over:

➥ their own characteristics (e.g. their knowledge of the world)
➥ the characteristics of the text (e.g. text structures and types)
➥ the goal to be achieved
➥ the strategies to be instituted in the event of comprehension breakdown.

In this early section on teaching skills and strategies at the meaning level, simple cognitive and meta-cognitive strategies will be modelled by the teacher in listening comprehension lessons (shared reading) and practised by the students when reading texts at a lower level of complexity (guided reading).

Cognitive strategies, such as activating background knowledge, integrating new vocabulary, prediction and review have already been a feature of the interactive text reading program (with literary/narrative texts) in the first school year. In the second school year, there will be greater emphasis placed on using appropriate cognitive strategies with different text types. The comprehension strategies with respect to these different text types will concentrate on establishing familiarity with text structure, research on which suggests positive effects for a wide range of students (Duke & Pearson, 2002). For example, story structure instruction has been found to be beneficial even for kindergarten students (Morrow, 1984a, 1984b, cited by Duke & Pearson, 2002). Similarly, students who are more knowledgeable about informational text structure recall more information than those who are less knowledgeable (Bartlett, 1978, cited by Duke and Pearson, 2002).

Meta-cognitive strategies introduced at the beginning of the second school year will emphasise the strategy of monitoring for meaning (evaluating and regulating comprehension) and fix-up strategies with respect to different text types. Additional components of the listening comprehension program in the second school year are:

➥ personal response to text
➥ grammatical concepts
➥ joint construction of text
➥ working in cooperative groups.

Personal response to text

In addition to the strategies already discussed, there will be a focus on a more personal response to texts on the part of the student, in order to foster reading/writing connections. Early forms of application, elaboration and evaluation relevant to different text types will be taught as a precursor to the higher levels of learning defined by Bloom (1956), which are pursued in the latter part of the students' second school year and in the third year.

Briefly, application requires students to use the principles of a story that has already been read, and apply them to a familiar situation of their own. For instance, in a literary (narrative) text about a dirty dog called Harry, children might discuss Harry's actions in relation to their own or a neighbour's dog.

With respect to elaboration, students are taught to alter certain elements in a literary text in an original way. In the preceding example, for instance, the students may be asked to devise a different ending for the story.

When teaching simple evaluation techniques at this very early stage, I have suggested an easy thumbs up/thumbs down rating system, allowing students, either individually or as a group, to respond personally to the text. Then, using criteria sensitive to different text types, students can be encouraged to articulate the reasons for their response.

Grammatical concepts

Through the medium of studying different text types, students' knowledge of different grammatical concepts can also be developed. A theoretical rationale for the introduction of grammatical concepts has been provided by Snow, Burns and Griffin (1998) in their text on preventing reading disabilities in young children. These authors have stated (p. 298) that effective teachers of reading must have knowledge about the grammatical structure of language in addition to knowledge about its phonology and the structure of English orthography.

Snow and her colleagues (1998) discuss the very rapid acquisition of the basic syntactic structures of their native language in young children in the pre-school years (p. 48). They go on to say that, by the time of school entry, most children produce and comprehend a wide range of grammatical forms although some structures are still developing. I was reminded of this when I visited a pre-school centre recently and heard a very linguistically competent child, who was almost five, ask her teacher, 'Why you are wearing a scarf?' indicating her still incomplete mastery of word order following the use of an interrogative adverb.

The introduction of grammatical concepts during interactive text reading has been supported by research (Snow et al., 1998, p. 49) showing that children learn new pragmatic functions of language (that is, how to use language appropriately and effectively) during book reading sessions. This finding suggests that the introduction of simple grammatical concepts in the context of shared book reading may make a positive impact both on the listening comprehension and the written expression of young readers and writers. Snow and her associates state that as time goes on, children will become critical readers as they 'begin to appreciate stories in which characters use language to deceive or pretend, to understand the point of fables, and to interpret metaphors and other figurative devices' (p. 49).

Grammatical concepts introduced during the study of different text types will facilitate the understanding of differences between the different literary and factual text types to which children are exposed during the listening comprehension program. In addition, 'as proficiency in the forms and functions of language grows, children will develop meta-linguistic skills. These involve the ability not just to use language, but to think about it, play with it, talk about it, analyse it componentially, and make judgements about acceptable versus incorrect forms' (Snow et al., 1998, p. 49). This latter skill has already been briefly introduced to children in syntactic awareness activities during interactive text reading in the first school year (*see* chapter 3).

At this point, however, it is only fair to note that research and consequent teaching implications in relation to grammatical or syntactical awareness are not nearly as advanced as those associated with phonological awareness (Nunes et al., 1997; Snow et al., 1998), even though it has been consistently found that children who score poorly on tests of syntactic awareness are also likely to make slow progress in learning to read (Tunmer & Bowey, 1984; Tunmer, Nesdale & Wright, 1987, both cited by Nunes et al., 1997). Similarly, Snow et al. (1998) have stated that comprehension can be enhanced through instruction about the syntax and rhetorical structures of written language (p. 6), but that there are still questions relating to the roles and dynamics of syntactic and semantic factors in beginning readers (p. 343). Thus, in weighing up this evidence, it appears to come down on the side of introducing grammatical concepts when teaching skills both at the word and at the meaning level, particularly if we are trying to instruct those children who do not easily access literacy concepts implicitly.

The grammatical concepts developed at this time will concentrate on the sentence and words/phrases associated with both nouns and verbs, concepts already familiar to students, as they have been and are continuing to be developed during the word level program. Consequently, during the study of different text types, three main grammatical concepts are introduced.

➻   the sentence
➻   words or phrases associated with nouns (these can be nouns, noun groups, adjectives or adjectival phrases which qualify nouns)
➻   words or phrases associated with verbs (these can be verbs, verb groups, adverbs or adverbial phrases which modify verbs).

Grammatical analysis will also lead naturally into the joint construction of text, or story-related writing of different text types, by teacher and students working together.

Joint construction of text

The purpose of this story-related writing segment, at this early stage, is to link reading and writing as the teacher records the ideas and opinions of the students about the story just read. This jointly constructed text can serve as a model for students when they come to write a literary or factual text independently in reading comprehension activities (*see* chapter 16).

Working in cooperative learning groups

Another feature of the meaning program which starts at the beginning of the second school year is student participation in cooperative learning groups. The purpose of these groups is to teach students to work together as members of a team and to become involved in student-to-student talk as well as teacher-to-student interaction (Duke & Pearson, 2002). There are a few simple rules which have been found to be effective when forming cooperative learning groups (Slavin et al., 1992):

➻   groups should always be selected by the teacher
➻   groups should be heterogeneous in ability, gender and ethnicity
➻   personalities of students should be taken into account when choosing groups
➻   groups should stay together for approximately ten weeks.

When forming groups or reassigning students to new ones, teachers can choose a brief team-building activity so students form a bond and can relate to each other as team-mates. To enhance the bonding procedure, students can choose a name for their team and create a team logo. It also appears that when teams are disbanded, an activity that signifies the end of a good cohesive group is much appreciated by the participants.

Towards the end of the second year of school and into the third year, higher-order comprehension skills involving analysis, synthesis and more complex evaluation will be discussed (*see* chapter 15). At this time also, visualisation techniques for literary texts and inferential skills will be explicitly taught to the students, leading directly into the writing instructional program.

While teachers should borrow and adapt freely from the suggested listening comprehension program, I have found that the following precepts have worked successfully in the classrooms that I have observed:

➤ teaching listening comprehension as a whole-class program in the home classroom
➤ delivering each lesson daily, if possible, for about 20 minutes
➤ using a variety of text types and exploring one text in detail each week
➤ using texts about one or two years above the class's reading level to allow for teacher modelling
➤ choosing appropriate texts to foster the teaching of comprehension strategies—if teaching prediction, for example, the text should be new to the children, have a sequence of events, and provide sufficient clues about upcoming events for the listener/reader to make informed predictions about them (Duke & Pearson, 2002, p. 211).

Practice

The purpose of interactive text reading is to create a learning environment in which teachers help students to respond to and interact with literature in a meaningful way. It also helps students to become aware of the strategies they need to use while listening to a story (and when reading themselves) in order to evaluate and regulate their text comprehension.

Let's examine a possible one-week program for teaching listening comprehension strategies using a literary text of the narrative type. The components of such a program could be:

✓ Introducing the story
✓ Reading the story
✓ Retelling the story
✓ Understanding the story: application, elaboration, evaluation
✓ Teaching grammatical concepts
✓ Story-related writing/joint construction of text

Introducing the story (pre-reading strategies)

When introducing a story there are three strategies involved:

➤ story preview
➤ student predictions
➤ purpose for listening.

The purpose of the story preview is to engage students in the story they are about to hear, to acquaint them with unfamiliar words and to give them an opportunity to predict what is going to happen in the story. Teachers can use the same procedures as in the earlier section on interactive text reading (*see* chapter 3) to preview the story. For example, they can show students the front cover of the book and tell them the title of the story. Background knowledge associated with the book's theme can also be activated and linked to the children's familiar experiences.

When it comes to discussing unfamiliar vocabulary, teachers could choose three or four key words, which might include characters' names, action words or the book title if appropriate. It's probably worthwhile looking back to Beck's discussion on vocabulary instruction (*see* chapter 3) to understand how in-depth this instruction should be in order to insinuate a new word into a student's vocabulary repertoire.

After the story has been previewed and the illustrations on the front cover examined, the importance of predictions can be discussed with students. Predicting a story's outcome keeps the reader engaged with the text, particularly when predictions are either confirmed or denied as the material is being read. For those pupils with established writing skills, simple predictions could be written down in writing books at this stage. For students at-risk, predictions could be written jointly with the teacher. These predictions could be discussed both in cooperative groups and with the teacher and then brought along next day for the actual story reading. The previewing and prediction stages provide a purpose for listening, a reason to read the story.

Reading the story (strategies during reading)

Like the pre-reading strategies, it is important to take the following into account when reading the story:

➤ discussing predictions
➤ teaching cognitive strategies: asking literal and inferential questions

➡ teaching meta-cognitive strategies: self questioning and fix-up techniques

➡ reviewing the story.

It makes sense to preface the actual story reading by a discussion or reading of the predictions previously made by the students. These predictions can become one of the purposes of listening to the story. As the teacher reads the story, the children can discover which, if any, of the predictions are confirmed.

Let's take a quick example from *Happy Birthday, Sam*, by Pat Hutchins (1978). While I would not advocate the use of this particular book at this level, because it is too short and too easy for a week's discussion, it can serve quite well as an illustration. When the children first made predictions, based on the title, the front cover and their own experiences, they may have predicted that the book was about a birthday party. As teachers start reading the book and discover, in the first few pages, that there seems to be an emphasis on Sam's inability to reach things that he wants, they could ask the children whether they still think that the story will only be about a birthday party or, perhaps, about something else. Take time to discuss the suitability of the predictions offered, then read on and let students see whether their predictions have been confirmed or not.

Even in this simple story, there is a possibility of asking inferential as well as literal questions (developing cognitive strategies), although inferential strategies will only be targeted explicitly in the third school year. Sam is given a toy boat by his parents as a birthday present, but he can't reach the sink to be able to sail it. You could ask the students whether they think Sam is happy with his parents' present and to justify their answer.

As an introduction to meta-cognitive instruction, you could now tell your pupils that you will show them how to check their understanding of the story by asking questions about it while the text is being read. Such questions are usually literal and can be asked at suitable junctures, often at the end of each page read. In the simple story that I have just mentioned, a relevant question could be whether Sam was able to reach the light switch.

Teachers could first model this procedure with the text being read through self-generated questions, and then show students how to apply fix-up strategies in the event of story comprehension difficulties (teaching meta-cognitive strategies). For example, if you answer a self-generated question incorrectly, indicating a comprehension hiccup, you could tell your pupils you will re-read the text more slowly this time, so the correct answer can be accessed more easily. Then suggest that re-reading the text or reading more slowly is a good technique whenever comprehension breaks down, explaining to children they should do the same when they are reading texts independently.

After the modelling procedure, it is often a good idea to call on a child who is likely to be having difficulty with text comprehension, so the meta-cognitive strategy routine can be practised by the student. You could continue in this way until the book is finished. Then teachers could discuss the original predictions with students and then review the main points in the text to prepare them for the next component, retelling the story.

Retelling the story (strategies after reading)

The purpose of the interactive group retell is to give students an opportunity to incorporate the story into their own schema, to learn the structure of a literary text, to enlarge their vocabulary, and to improve their oral language skills. This procedure also provides a good opportunity to encourage students to work as members of a team and to promote cooperative learning. Some suggestions for group retell activities, both as a whole-class exercise and in small cooperative groups are:

➤➤ interactive story circle
➤➤ sequence cards
➤➤ story dramatisation
➤➤ story maps.

These should in no way constrain teachers from using other or additional activities that they have found to be useful.

Interactive story circle

This is usually performed as a whole-class activity because it is difficult for teachers to supervise small groups engaging in this exercise. One student is asked to start the story off. The next child can add some detail to this beginning sequence, if anything has been omitted. A third can continue with the next event, and so on until the sequence of events that constitutes the text is completed. Needless to say, the teacher will be facilitating the process, ensuring the discussion remains on track and children remain on task.

Sequence cards

These have been mentioned before in an earlier section on meaning-related skills (*see* chapter 3). Now students as well as teachers can be involved in the use of sequence card procedures. These are very suitable activities for students to engage in small-group cooperative learning under teacher supervision. As previously, in interactive text reading, teachers can either cut up an extra book to make sequence cards or make them themselves to use in teacher-directed activities. Students can be divided into their cooperative learning groups and either prepare one sequence card suggested by the teacher, or one that illustrates their favourite part of the story after negotiation with the teacher and other students. At the end of the session one member of each group can join with the others in forming the correct story sequence to discuss the card made by his/her team.

Story dramatisation

Once again, this procedure lends itself to group cooperation as well as to whole-class participation. If the former procedure is chosen, each group may decide, with teacher assistance, how much of the story will be dramatised and in what way the dramatisation will be organised. The teacher will still be responsible for the props, sequence cards, etc. that each group will use.

Story maps

Another important way to retell a story is to construct a story map that allows students to use the structural features of a literary text of the narrative type to organise the sequence of events and understand how the elements of a story fit together. The main structural features of a narrative text are:

➼   the characters
➼   the setting
➼   the problem
➼   the resolution
➼   the coda or moral, if applicable.

With these features as a guide, teachers and students can build a story path or map when retelling the story, to illustrate the way in which the story components are organised. This form of retelling a story helps students to develop meaningful connections among story elements, and then use this knowledge to enhance listening and reading comprehension. Having access to a defined pattern or structure facilitates both the reading and writing process for children. Teachers could draw an outline of the story map on the board and complete it with their students, the first instantiation of visual literacy. While at this early stage this could probably be a whole-class activity, later in the year students could be encouraged to complete their own story maps in cooperative groups.

It is encouraging to know that story structure instruction shows positive effects on comprehension for a wide range of students including kindergarten children (Morrow, 1984a, 1984b, cited by Duke & Pearson, 2002) and students identified as struggling readers (Fitzgerald & Spiegel, 1983, also cited by Duke and Pearson, 2002).

Understanding the story

The aim of this component of the literary text is to give students a variety of ways in which to react to literature and to help them develop critical thinking strategies. I suggest that after reading the text interactively, and before re-reading the story to your children without a break, you have some questions prepared that will promote their learning the specific skills of application, elaboration and evaluation.

If, for instance, *Harry, the Dirty Dog* (Zion, 1956) is the text under discussion, teachers could ask students to use the principles of this story (a dog who does not want a bath) to apply them to a familiar situation of their own. This should help children to develop the skill of application and to ground the story within their own experience.

To develop the skill of elaboration, students could use some of the elements of the story just read to arrive at a different outcome. This, of course, can easily be the springboard for the story-related writing activity (joint construction of text).

Finally, to promote the skill of evaluation or personal response, there are a couple of possibilities to be considered. First, if the literary text contains a coda or moral, you could ask the students to discuss it. Let's take *The Cat in the Hat* (Seuss, 2003) as an example. This wonderful story describes a frenetic day in the lives of two bored house-bound children who watch with both horror and delight as the Cat in the Hat takes their home apart and then puts it back together. The story ends with the question of whether the children should tell their mother what has happened in the house during her absence—an instructive dilemma for the students to discuss and to personalise.

Students could also be given an opportunity to share their opinions about the story. Maybe a thumbs-up or thumbs-down to show either their appreciation or their dislike would suffice as an early form of critical analysis. Pupils could give a more refined rating based on characterisation, general interest and illustrations, with a star rating for each book studied displayed on a wall chart. Obviously, these ratings are only meant as a guide and will change with the complexity of the book and the maturity of the students.

Teachers could engage the whole class by asking several students to give their opinion of the story and whether or not they would recommend it to a friend. Some of these opinions could be written down and displayed in the classroom. Once these routines are firmly established with the students, cooperative group responses could easily be encouraged.

Teaching grammatical concepts

I've chosen to introduce the teaching of grammatical concepts at this point because it flows quite naturally from interactive text reading and can be practised during the final component of literary text instruction, story-related writing.

In the listening comprehension program during the second school year, the following grammatical concepts are discussed in the context of literary texts:

➤ the sentence as a statement (indicative mood), as a question (interrogative mood) and, possibly, as a command (imperative mood)
➤ nouns/naming words that usually include people, places and things, e.g. *James* saw a *boy*—subjects of verbs tend to be introduced before objects
➤ adjectives that often describe size, colour, shape etc. of characters in the story or literary recount, e.g. The *little* boy ran home
➤ adjectival phrases that give a fuller description of the noun, e.g. The boy *with the red hair* ran home
➤ verbs that in narrative text are often about an action and in the past historic tense, e.g. Jack and Jill *ran* up the hill
➤ verbs can also be about the speech and thoughts of character, e.g. Cinderella *thought* she *was* ugly
➤ adverbs which give more information about the verb, e.g. James ran *quickly* in the race
➤ adverbial phrases which modify verbs and tell you how, when and where an action takes place, e.g. Jack and Jill went *up the hill*.

At the beginning of the second school year, it probably makes sense to revise the concept of a sentence as a statement, as a question and, possibly, as a command.

Remembering that familiarisation should precede recognition, which in its turn is easier than production, teachers could first take a sentence from the text that has just been read e.g. 'Harry eats dog biscuits'. Writing it on the board and reading it out highlights the capitalisation and punctuation for children.

You could explain to your students that this is a sentence because it carries a coherent or fully understandable message. Give the children more examples from the text or make up other sentences from other books that you have read together. Maybe you can give the children examples of non-sentences, like 'Harry, the Dirty Dog' and explain that because the information is incomplete, this is not a sentence. You could then ask your pupils for suggestions for simple sentences and discuss their replies.

Perhaps at this point teachers could introduce the interrogative form of a sentence e.g. Does Harry eat dog biscuits? Go through the same procedures as before to familiarise your students with the new concept. If you think that the command form of the sentence, 'Harry, eat the dog biscuits!' is too difficult, then, of course, this can be introduced at a later date (most easily when discussing procedural texts). If, however, it appears in a text that has just been read, it could at least be introduced. After all, most children are used to orders!

When teachers feel they have exhausted familiarisation and recognition (and the children are still on side), they could divide the class into its cooperative groups and play a grammatical game along the following lines. One group could be asked to generate a sentence in the indicative mood, and explain to the rest of the class the defining characteristics of a sentence. Another group could be given a similar task, this time producing a sentence in the interrogative mood, and a third could be requested to turn a sentence into a command (imperative mood), if this concept has already been covered. Alternatively, a group can be encouraged to produce an example of a non-sentence.

When all the groups have finished their task, select a spokesperson from each group to present the generated sentence and explain its distinguishing attributes. Adaptations and no doubt superior versions of this procedure can be used as teachers systematically introduce new parts of speech into the listening comprehension program.

Story-related writing/Joint construction of text

The last suggested component of the literary comprehension program is a joint construction of text. This procedure can serve to link reading and writing as the teacher records the ideas and opinions of the students about the story just read. It can also provide students with a model for independent writing described in the subsequent reading comprehension program.

In order to facilitate the students' understanding of story structure, the elaboration activities could easily be used as a springboard for the joint writing session. As teachers construct the story with their pupils, they could also draw attention to the grammatical concepts discussed during the past week. If there are students in the class who do not need such modelling for story-writing, they could either work individually or in a small group before telling their story to the rest of the class. Then, at the end of the session, the story could be edited, printed and distributed to each student as a model for writing a narrative text.

Under the rubric of literary text, I have concentrated mainly on the narrative. Other texts, such as the literary recount, are also subsumed within this category, and could be explored in a similar manner. With a literary recount, however, the sequence of events tends to establish a relationship between the writer and reader (or speaker), and the characterisation may be downplayed in discussion.

Summary

This chapter illustrated the power of instruction in helping children to develop skills and strategies at the meaning level. First, a theoretical rationale was presented to argue the case for explicit instruction in listening comprehension in the early school years. Then a suggested sequence of activities for studying a literary text of the narrative type was discussed in some detail.

In the next chapter, we move to a discussion of the factual and procedural text.

12 Factual and procedural texts

Teaching skills and strategies at the meaning level

Factual texts

This chapter presents a suggested sequence for exploring factual and procedural texts in the second school year. The factual texts under discussion subsume factual descriptions and information reports.

The theoretical rationale for explicit instruction in listening comprehension strategies was delineated in the previous chapter. I am now going to discuss a factual text instructional program in which comprehension strategies, modelled first by teachers, can be generalised to independent reading on the part of students.

A possible weekly program for teaching listening comprehension strategies using a factual text could contain the following components:

✓ Introducing the text
✓ Reading the text
✓ Retelling the text
✓ Understanding the text: application, elaboration and evaluation
✓ Teaching grammatical concepts
✓ Joint construction of text

Introducing the text (pre-reading strategies)

The same procedures described earlier in interactive text reading (*see* chapter 3) and in the previous chapter on literary texts can again be invoked here:

➼ text preview
➼ student predictions
➼ purpose for listening.

The purpose of previewing a factual text is to engage students with the topic of the book that is about to be read to them. Teachers can show students the front cover of the book, give them the title of the book, fully discuss and write on the board key unfamiliar words, and activate prior knowledge. Such a preview will assist students to bring relevant knowledge to the reading of a factual text.

After the book has been previewed, teachers can initiate a discussion about the topic of a factual text. They can explain that this joint discussion, before reading, can facilitate comprehension of the factual material contained in the text. Such discussion, of course, can model for students the important meta-cognitive strategies of being active readers and exercising self-knowledge about their own characteristics and those of the text.

At this point, teachers can write the topic of the text on the board. If, for example, the topic is about domestic animals, children can be encouraged to provide information (supporting details) about cats, dogs, rabbits etc., which can then be tabulated under the appro-priate categories. More advanced students could write down the information themselves, while others, including those at-risk, can be given a photocopy to be pasted into their writing books to reinforce the structure of a factual text.

The purpose of listening to a factual text is more self-evident than for a literary text, since it involves gaining more information about a topic that should be of intrinsic interest to the prospective readers. Nevertheless, making predictions about a factual text's content will also help students to engage with the book about to be read and provide a purpose for listening/reading.

Reading the text (strategies during reading)

Once pre-reading strategies have been completed, teachers could start reading the book with a view to:

➼ teaching cognitive and meta-cognitive strategies
➼ discussing predictions
➼ reviewing text.

The teacher can stop in strategic places to ask students what they have learnt about the topic. This new information can be added to the list already written on the board or on chart paper. If appropriate, teachers can ask predictive questions as well as literal ones (cognitive strategies) during interactive text reading. This allows children to integrate new concepts with existing schema and to maintain their involvement with the text.

A correct response from students allows teachers to continue reading the text, as the children have obviously understood what has been read. If responses are generally incorrect, pupils can be told that the section will be re-read, more slowly this time, in order to give them another opportunity to answer the questions correctly. This should be a priming device for future self-correction on the part of the students, when they are actually reading texts themselves.

As with literary texts, teachers can stop at strategic intervals to discuss the suitability of each prediction provided by the students as text reading continues. Confirmation or denial of predictions will often engender a spirited class discussion. When the book reading is finished, review the facts and discuss what the students knew before the text was read and what additional information they have learnt. Once again, a visual display can reinforce acquisition of new information.

Retelling the text (strategies after reading)

The purpose of the already familiar interactive retell is to give children the opportunity to recount the information gleaned from the text and to internalise factual text structure (topic and supporting details). This is important, since research from the 1970s and 1980s suggests that almost any approach to teaching the structure of a factual text improves both the comprehension and recall of key text information (Duke & Pearson, 2002, p. 217). The following is a suggested list of procedures that teachers could use for group retells:

- interactive circle
- sequence cards
- pictorial/diagrammatic representation.

Using an interactive circle, pupils could take turns talking about the facts they have learnt about the topic from the previous day's reading. They could also get the teacher or another student to answer questions about the topic.

Sequence cards could be used to demonstrate that factual texts of the type described in this section do not necessarily have a sequence of events in the same way as a literary text. With this type of activity, students can be clearly shown that there is usually no defined temporal order for a factual description or information report. Students can easily work in their cooperative groups for this type of text retelling procedure.

The study of factual texts can also lend itself to pictorial representation of information acquired (visual literacy). Students can be encouraged, either individually or as a group, to illustrate the facts they have learnt about a topic or to draw a diagram to represent that information.

Understanding the text

The purpose of this component is to help students develop critical thinking strategies in order to generalise the information gained from the factual text that has just been read to them. As with literary texts, questions could be prepared in advance to promote the skills of:

➠ application
➠ elaboration
➠ evaluation.

Having read the book through, this time without stopping to ask questions, teachers and students could now discuss the text together with a view to developing these specific comprehension skills.

With respect to application, a book describing a visit to a farm could easily be used to encourage students to generalise the new information to similar situations e.g. a visit to an orchard. In order to develop elaboration skills, a discussion of a text about prehistoric animals could be extended to determine how more information about the topic could be obtained for those students interested in increasing their knowledge.

The same criteria for evaluation could be used as for literary texts, although the emphasis will now be on the type of information presented and the mode of presentation, rather than on character portrayal and problem resolution. Children can also be asked to provide a critique of the text, 'I liked the book because'/'I disliked the book because', or whether they would recommend it to a friend. These suggestions for text evaluation are presented only as a guide to teachers, in the expectation that they will be modified and revised as the year progresses.

Teaching grammatical concepts

As I have mentioned before, grammatical concepts introduced during the study of literary and factual texts appear to help children understand the essential differences between the text types, which may result in improved listening comprehension ability. The following grammatical concepts are typically taught in the context of factual texts:

➡ the sentence as a statement, question and command
➡ nouns/naming words that tend to include places and things rather than people, e.g. 'The *kangaroo* lives in *Australia*'
➡ adjectives that often describe size, colour, shape etc. of things or places in the text, e.g. 'The *grey* beaver can often be found in a *muddy* creek'
➡ adjectival phrases that give a fuller description of the noun, e.g. 'Parents with *children* are allowed to board aeroplanes before other passengers'
➡ verbs in factual texts are often about a condition and in the present tense, e.g. 'When an animal *is* ill, its owner *takes* it to the vet'
➡ adverbs which give more information about the verb, e.g. 'The hare runs *quickly*'
➡ adverbial phrases which modify verbs and tell you how, when and where an action takes place, e.g. 'Beavers live *in a confined space*'.

Re-reading a number of sentences from the factual text, once it has been completed by the teacher and retold by the students, gives teachers an opportunity to revise the concept of a sentence. Then, using a familiar sentence, teachers could institute a cloze activity, beginning with the omission of the noun subject. For example, if a book describing circus animals has just been read, and specific sentences have been discussed, you could present students with the following sentence '_____ jump through hoops in a circus ring', omitting the noun subject. Teachers could also ask their pupils to provide the answer to the question 'Who or what jump through hoops in a circus ring?' When the correct answer is provided either by a student or by the teacher, the function of the noun subject in the sentence can be explained (teaching of terminology is probably unimportant at this early stage).

Teachers could point out that in factual texts, proper nouns associated with the names of characters are used less frequently than proper nouns associated with the names of places, and common nouns (the names of things) tend to be used more frequently. This could be illustrated by citing an example of a proper noun subject used previously during a literary text discussion, contrasted with a common noun used in the factual text just read. Similarly, verbs in a factual text usually describe an action rather than a thought or feeling. Once again, comparing verb usage from a literary text that has been studied, with verbs from a factual text under discussion can particularise this grammatical concept. These grammatical concepts can then be practised by teachers and students together in text-related writing.

Joint construction of text

The purpose of text-related writing or a joint construction of text is to expose students to another medium by which to express their knowledge. At this early stage, the teacher will probably act as a scribe, and can thus provide a model for writing a factual text. As a starting point, the application activities could be reviewed and used as a basis for writing about the topic. Together the teacher and students can construct a text using the original factual text as a model. During the writing activity, attention could also be drawn to the grammatical concepts that have just been taught in relation to a particular factual text. Teachers could point out that a factual text is written in the continuous present (use examples of sentences from the text rather than teaching terminology at this stage) and contrast this with sentences from a literary text, which tends to be written in the historic past. The more competent students could work either as a group or individually to write their own text instead of participating in the teacher-led writing exercise. Once the joint construction of text has been finished, the description or report could be edited jointly, then printed and distributed, so all students have a working model of how to write a factual text.

To give students additional practice with writing a factual text, teachers could choose a topic similar to the one just used for the joint construction of text. For example, a writing activity about pet dogs could easily morph into another writing activity about pet fish. Teachers could first brainstorm the new topic, writing key facts and supporting details on the board in diagrammatic form, before commencing writing. Then the process could parallel the one used for the joint text construction.

At this early stage, only two types of factual text (factual description and information reports) have been discussed in detail. Since a procedural text exhibits a different text structure from these two types of factual text, but is accessible and fun for young students, it is dealt with separately.

Procedural texts

The following suggested activities for shared reading of a procedural text are similar to the ones already presented for factual text discussion:

- ✓ Introducing the text
- ✓ Reading the text
- ✓ Retelling the text
- ✓ Understanding the text: application and evaluation
- ✓ Teaching grammatical concepts
- ✓ Joint construction of text

Introducing the text

➤➤ text preview

➤➤ student prediction

➤➤ knowledge of procedures.

In the preview activities, when introducing the book, the listening comprehension strategies to be used before reading a procedural text can be modelled by the teacher. The purpose of this preview is to engage the attention of students for the procedural text they are about to hear and to acquaint them with a slightly different text type. The routine for the preview section is fairly familiar by now, based as it is on the original interactive text reading procedure. Once again, teachers could show their students the book's front cover and tell them the title of the book. Relevant background knowledge about familiar procedures, such as baking a cake or going to see a doctor, could be activated to facilitate children's ability to follow the procedure featured in the text. A few key words could then be discussed fully and written on the board, and an opportunity provided for students to predict the procedure that will appear in the book.

Pupils could then list the ingredients or materials that might be required for a particular procedure or routine, as well as the steps involved, all of which could be written on the board. Student satisfaction with the temporal order of the steps could be canvassed and the order revised if necessary. Once there is general satisfaction in the classroom about the order of the steps in the procedure, the list could be kept as a reference to be employed during the actual book reading. The predictions about the relevant steps in the procedure can become the purpose for listening to the text, as students anticipate either their confirmation or their denial.

Reading the text

At this junction the teacher will be:

➤ teaching cognitive and meta-cognitive strategies
➤ discussing predictions.

While the book is being read, students not only become acquainted with a procedure but can also develop cognitive and meta-cognitive strategies that are being constantly modelled by the teacher. For example, during text reading, teachers will be asking literal and inferential questions (cognitive strategies) to keep students involved with the book. The type of summative questions relevant to this type of text relate to the ingredients/materials and procedural steps that appear on each page. Where possible, predictive questions about the theoretical next step in the procedure can also be asked. Any prediction supplied by a child can be discussed in terms of its relevance. Then as teachers reach the end of each page, they can stop and model the meta-cognitive strategy of monitoring for meaning, as has already been discussed during literal and factual text exploration. Finally, throughout text reading, the confirmation or denial of student predictions can lead to vigorous group discussion, which should help maintain class enthusiasm.

Retelling the text

At this point you need to consider:

➤ text structure
➤ performing or illustrating the procedure.

In order to carry out or illustrate the procedure, children should be made aware of the following characteristic structure of a procedural text:

➤ an aim or goal describing what will be accomplished
➤ a list of ingredients/material required
➤ a series of steps or actions to be taken
➤ an optional summary about the finished product.

The main reason for either performing or illustrating the procedure is to give students the opportunity to learn the structure of a procedural text. If teachers are going to carry out the procedure as a retelling device, they can first discuss the goal or the finished product, the necessary materials/

ingredients, and the correct sequence of steps for the procedure. Then the class can be divided into its cooperative groups, so that each group member can work out what needs to be brought to the classroom for the demonstration, before the procedure is performed. If teachers believe in a merit system, points could be awarded to the groups who carry out the best procedure and the reasons for the award can be discussed.

If the procedure cannot be performed in the classroom, teachers could, once again, divide the class into cooperative groups and get the children to illustrate the materials/ingredients and the steps in the procedure. The students could then use the illustrations to recount the procedure, ensuring the procedural steps are in the correct sequence.

Understanding the text: application and evaluation

While elaboration may be less relevant when discussing a procedural text at this early stage, an activity involving application (preparing the evening meal, going to the dentist) and evaluation of the procedural text could easily be included. The only difference between the evaluation of a procedural text and a literary/ factual text lies in the rating criteria. For a procedural text, for instance, students could rate:

➤➤   the appropriateness of the materials/ingredients listed
➤➤   the ease of following directions
➤➤   the enjoyment of carrying out the procedure.

Teaching grammatical concepts

There are a number of new grammatical concepts associated with procedural texts which can easily be introduced and then generalised during a joint construction of a procedural text. When discussing naming words with regard to procedural texts, teachers can explain that they are generally the name of things rather than people and they tend to appear as noun objects rather than noun subjects, e.g. 'Put the *eggs* in a bowl' (asking who or what after the verb).

The concept of words used to describe nouns (adjectives) in a procedural text can also be introduced. Adjectives tend to give more information about a noun or noun group, as in, 'Put *six* eggs in a bowl', or 'Take a *big* bowl'. Once again, it is the function of the word in a sentence rather than the terminology that teachers can emphasise at this stage.

Procedural texts also give teachers a good opportunity to introduce students to the sentence as a command (imperative mood), through the use of bossy verbs. '*Put* the eggs in a bowl' is an example of a sentence which is a command or directive. Even though the subject of the verb has been omitted, the sentence is coherent because the omitted subject is understood as (you). Verbs used in procedural texts tend to be action words as in factual texts rather than thoughts or feelings, which are more characteristic of a literary text.

Single words that provide more information about or modify verbs (adverbs) are also often employed in a procedural text. Adverbs usually give information about where, how and when an action should take place. For example, '**Put six eggs** *carefully* **into a bowl**', explains how the action of putting should take place. A group of words that amplify a verb (where, when and how), variously called adverbial phrases, prepositional phrases or circumstances, can also occur, e.g. '**Put six eggs** *in a bowl*', informing the reader where to put the eggs.

I am not suggesting that all these grammatical concepts should be introduced in the first discussion on procedural texts. I'm simply trying to show how over the year, the grammatical concepts outlined in a state or district syllabus, can be fairly painlessly introduced in the context of exploring different text types.

Joint construction of text

Having revised the structure of a procedural text with your students, choose a topic for writing that is related to the procedure that you have been discussing during the week (application activities). Thus '**How to bath a dog**' might become '**How to bath a baby**'. With the teacher acting as a scribe, students could contribute new materials and a new series of procedures which they think will be needed for the new topic.

During this joint construction of text, teachers could draw attention to some of the new grammatical concepts as they occur in the written text. The use of the imperative form of the verb (order or command) in procedural texts, with the subject omitted, could be particularly emphasised. Copies of the edited text could be distributed to the children, while more competent students could use their own written and corrected efforts as a model for a procedural text.

A suggested program at the meaning level for the second school year appears on the following page:

Literary text

Day 1
- ✓ Introducing the book
- ✓ Story predictions
- ✓ Student predictions

Day 2
- ✓ Reading the book
- ✓ Prediction review
- ✓ Story reading

Day 3
- ✓ Retelling the story
- ✓ Group retell activities
- ✓ Teaching grammatical concepts

Day 4
- ✓ Understanding the story
- ✓ Teacher re-reading the story without a break
- ✓ Teacher-prepared questions to foster application, elaboration, evaluation
- ✓ Revising grammatical concepts

Day 5
- ✓ Joint construction of text

Appropriate adaptations for factual and procedural texts

Summary

This chapter first showed the means by which teachers can assist children to develop skills and strategies at the meaning level in the context of factual text discussion. A suggested program for studying factual description/information reports and procedural texts was then presented in some detail.

A balanced approach to literacy instruction continues in the next chapter as the focus switches from comprehension strategies to the examination of skills and strategies taught at the word level in the second year of school.

13 Word building and morphological awareness

Teaching skills and strategies at the word level

Theory

This chapter presents a rationale for introducing a word building program, the self-teaching mechanism and morphological awareness into the word level program in the second school year. More complex sound/symbol correspondences, fluency practice in connected text and spelling homework are also added to the word program, and are discussed in detail.

At the same time as children are gaining listening comprehension skills, it is vital that they continue to develop their skills at the word level so that they learn to read all types of books independently with both accuracy and fluency. A quick review of some of the concepts addressed in the word level program in the first school year will probably clarify the objectives of the word recognition program in the second school year. At that time, I outlined four ways suggested by Ehri and McCormick (1998, p. 137) to achieve word recognition:

➼ by decoding (c-a-t = cat)
➼ by analogy (knowing 'light' and /f/, therefore recognising the unfamiliar 'fight')
➼ by prediction
➼ by sight, when the sight of the word immediately activates its spelling, pronunciation and meaning in memory.

Sight word reading is the automatic stage of word recognition and our ultimate aim, because it is effortless and allows the reader to expend energy only on the meaning of the print.

In the first school year, skill and strategy instruction at the word level emphasised decoding (together with phonemic awareness) and, to some degree, analogising through word family activities, to achieve word recognition. This approach was considered necessary because most children, at school entry, were only at the pre-alphabetic phase of reading, with very little awareness of the alphabetic spelling system (Ehri & McCormick, 1998). Consequently, the aim of the first school year was to move pupils from the pre-alphabetic phase of reading to the partial alphabetic phase when they are typically using letter/sound associations to some extent and have a rudimentary grasp over analogising.

In the second year of school, with respect to teaching skills at the word level, I will concentrate on moving students to the full alphabetic phase of reading development, through both further instruction and the use of the self-teaching mechanism (Share, 1995, 1999). When this phase is reached, children will have achieved complete mastery over the major grapheme/phoneme correspondences.

The word building program

In order for children to move from the partial alphabetic phase of reading into the full alphabetic phase, they must successfully apply decoding skills to each letter in a word. Until they apply such an exhaustive decoding strategy during reading, they will fail to benefit from the self-reinforcing aspect that typically comes from continually applying alphabetic decoding skills across all letters in a word (McCandliss et al., 2003, p. 100). Thus the self-teaching mechanism (Share, 1995, to be discussed shortly) that enables children to progress from 'early attempts at novel words toward identification of familiar words in a way that captures all the important orthographic content necessary to specify a word fully' (McCandliss et al., p. 99) may be beyond the grasp of children who are only able to successfully decode the first sound of a novel word.

The word building program, developed by Isabel Beck (Beck, 1989; Beck & Hamilton, 2000), has been found to be extremely effective for low progress readers in terms of significantly improving their ability to decode in the onset, vowel and coda (see Glossary) regions of the word form. Furthermore, participation in such a program has also resulted in significant gains in both phonological awareness and reading comprehension abilities (McCandliss et al., 2003). While this intervention program specifically targeted students at the lower end of the literacy distribution, I believe the use of such a program could be of great benefit to many children in inclusive classrooms, for whom the transition from the partial alphabetic to the full alphabetic phase of reading is likely to be problematic.

A core aspect of the word building program is an instructional activity called progressive minimal contrasts (McCandliss et al., 2003, p. 78) which enables children to form a chain of words, differing only by a single grapheme, through the use of letter cards. This activity is designed to help children attend to the subtle impact of a single grapheme change on the appearance and pronunciation of each word. The authors state that focusing attention on each individual letter unit within words may play an important role in developing fully specified representations of printed words (p. 78).

Briefly, a word building activity works in the following way. Children are given a small set of letter cards, using taught sounds, from which they build words as directed by the teacher. After they have formed a word and successfully read it out aloud, the children are instructed to insert, delete or substitute a specific letter, which results in transforming the current word into the next word in the sequence. This new word is then read both in isolation and in a meaningful sentence. Thus a sequence of word transformations could look something like this (adapted from McCandliss et al., 2003, p. 24):

sit
si**p**
tip
to**p**
stop
top**s**

As can be seen from the highlighted grapheme, each new word transformation focuses a child's attention on different positions in the word form by holding constant other letters from the previous word.

The way in which the word building program differs from the traditional phonemic awareness substitution activities already encountered in the first year word program, is its insistence on drawing attention to letters in each position within a word form, that is, to the initial consonant, final consonant, vowel, and initial or second consonant within an onset or coda cluster (McCandliss et al., p. 84). Furthermore, the letter changes are designed, as much as possible, to ensure the same letters that appear in the initial position of words also appear in other positions.

If a word building program, along the lines outlined, is incorporated into the word program in the second school year, particularly when the emphasis is on the medial vowel sound and the second sound in a consonant cluster in the onset or in the coda, then children's entry into full alphabetic decoding, via the self-teaching mechanism, may be appreciably facilitated.

The self-teaching mechanism

While explicit instruction in sound/symbol correspondence has been emphasised as critical to most children's acquisition of literacy, the self-teaching mechanism enunciated by Share (1995) should also be addressed because of its emphasis on how children themselves learn to read (see Bryant, 2002 for an illuminating account on the importance of children as learners). According to Share's self-teaching principle, children do not play a passive role in learning to read and spell, but induce reading and spelling rules themselves through exposure to text. However, Tunmer and Chapman (1998) in accepting this principle have stated that only children with reasonable mastery over sound/symbol correspondence and syntactic awareness can increase both their word-specific knowledge and their knowledge of grapheme/phoneme correspondences, when reading connected text containing unknown words at their independent level. That is why prediction or guessing an unfamiliar word from context or picture cues, was not considered a useful strategy in the first school year for students with minimal mastery over sound/symbol correspondences and inability to pay attention to letters in each position within a word form. Furthermore, at-risk children, at the beginning of their literacy career, tend not to read enough text, nor to be sufficiently successful at decoding to induce literacy rules without some direct instruction (Reitsma, 1983; Ehri & Saltmarsh, 1995).

In the move from the partial alphabetic phase to the full alphabetic stage in the second year at school, children who have acquired reasonable mastery over phoneme/grapheme translations and can focus on each individual letter within a word form could be encouraged to increase their word recognition skills by employing a self-teaching strategy when reading text containing words that are unfamiliar.

Share (1999, p. 96) explains his self-teaching hypothesis in the following way. He states that:

Each successful identification (decoding) of a new word in the course of a child's independent reading of text is assumed to provide an opportunity to acquire the word-specific orthographic information on which skilled visual word recognition is founded. Relatively few exposures appear to be sufficient for acquiring orthographic representations, both for skilled readers and for young children (see also Reitsma, 1983, 1989; Manis, 1985; Ehri & Saltmarsh, 1995)

It needs to be stressed, however, that low progress children will need additional exposure opportunities to fix the word form in memory.

A series of four experiments conducted by Share in 1999 indicated that phonological recoding (as opposed to pure visual exposure) was critical to the acquisition of word-specific orthographic representations as proposed by the self-teaching hypothesis. Thus, 'phonological recoding acts as a self-teaching device or built-in teacher enabling a child to independently develop the word-specific orthographic representations essential to skilled reading' (Share, 1999, p. 96).

If we combine the input from both Share (1999) and Tunmer and Chapman (1998), one of the main aims of the word level program in the second year of school becomes clear. It is to give students enough knowledge of letter/sound correspondences and the constraints of sentence context to enable them to generate a plausible candidate for a novel string of sounds when reading texts independently. Accordingly, in the word level program I am suggesting commercial readers that are less phonically constrained than 'little readers' could be introduced. These texts allow students to extend their word-specific knowledge through the self-teaching principle, develop fluency and more easily access the levelled readers in their classrooms. The importance of a variety of levelled readers in the classroom to which students have ready access cannot be overstated, even at this early stage of reading. Such classroom texts with different language patterns and themes can be used both for guided reading lessons and for independent reading, provided students are carefully matched to their text level.

Morphological awareness

Another major aim of the second year word level program is the development of spelling proficiency. The rationale for introducing spelling into a beginning reading program was made earlier, since reading and spelling are considered interdependent and phonology mediates them both (Bosman & van Orden, 1997, p. 188). In the spelling program, during the first school year, the phonological connection between words read and spelt was stressed because this connection is at its most important when children are first introduced to the alphabet (Nunes et al., 1997, p. 152).

However, written orthographies convey not only phonological but also morphological information, word roots, syntactic inflections and derivational relations that constitute the minimal semantic and grammatical units of a language (Verhoeven & Perfetti, 2003, p. 209). The authors further note that morphological information can be either derivational (e.g. dark, darkness, darken, which all derive from a single base morpheme) or inflectional (e.g. look, looks, looked, which provide grammatical information to the reader) and that some morphological awareness seems necessary for children to be successful readers and spellers. Indeed, the work of Carlisle (1995) suggests that 'morphological awareness, like phonological awareness may bear a privileged relation to reading achievement in the early school years' (p. 206).

Consequently, as students move into their second year of school, they will also have to encounter the grammatical connection in written language in order to understand that the phonological connection does not always underlie the spelling of every word. They will have to learn, as an example of inflectional morphology, that the ending of plural nouns is usually spelled with an 's', despite the fact that this 's' often has a /z/ sound (Nunes et al., 1997, p. 163), as in the well-worn example 'dog', 'dogs'. The importance of inflectional morphology knowledge has also been stressed by Green and her colleagues (Green et al., 2003), as it has been found to relate to academic progress in the second and third years of school.

Some time later in children's reading and spelling career in the upper primary/elementary years, they will also have to learn, as an example of derivational morphology, that **'heal'** and **'health'** have the same base spelling, even though the phonological connection would dictate a different one. Such distinctions in spelling depend on children's grammatical, or more specifically, their morpho-syntactic awareness, and so eventually children will have to draw on their grammatical knowledge to understand which spelling to adopt. Indeed, they must understand that particular morphemes may be spelled in a specific or distinctive way (Bryant et al., 1997, p. 221). Thus, when looking at skills and strategies at the word level, the phonological and grammatical connection (particularly with respect to inflectional morphology) will both be a part of the second year spelling program.

Practice

By the end of the first school year, students had learnt the single consonant sounds /m/, /s/, /t/, /p/, /n/, hard 'c' (/k/), /d/, /r/, /h/, /l/, /b/, /f/, hard /g/, /k/ and the two short vowels /a/ and /i/ (or, possibly, all single consonant and short vowel sound/symbol correspondences). Regular oral blending and segmenting of untaught sounds gave students practice in phonemic awareness activities. Furthermore, phoneme identity activities, as well as blending, segmenting and manipulation of taught sounds facilitated reading and spelling through emphasis on the phonological connection.

Reading by analogy, using simple word families consisting of taught sounds, was also a feature of the first year program at the word level. In addition, most students should now be able to read a number of common exception/irregular words encountered either in their 'little readers' or in other guided reading texts chosen by teachers. Simple text features (grammatical concepts and punctuation conventions) were also introduced during word recognition lessons. Moreover, fluency practice at both the lexical (regular and exception words) and the sub-lexical (rimes from familiar word families) was instituted in the first school year to obviate possible naming speed difficulties (Wolf et al., 2000). Finally, spelling of regular monosyllabic words was also a feature of the word recognition program, and at the same time, children were taught orthographic constraints to expose them to both permissible and non-permissible letter combinations.

Now, at the beginning of the second year at school, it makes sense first to assess students as quickly as possible to see whether they have mastered the word-level skills and strategies taught in the first year program (*see* Section 6 for assessment suggestions for testing phonemic awareness, real word reading in both context and in isolation and pseudoword reading).

In an ideal world, children would arrive with records from the previous school year but, in practice, teachers are rarely provided with this luxury. Consequently, early assessment enables teachers to organise their pupils into the homogeneous literacy groups based on students' word level knowledge, which was a feature of the first year classroom organisation. Four or five weeks into the second year program, formative assessments should be undertaken again (particularly for students new to the school), so that teachers can rearrange their groups, if necessary, and identify those children who may need additional individual assistance, extension or promotion.

In the word recognition program in the second school year, the basic components introduced in the first year remain the same (*see* chapter 6), but a number of refinements are added in order to move students into the full alphabetic phase of reading. The new components are:

➻ morphological awareness
➻ complex sound symbol correspondences: consonant clusters, digraphs
➻ word building to promote full alphabetic decoding

➡ spelling homework
➡ fluency practice in connected text
➡ self-teaching mechanism.

Once children have been appropriately placed in their homogeneous groups, I would suggest starting the year with a review of all sounds learnt, together with appropriate phonemic awareness, spelling and guided reading activities. It is possible that not all children will be ready to start immediately on the second year word recognition program, and they will need consolidation of the first year word level program.

Morphological awareness

Because no new letter/sound translations or new phonemic awareness activities are introduced during the review period, this could be a good time to begin developing morphological awareness in children by introducing them to the inflection 's' (/s/, /z/) as the plural ending of nouns. Teachers could start by using key pictures with objects that end with the soft sound /s/ as in 'rats'. For example, a picture showing one **cat** (**cap, bat, sack**), followed by a picture showing several **cat/s, cap/s, bat/s, sack/s**, would work well. Vary the number of objects used to illustrate the plural noun so that children do not automatically associate the plural /s/ with only two objects.

This sequence could be followed by showing pictures of objects that end with the hard /s/ (/z/) as in '**prams**'. Pictures of **dog/dogs** and **pig/pigs** would fit the bill. Children can also be encouraged to suggest singular and plural nouns themselves, and draw them, if appropriate. The phonological and morphological connection can then be discussed with respect to the objects that the children have volunteered.

As children articulate 'cats' and 'dogs' teachers can encourage them to talk about their mouth and teeth positions and feel their larynx to underscore the differences between unvoiced (/t/ in **cat**) and voiced sounds (/g/ in **dog**) and how this final consonant in the singular form influences the sound of /s/ in the plural form. By writing familiar words in both the singular and plural form on the board, students will be able to read them (blending practice), to use them in sentences (vocabulary practice) and to re-read them again quickly for fluency practice at the lexical level.

The flip-side of this activity, segmenting and spelling, could be introduced for singular and plural words, using a mix of words that differ in the pronunciation of the final /s/ sound to reinforce the morphological connection.

The use of 'little readers', which complement the introduction of the morpheme 's' (preceded by word and sentence practice), provides connected text reading and avoids decontextualisation. Of course, any appropriate reader with a mix of plural nouns can be substituted for 'little readers'.

While still reviewing first year sound/symbol correspondences, teachers could concentrate on the morpheme 's' in relation to verb inflections. Fortunately, English grammar is kinder than that of many other languages, and the only inflected verb that needs to be demonstrated, at this stage, is the one that accompanies the third person singular subject, 'he', 'she' or 'it' in the present tense—children in France or Germany are not let off so lightly. As many games can be devised to illustrate this principle, this can end up by being quite a noisy activity. Checking lip, tongue and teeth position as well as feeling the larynx can calm the students down and, once again, can reinforce the morphological rather than the phonological connection.

At this point, grammatical analysis using nouns/noun groups as subjects and objects of verbs/verb groups can be introduced. This gives the children an opportunity for grammatical revision, and practice in noun and verb inflections.

Some time later in the year, when the rime 'ing' has been introduced in words like 'wing' and 'ding' in sound/symbol correspondence instruction, 'ing' will also need to be reintroduced as an inflectional morpheme (a marker for the present continuous tense of a verb). Be prepared for some noisy activities as students are encouraged to start 'jumping' and then to stop 'jumping'. Teachers can discuss the action of the students using a complete sentence. Uninflected verbs (**look, help, call**) can then be presented to children who can turn them into appropriate actions using the verbs' inflected form. Teachers can discuss the difference between '**Ahmed jumps**' and '**Ahmed is jumping**' and remark on the auxiliary verb '**is**'. This grammatical lesson could obviously be tied in to the lesson on verbs/verb groups that is taking place in the listening comprehension component, so that the grammar activities taking place both at the meaning and at the word level reinforce each other.

Complex sound/symbol correspondence instruction

If teachers are following my suggested sequence of sound/symbol instruction, the short vowel 'o', /o/, final double consonants of the 'vcc' (vowel/consonant/consonant) type, the single consonant 'w', /w/ and initial consonant blends of the 'ccv' variety could be introduced at the beginning of the second school year. Moreover, each new single sound introduction should attract the same panoply of phonemic awareness activities that were a feature of the first year program.

If teachers have already introduced all single consonant sounds and short vowels in the first school year, they would probably plunge straight into the introduction of final double consonants and initial consonant blends at the beginning of the second year (and can ignore the next few paragraphs).

When introducing the third short vowel, 'o', /o/ (more often found in the medial than in the initial position), teachers could use the visual vowel picture as before to accompany the presentation of the letter. A suitable and amusing text to supplement the 'little readers' for this vowel could easily be *Hop on Pop!* (Seuss, 2003). The recommendation for vowel introduction has always been to double the time spent on single consonant introduction. However, with a relatively easy vowel sound, such as the short /o/, less time could be devoted to it than to the harder short vowel sound /e/, to be introduced shortly. All associated activities connected with the introduction of /o/ can be carried out as before, remembering you have the added luxury of the morpheme 's' both as a noun and verb inflection. The introduction of this new vowel also enlarges the number of word families for the classroom chart (e.g. 'ob', 'og', 'op', 'ot') and the opportunity for word building activities.

The way has now been cleared for the introduction of final double consonant clusters in words like 'sand', 'silk' and 'cost', which involve the nasal 'n', the liquid 'l' and the fricative 's'. There is research evidence (Read, 1975; Treiman, 1993) that first graders tend to omit the interior phonemes of final phoneme clusters, spelling 'hand' as 'had'. A possible explanation is that children analyse certain spoken syllables differently from literate adults (Treiman, 1998a, p. 382) and given 'ant' to segment, children would be inclined to produce only two sounds, /a/ /t/. According to Treiman, the most efficient way for children to reconsider their analyses of spoken words, and consequently their spelling of them, is through direct instruction. She suggests games could be played with spoken words in which children are asked to remove the first sound of an initial cluster or the last sound of a final cluster in an enjoyable way. They can be corrected if they remove two sounds instead of one.

Teachers could then reintroduce counters into the phonemic awareness activities based around the new sounds, to show students more clearly that 'and' contains three phonemes and not two. Even at this early stage, sufficient consonants and vowels have been taught to give children plenty of practice in putting out the correct number of counters for a large variety of words ending with a double consonant cluster. I have emphasised the specific difficulty, for children, of learning consonant clusters, so that teachers can pay particular attention to phonemic and spelling activities when they are introducing either final or initial consonant clusters or doublets. Once again, a word building program to direct children's attention to each grapheme position within a word, could be of great benefit here.

Because I tend to err on the side of caution, I have suggested introducing the single consonant, 'w', /w/, before dealing with initial consonant clusters in order to separate the teaching of final and initial consonant clusters. Some teachers will already have introduced this single consonant /w/ in the first school year, and could intersperse some other activity to obviate possible confusion.

The next suggested group of sounds to be introduced are the initial double consonant clusters, involving consonants combined with the liquids 'l' and 'r' as in the words '**slip**' and '**frog**'. (I have left the liquid /r/ as a final phoneme or phoneme cluster until later in the program.) Different combinations of initial double consonant clusters in word like '**spin**' and '**swim**' could also be discussed. Once again, particular attention needs to be paid to the second consonant of two-consonant syllable initial clusters, since young children also tend to omit these both in spoken speech and in written transcription. The spoken games suggested by Treiman (1998a) and the re-introduction of counters into phoneme awareness activities can go someway to obviate these difficulties, while word building, segmenting and spelling, together with spelling homework (discussed a little later), may also be of assistance.

As I have suggested before, a review week after every group of new sounds introduced could be instituted, for revision and assessment, before the next group of unfamiliar sounds is presented to students.

The proposed sequence continues with the short vowel '**u**', /u/ (both in the initial and medial position), the consonant digraph '**sh**', /sh/ (at both the beginning and end of the word), the single consonant '**j**', /j/, and consonantal '**y**', /y/ (as in yam). The same activities outlined before should enable the children to incorporate these novel letter/sound translations into their repertoire, while the use of 'little readers' or other appropriate texts gives children the opportunity to read new sound/symbol correspondences in connected text.

In concluding this group of sounds, it is probably worthwhile to point out one variant in the program. When teaching the digraph /sh/ at both the beginning and end of words, you could reinforce the fact that the digraph is a single spoken sound, through phonemic awareness activities using counters, while highlighting the representation of the single sound /sh/ by the two letters 's' and 'h' in reading and spelling activities.

The next set of sounds which is introduced consists of the short vowel /e/ in the medial position, the digraph /ch/ as both an initial and final sound, the single consonants /v/ and /z/, and the consonant digraphs /th/ and /wh/. In addition to the activities already outlined to teach these sounds both in isolation and in context, a couple of specific comments should be made here.

While short vowel sounds have been generally considered more difficult to learn than single consonants because they occur in both the initial and medial position, Treiman (1993, p. 125) has also indicated that some short vowels are more difficult to acquire than others. This appears to be the case for the short vowel /e/, as in 'egg', so more time probably needs to be devoted to teaching it than to the others to distinguish it quite clearly from /a/ and /i/. The short /e/ is introduced primarily in the medial position with phonemic activities, reading and spelling, but children are still exposed to /e/ in the initial position during matching games with pictures and letter cards.

The consonant digraph /ch/ presents the same difficulties as the ones outlined for the consonant digraph /sh/ and thus could be treated in the same way. Activities with the /ch/ sound in this section concentrate on the sound in the initial position because, in combination with a short vowel, the final /ch/ sound is usually represented by 'tch' as in 'patch', 'fetch', 'pitch', 'notch' and 'hutch'.

The digraph /wh/ is only introduced in the initial position, but the problems children may face with this sound are twofold: first, a single spoken sound is represented by two letters when written and, second, it may sound almost identical to the sound represented by the single consonant 'w' recently introduced. To minimise the first difficulty, phonemic awareness activities could emphasise the fact that the digraph is a single spoken sound, again through the use of counters, while reading and spelling activities could high-light the representation of the single sound /wh/ by the two letters 'w' and 'h'. To minimise the second difficulty, teachers may need to invoke the grammat-ical connection, by pointing out that many words starting with the sound /w/ and represented by the digraph /wh/ are interrogative adverbs introducing a question, such as 'What is this?', or interrogative adjectives, as in 'Where are you going?', 'Which shop will we go to?' (even if grammatically incorrect!). This also provides a good opportunity to revise the three different sentence forms discussed earlier in the text during listening comprehension activities.

Unfortunately, words like 'whip' and 'whizz' cannot be explained away in a similar manner, but must be attacked through reading and direct spelling instruction. That is why teaching too many rules to children about English orthography does not always pay dividends.

As we move on, the introduction of the consonants /v/, /z/ in the initial position should present no particular problems, but children could be shown that they are the voiced equivalents of the two familiar sounds, /f/ and /s/, respectively.

The next digraph which is introduced, /th/, is quite idiosyncratic in that its dominant pronunciation is unvoiced as in 'thin', but in about fifteen highly familiar words, like 'the', 'they', 'this', 'there' and 'though', the /th/ sound is voiced. As this is a difficult concept for young students to grasp, it is probably not worth mentioning to the students at this stage. However, as no particular problems in the acquisition of this digraph are envisaged, teachers could include both voiced and unvoiced /th/ sounds in spelling homework. This group of sounds could end with two sets of rimes /ank/, /ink/, /onk/, /unk/; and /ang/, /ing/, /ong/, /ung/. The /ing/ rime is then considered further as a morphological inflection, associated with a verb tense, as previously discussed.

As we already know (Read, 1975; Treiman, 1993) that first graders tend to omit the interior phonemes of final phoneme clusters, and tend to both segment and spell 'sink' as /s/ /i/ /k/, particular attention must be paid to these words in phonemic awareness activities using counters, as well as in the segmenting and spelling component. Children can be easily shown the difference between these two words (orally and in written form), and this difference can be reinforced through the addition of word families using the new rime combinations. 'Little readers' and appropriate levelled books will also facilitate the orthographic connection when children read these words in connected text. Finally, another advantage of introducing these rimes and getting children to read word family charts, first by combining onset and rime, and then reading the word quickly, is to move them from single sound decoding to word recognition by analogy.

Spelling homework

In this second school year, while the spelling component is recommended as before, a spelling homework section has now been added, in which children are given a spelling list for about a week before a regular spelling assessment is administered in class. This spelling list contains familiar phonically regular words, familiar words that involve both the phonological and ortho-graphic processor (*see* Glossary)—'wall', for example—words that involve the morphological processor ('dogs'), and words most reliant on the orthographic processor (familiar exception words like 'the', and as yet undecodable words). Once final and initial consonant clusters are introduced into the word level program, the spelling homework list should begin to include some familiar examples to reinforce the presence of the second consonant in the cluster.

Practising fluency in connected text

Decodable texts like 'little readers', or other appropriate readers used in guided reading are also a perfect vehicle for developing fluency at the sentence level. This was not a feature of the first year program because most children were still at the pre-alphabetic phase of reading. While more will be said about fluency development in the following chapter, repeated reading of 'little readers' or other appropriate texts that are pitched at the students' independent level of reading (about 95 per cent accuracy, or 1 in 20 unfamiliar words) is an ideal way to commence fluency acquisition.

Time can be scheduled in the classroom for students to read familiar 'little readers' to the teacher or to each other, with one child acting as teacher while the other becomes the reader. As students are expected to take the 'little readers' home, an emphasis on fluency as well as accuracy can be placed in the take-home homework sheet. Furthermore, as fluency is being developed, reading comprehension of any easy texts (95 per cent accuracy) can also be encouraged both in class and at home.

Promoting the self-teaching mechanism

While decodable texts can be used to promote fluency, levelled texts in guided reading (where word accuracy may only be at the instructional level of about 90 per cent) can be used to promote the self-teaching mechanism in the second school year. At some point during this year, those students with sufficient phoneme/grapheme proficiency can use their increasing knowledge of the alphabetic system and the surrounding text to generate a plausible word from a novel string of sounds. Each time a child successfully decodes a new word during independent reading, she 'is assumed to be developing the word-specific orthographic representations essential to skilled reading' (Share, 1999, p. 96).

A suggested program for teaching skills and strategies at the word level in the second school year appears below:

Suggested program at the word level for the second school year

Day 1 (once little readers are introduced)
✓ **Reading revision:** Reading of previously introduced little reader
✓ **Sound/letter revision:** Revision of previously learnt sounds and letters
✓ **New sound/letter introduction:** For new little reader
  – The reason for sounds and letters
  – Introducing the sound (with relevant activities)
  – Phoneme identity activities (beginning, end and medial positions)
  – Introducing the letter
  – How is the letter made?
  – Writing the letter
✓ **Re-reading little reader**

Day 2
✓ **Re-reading previously introduced little reader**
✓ **Phonemic awareness activities**
  – Blending, segmenting and counting unlearnt sounds (oral)
  – Blending, segmenting and counting learnt sounds (with letter cards)
  – The quick-change game
  – Using blended and segmented words in sentences
✓ **Word building**
✓ **Segmenting and spelling**
✓ **Fluency training with word families**
✓ **Fluency training with decodable/sight words**
✓ **Text features**
✓ **Orthographic constraints**
✓ **Sight/decodable word practice for new little reader**
✓ **Introduction of new little reader**

Review week and assessment after the introduction of four or five new sounds

Students should now be approaching the second half of their second year, progressing toward the full alphabetic phase of reading development. At this point, commercial readers are added to the program (see next chapter) to promote speedy and fluent word retrieval, and to prepare students for the final consolidated phase of reading development. This is, of course, the automatic stage of word recognition and our ultimate aim, because it is effortless and allows the reader to expend energy only on the meaning of the print.

Summary

This chapter presented a theoretical rationale for including a word building program, the self-teaching principle enunciated by Share (1995, 1999) and morphological awareness in the second year word level program. New single consonant sounds and the remaining short vowels were then introduced, although they may have already been covered in the first year of school by teachers using a different sequence. In addition, complex sound/symbol translations and new word families were also discussed. Fluency practice in connected text as suggested as well, together with the need for formal spelling homework.

In the following chapter, which combines the teaching of skills and strategies at the meaning and word level, most of the remaining phoneme/grapheme translations are introduced. Commercial readers for fluency practice become a feature of the word program, and as children start to read text themselves, reading comprehension strategies are discussed.

14 Beginning fluency and reading comprehension

Teaching skills and strategies at the word and meaning level

This chapter introduces the use of commercial readers with familiar sound patterns to develop fluency acquisition and reading comprehension in the second school year. More complex vowel and consonant digraphs are also presented to the children, together with additional morphological processes to assist reading and spelling.

Most children, mid-way through their second school year, should now have mastery over a significant number of phoneme/grapheme correspondences, a growing number of words they can identify by analogy and a defined number of exception words. As a result of this and developing levels of syntactic awareness, they can also make use of the self-teaching principle to access an increasing number of unfamiliar words in connected text. Consequently, they should be able to decipher print reasonably accurately, but they may still be unable to access many words by sight. That is, the sight of a word does not immediately activate its spelling, pronunciation and meaning in memory.

In order to access the majority of words by sight, and thus enter the automatic or consolidated phase of reading (Ehri & McCormick, 1998, p. 137), we now need to develop children's acquisition of word fluency in addition to word accuracy acquisition during connected text reading. While I touched on developing fluency in connected text in the previous chapter, the acquisition of reading automaticity becomes the focus of instruction in the second half of the second school year.

What is reading fluency and why is it important?

According to Samuels (2002, p. 167), 'fluent readers are characterized by the ability to read orally with speed, accuracy, and proper expression'. Fluency is important because of the influence it exerts on comprehension. Unless students can identify words both accurately and quickly, text comprehension will be compromised. The reasoning behind this is because individuals possess limited amounts of processing space, and the more space devoted to word identification, the less space is available for comprehension (Fleisher et al., 1979, quoted by Samuels, 2002).

Samuels (2002) goes on to say 'that the beginning reader finds the dual tasks of decoding and comprehension require more attentional energy than is available' (p. 169). To overcome this problem, the beginning reader 'first directs his/her attention to decoding the word in the text and then switches attention to comprehending the passage just read. This attentional shift places a heavy burden on memory and impedes text comprehension' (Samuels, 2002, p. 169). Only once the reader reaches the stage of sight word recognition (fluency or automaticity) can total attention be directed at print comprehension, the ultimate goal of reading.

How will fluency be best achieved? According to Samuels (2002, p. 173):

> It appears that this will happen by a lot of reading, so that the same common words are encountered repeatedly. As a result of these repeated encounters, the size of the visual unit increases with practice, so that the entire word can be processed as a single unit.

While attentional space is now readily available for deriving meaning from print, once fluency has been attained, the motivation for reading and expending this energy directly on text comprehension must not be neglected.

Teachers should be aware that some children need not only to be led to water, but also encouraged to drink. For children unengaged with print, the accumulation of repeated unsuccessful efforts to read and understand literary and, particularly, factual texts, decreases their motivation to persist with learning (Gersten et al., 2001, p. 287). These researchers suggest that to promote task persistence, both extrinsic and intrinsic motivators should be employed, together with increased rates of peer-mediated instruction (p. 287). They also point out that teaching approaches that actively encourage students to try to work out the meaning of text appear to be an important development in comprehension instruction (*see also* Beck et al., 1996).

These issues, developing fluency in connected text and the motivation for reading, are the main features of the second half-year program, as well as the introduction of new complex vowel and consonant grapheme/phoneme correspondences. Thus, in the latter half of the second year, a new format for teaching skills at both the word and meaning level is adopted.

In order to enable children to acquire automaticity, commercial readers with familiar letter/sound patterns, which are less phonically constrained than 'little readers', are introduced into the program, while decodable texts are still used to practise novel sound/symbol correspondences.

A further addition to the instructional program entails the formation of partnership pairs between compatible students. The main benefit of establishing such dyads is the greatly increased provision of opportunities for children to read appropriate connected text together. Working in pairs can promote task engagement, as children cooperate to improve their word accuracy and fluency and consequent reading comprehension. From a practical point of view, it also halves the number of commercial readers that need to be bought!

The introduction of commercial readers

I have suggested including the six titles from the Bangers and Mash series (Groves, 1989) early in the second half-year to consolidate familiar sound symbol/correspondences, before new ones are introduced into the program (see box below for book titles). This is because recommended readers like these (or any other appropriate ones) give students the opportunity to develop their fluency with easily decodable words, as well as to learn 'new word-specific orthographic representations essential to skilled reading' (Share, 1999, p. 96), as a result of novel vocabulary.

Bangers and Mash series of readers by P. Groves

First Series

The Hat Trick
Eggs
Wiggly Worms
The Clock
The Best Duster

Second Series

Ding Dong Baby
Indians and Red Spots
The Bee and the Sea
Wet Paint
Toothday and Birthday
Bikes and Broomsticks

Students can now spend much of their time reading these commercial texts with a partner. If each member of the dyad alternates between a teacher and a student role when using these readers, both children are getting repeated practice with reading connected text. There is evidence (O'Shea et al., 1985) that most of the gains in reading speed, word recognition, error reduction and expression in oral reading, are acquired by the fourth reading of the same text and any additional readings of the same text appear to be redundant. This should not be too difficult a goal to which to aspire, with both partner work in class and caregivers at home listening to children read.

No new phoneme/grapheme translations are introduced in the first few weeks, so the format when using these commercial readers is modelled on the interactive text reading routine, with about two readers per week being studied with teacher and partner support. The book is first introduced, background knowledge is activated and predictions about the text can be canvassed. When introducing new vocabulary, teachers can make appropriate instructional decisions based on the ability level of their students. If they feel that their students can use the self-teaching principle and sentence constraints to decode words containing new sounds and still develop fluency with repeated readings, there need be no pre-teaching of new vocabulary, since the printed words in these readers should be in the students' spoken lexicon. However, for less able pupils, some pre-teaching of new exceptions or as yet undecodable words may be necessary. Fortunately, even new exception words can be made more familiar by stressing the sounds already known when encountering a novel word (e.g. 'puts'). It is also a good idea to encourage the use of the new words in a sentence to reinforce their meaning.

Strategies for reading difficult new words can also be taught in this component, although the difficulty level of words will vary directly, of course, with the ability level of the students. Students can be encouraged to look for familiar letter/sound correspondences, particularly at the beginning and end of words. They can then try to articulate a word containing those sounds and see whether it makes sense in the context of the passage they are reading. A wall chart containing these new words can be created and the words read regularly for fluency practice.

Once students have been assigned to pairs, guided reading can commence, with the teacher first reading the text aloud to the class. In this first reading, teachers can model expression (prosody) and also stop to ask summative, predictive and evaluative questions. Inferential questions, which will be discussed in detail in a later section, can certainly be addressed to more able students. The text reading can conclude with a discussion of the accuracy of student predictions. During partner reading, as students re-read the text alternately, the teacher has an opportunity to encourage students to help each other with troublesome words before seeking assistance from the teacher. Children could take turns in taking the book home to read to care-givers, but if this is not possible, perhaps a system of tutors from higher grades or parent volunteers could be established.

The second day devoted to text reading can commence with students re-reading the book. Then a vocabulary review of difficult words encountered can become a basis for some grammatical analysis. At this juncture, this activity could investigate the function of a new part of speech, the adjective, if this parallels the text features being discussed in the listening comprehension lessons.

Resuming partner work, students can re-read the book to each other, and then work together on their worksheets (*see* example of worksheet for 'little readers' in Appendix) to summarise the basic points of the story (practising reading comprehension). Different pairs of students can then present their summary to the rest of the class.

A story-related writing activity is also included in this new format, with partners discussing the topic that appears on their worksheets. Students are then encouraged to write two or three sentences on the topic, helping each other to spell familiar words correctly, and using invented spelling for those words not yet in their spelling repertoire. The worksheets conclude with a story quiz, which can easily become the basis for a whole-class discussion.

I suggested discontinuing the commercial readers during the introduction of new sound/symbol translations, but propose their reintroduction when all novel sounds have been taught, so that fluency practice and reading comprehension continue to be developed.

The return of the decodable text

As soon as novel sound/symbol correspondences are introduced into the program, decodable texts (little readers) are substituted for commercial readers to give students the opportunity to practise new sounds in connected text. However, the format for the use of little readers changes from that used in the first school year and the first part of the second year. Now students can work in partnership dyads for the story-reading component, replicating the procedures used with the commercial readers, since there is a much greater emphasis on acquisition of fluency and reading comprehension than simply on the development of word accuracy.

Once students revert back to the decodable texts, rather than the commercial readers, an individual copy of the text, cheaper of course than commercial readers which cannot be photocopied, is recommended once again.

In addition, a new comprehension strategy, monitoring for meaning/ thinking aloud is introduced when using little readers (or any other appropriate text). First discussed by the teacher in the listening comprehension segment, it can now be practised by students as they read the text for themselves. To facilitate this transfer, teachers can first read the text aloud. During this read-aloud, as the rest of the class acts as a reading partner, teachers summarise what they have just read, through self-questioning techniques, and let the class check their text comprehension. When class members decide that the teacher has understood what has been read by correctly answering the self-generated questions, they allow the teacher to continue reading the next page or section. To model the procedure needed for their students to learn 'fix-up' strategies, teachers can intentionally produce an incorrect answer, and suggest that this can be rectified by their re-reading the text more slowly. This monitoring for meaning/thinking aloud strategy is then adopted in turn by each pair of student readers when they start their new little readers.

If the current story also happens to be a narrative, students at this point can be encouraged to discuss an aspect of characterisation, as a prelude to the more complex character appraisal that will be addressed in the following section. Once characterisation becomes a feature of little reader discussion, a review of the function of adjectives in the sentence could easily be instituted to parallel grammatical activities taking place in the listening comprehension component and in vocabulary discussion. Every opportunity should also be taken to promote fluency as students read their little readers to their partners, to develop skills and strategies at the meaning level. However, at this point, let's also take a look at word level instruction, which is now integrated with teaching meaning level skills in the latter part of the second school year.

New sound/symbol correspondences

Once the first series of commercial readers designed to develop automaticity is completed, the next suggested group of sounds to be taught in the second half year, in conjunction with little readers, include the long vowels 'a', 'i', 'o', 'u', the vowel digraphs 'oo', 'ee', 'ea', 'ai', 'ay', the 'r' controlled vowels 'ar', 'er', 'ir', 'or', 'ur', the less common single consonants, soft 'c', 'y', 'q', 'x' (if not covered in the first year) and a new morpheme, the past tense marker 'ed'.

Since regular assessments have been recommended at the end of each new group of sounds introduced, some or all of these phoneme/grapheme correspondences may be redundant for a number of students who can proceed to the next series of commercial readers for fluency and reading comprehension practice.

As a number of difficult concepts are introduced here, and students are becoming more sophisticated, the format changes a little from the one that has previously been suggested in the word level program. Furthermore, as morphological instruction, extended text reading and reading comprehension are now integrated into the word recognition program, instruction in each new complex phoneme/grapheme translation, for the average and at-risk student, could take up to a week.

With the introduction of these new sound/symbol combinations, a mystery game, in which a detective card is held up whenever a long vowel sound is heard, is substituted for the Yes/No game used previously. In addition, students are no longer expected to use individual letter cards or blocks with activities involving phoneme manipulation. These are done as a whole-class group, with the teacher writing the changes on the board. All other activities for the introduction and practice of new sound/letter combinations can remain the same as before. These programmatic suggestions are put forward only as a guide, since teachers themselves are generally much more adept than researchers at translating theory into practice.

When the long vowels and non-invariant consonants are introduced, I have suggested using some phonic rules which may prove helpful in decoding the majority of words in which these graphemes appear. For example, the following rule is quite useful and appealing to students when decoding long vowels, even though it applies in only 64 per cent of cases (Clymer, 1996). Whenever an 'e' follows 'a', 'e', 'i', 'o' or 'u' and a single consonant, it becomes bossy and makes the vowel sound like its letter name. Like a typical boss, it makes others work, but stays silent itself. Many examples come to mind, such as 'hat', 'hate'; 'pet', 'Pete'; 'bit', 'bite'; 'not', 'note'; 'shut', 'shute', but not 'done'.

To provide some variation, the previously mentioned detective game has been devised to assist students to identify words with a bossy 'e' and those without, using visual cues at first, and then just presenting the oral stimulus. Each word can then be used in a sentence and also committed to a spelling and dictation list. Teachers will also notice a large increase in the number of word families with the introduction of long vowels and the bossy 'e'.

While an example of the long /e/ has been given here, more time could be spent introducing long /a/, /i/, /o/ and /u/, since words with the long medial

/e/ are relatively rare. There would thus be only limited opportunity for teachers to play the two-picture game and the mystery game, or to carry out the phoneme manipulation and spelling components that typically accompany the regular decoding program. Furthermore, confusion could easily arise between the long /e/ and the vowel digraphs /ee/ and /ea/, to be introduced shortly.

Compound or multi-syllabic words are also introduced into the program at this point because they start to appear in the decodable texts that accompany the new sound/symbol translations. Students can be introduced to these words gradually, as teachers highlight familiar compound words such as 'into' and 'cannot', now occurring in text reading. Children can be given strategies to read compound words by suggesting they look to see if such apparently complex words contain any shorter familiar words (**'grand-mother'**, for example). A very exciting game for children with multi-syllabic words is to see how many shorter words can be derived from one long word, a game which children can enjoy right through their elementary school career, even if it needs modelling at first. **'Grandmother'**, for example, can yield at least thirty shorter words. When further derivational and inflectional morphology instruction is provided towards the end of the second school year and into the third, children will have additional ammunition for decoding multi-syllabic words.

The next suggested group of sounds to be studied in detail are the vowel digraphs /oo/ as in **'soon'**, and /ee/, /ea/ as in **'feet'** and **'meat'**. While these sound introduction lessons follow the same format as the one for long vowels, there is a caveat for the spelling section involving /ee/ and /ea/. With respect to spelling, when the emphasis on the new sounds is, at first, phonological, it may be too difficult for children to choose between the alternative spellings of words in which the long /ee/ or /ea/ occurs. As their orthographic skills in relation to these sounds may still be weak, they could be given a set of words containing the /ee/ sound to learn first, followed by a separate set containing the /ea/ sound. Once children encounter these words repeatedly in text (Bosman and de Groot, 1991, quoted by Bosman & van Orden, 1997 suggest nine exposures in reading are necessary before spelling performance improves), then the orthographic processor tends to override the phonological one for young students. From that point, children should have little trouble selecting the correct spelling.

The next proposed group of sounds are the vowel digraphs /ai/, /ay/ and the soft consonant 'c'. Teachers could write a number of words on the board featuring /ai/, such as **'rain'**, **'aim'**, **'paint'**. When these have been read and used in sentences, the same could be done for a number of words spelt with

/ay/, such as 'day', 'stay'. Maybe students will be able to induce the rule that /ai/ can occur in the middle of a word, while /ay/ can only occur at the end. A slightly more sophisticated explanation for distinguishing words that use /ai/, /oi/ from words that use /ay/, /oy/ is the following (adapted from the orthographic constraints test of Treiman, 1993): dain, dayn; poyt, poit. Digraphs ending with y do not usually occur before consonants. Thus, while the non-words **dain** and **poit** are permissible, the non-words **dayn** and **poyt** are not. Once the rule has been discussed, a brief orthographic constraints segment could be easily introduced, using different pseudowords in order to reinforce it (*see* chapter 10).

Unfortunately, while the students have been helped to distinguish between the use of /ai/ and /ay/ by this orthographic rule, it does not assist them in the case of words like 'aim' and 'game'! So while the spelling component for the words that involve only /a/ and /ay/ can be used in this lesson, you may need to wait for the results of spelling homework, as well as for the orthographic processor to kick in, before you can expect correct spellings for all three forms of the long /a/ sound in creative writing.

The introduction of the soft 'c' can be prefaced by the phonic rule that 'c' is pronounced like /s/ when it is followed by the vowels 'e', 'i' or 'y'. (I have tried hard to think of an appropriate word that could be a mnemonic for these three vowels and have failed! 'Feisty' or 'dicey' may be suitable at a later stage.) However, 'c' retains the /k/ sound when it is followed by the vowels /a/, /o/ or /u/, the vowels in the word 'about'. The same rule also applies to soft and hard 'g'. Although examples where 'e' follows 'c' are plentiful, words containing 'c' followed by 'i' that are easily decoded at this stage are rarer. However, '**cinema**' (with its unfortunate medial /e/ sound) and '**cinch**' do give children practice with multi-syllabic words and recently introduced sounds, respectively. It's quite easy to follow these examples with words where 'c' retains its original sound, for example, '**cot**', '**came**' and '**cute**'. Thus spelling homework could easily include the three different forms of /a/, as well as the two different pronunciation of 'c'.

At this point, both inflectional and derivational morphology instruction are introduced into the word level program. Previously, morphological instruction concentrated on noun and verb plurals, as well as the suffix '**ing**', denoting the continuous present tense of the verb. Now, as the end of the second school year is approaching, I am suggesting that the past tense of the verb and the morpheme '**ed**' be introduced to students.

Once again, phonology will have to yield to morphology as grammatical rules, rather than sound structure, begin to dictate the spelling of the verb.

Teachers could easily commence this segment by asking a student to open a book placed on the desk. Once done, teachers could ask other students what action was taken by the student. With luck, the answer will be, '**Mohammed opened the book.**' Then another child can be told to jump over a book placed on the ground in the classroom. When Mira has done this, teachers could ask other students what action was taken by this energetic pupil and the reply might be, '**Mira jumped over the book.**' This procedure could be repeated with other suitable verbs ('**call**', '**fill**' for /d/ sound ending and '**lick**', '**help**' for /t/ sound ending).

After all the physical exertions are over, and the implications of the verb in the past tense, using the /ed/ marker, have been discussed, the base verbs and the '**ed**' morpheme (perhaps highlighted) can be written on the board. As teachers and students read the words aloud, you may need to explain that sometimes '**ed**' to mark the past tense is pronounced with a /d/ sound and sometimes with a /t/ sound. Pupils can be told to watch for these endings in their reading and that it will take a considerable time before they will be able to transcribe them correctly in their spelling. However, by teaching the rule that underlies the use of the morpheme '**ed**', teachers may be able to reduce children's tendency to overgeneralise '**ed**' endings to other inappropriate parts of speed, for example '**sofed**' (Bryant, 2002, p. 20).

It's now opportune to reintroduce the single consonant /y/, this time at the end of a morpheme, which is now pronounced like the short vowel /i/. In this position, '**y**' often represents a change from one part of speech to another. For example, by acting as a suffix to the noun stem, it transforms the original noun into an adjective. Think of '**rain**', '**rainy**'; '**luck**', '**lucky**'; '**rust**', '**rusty**'. No doubt, children will be able to provide many more examples, which can be used in sentences to delineate the function of different parts of speech. Do be wary, however, of a response that was once offered to me by a most creative young student who produced '**phone**' and '**phoney**'. This could also be a good time to discuss the role adjectives play as a descriptor vis-a-vis the noun, particularly if adjectives are also being discussed in the grammatical analysis section of the listening comprehension lessons.

Although the role of adverbs in sentences may not have yet been discussed in listening and reading comprehension lessons, it could be introduced here as students are exposed to the '**ly**' suffix, with adjectives now forming the base word. They could also be shown words like '**slow**', '**slowly**'; '**faint**', '**faintly**'; '**sad**', '**sadly**', and their function in sentences discussed as before. Prepared sentence strips could be used for practising the new sound as it appears in adjectives and adverbs, as well as in uninflected words such as '**silly**' and '**city**'.

In order to reinforce the distinction between the consonant /y/ and the short vowel /i/, you could make use of another example from the orthographic constraints list adapted from Treiman (1993): **bli, bly**—i does not usually occur at the end of morphemes; y does not usually occur at the beginning or in the middle of morphemes: **yg, ig, shyd, shid.** In addition, as was suggested before, different pseudowords, based on this principle, could be prepared to reinforce the concept.

The penultimate sound/symbol correspondences at the word level introduced to students in the second school year are the 'r' controlled vowels. Pupils can first be told that when 'r' follows a vowel in a word, the pronunciation of that vowel sound is altered e.g. 'girl', 'shirt' and 'first'. To make this new sound/letter combination more accessible, teachers could explain that when a vowel and the consonant 'r' occur together, 'r' changes or controls the sound of the vowel. Children can also be shown how 'r' controls the sounds of the vowels /e/ and /u/ when they precede it in a word. Interestingly, 'r' forces all three vowels to sound alike. Maybe '**burp**' will provide a useful mnemonic. Examples like '**bird**', '**burn**', '**fern**', '**girl**' will clarify the power of 'r' and can be included easily in the spelling activity. Students can then be introduced to 'r' controlled words containing /or/ and /ar/ with appropriate procedures instituted to give children practice in seeing, hearing, feeling and writing the new sounds.

The final phoneme/grapheme translations in this group introduce the single consonants 'q' and 'x'. An appealing way of teaching 'q' is to characterise it as a '**borrower**', as it borrows the familiar sounds /k/, /w/ for its pronunciation and 'u' for its written form.

With the introduction of these two infrequently used consonants and additional commercial reader practice using about six new texts in which students will encounter the rime '**ight**' and the vowel digraphs '**oa**' and '**ou**', we have completed the meaning and word level program in the second school year. For many students, this may only be about three-quarters of the way through the year, as they are ready to leave the 'learning to read' stage and enter the exciting stage of 'reading to learn' (Chall, 1983, p. 26). However, for students at-risk, a more slowly paced program may need to continue until the end of the year to ensure that they become 'unglued from print' (Chall, 1983, p. 26).

Summary

One of the key features of this chapter was the introduction of commercial readers with familiar sound patterns to develop fluency acquisition. In addition, strategies to promote reading comprehension were also taught, modelled first by teachers and then practised by students, working in pairs, to facilitate their progress towards the 'reading to learn' phase of literacy instruction that is the focus of the next section. Furthermore, more complex vowel and consonant digraphs were also presented to the children and practised both in isolation and in connected text, while additional inflectional morphological processes (that is, the past tense of the verb) in learning to read and spell were also introduced.

Conclusion to the *second* year at school

By now we will have almost completed the second year at school. Children will have been taught early listening comprehension strategies for both literary and factual texts to prepare them for 'the reading to learn' phase of literacy instruction. If teachers wish to access specific comprehension lessons, they could also consult Teaching Reading Comprehension: Narrative and Transactional Texts (Dymock & Nicholson, 2001). Now that the focus of literacy instruction is moving away from the acquisition of word recognition to automatic and seamless sight word reading in order to derive meaning from print, we are also ready to move on to the third year at school.

THE *THIRD* YEAR
at school

Once it clicks, decoding sticks: Understanding keeps expanding

15 Listening comprehension

Teaching skills and strategies at the meaning level

This chapter introduces strategies for extending listening comprehension ability in young students in their third year at school. A suggested program for improving the listening comprehension of students with respect to literary texts of the narrative type is then explored, followed by a suggested program for factual and procedural texts.

The third year in school marks the transition from 'learning to read', the focus of the previous two years, to 'reading to learn' (Chall, 1983, p. 26). Thus the emphasis in this third year shifts from instruction at the word level to instruction at the meaning level. The aim is now to extend listening comprehension skills and strategies (during shared reading), and to teach reading comprehension skills and strategies (during guided reading). However, as may be anticipated, word level strategies are not neglected but are now more appropriately situated within the reading comprehension program.

By the third year at school, most students will have reached the full alphabetic phase of reading. They should thus be phonemically aware and have a good grasp of the major grapheme phoneme correspondences, so that they can decode unfamiliar words and add them to the familiar ones already stored as sight words in memory (Ehri & McCormick, 1998, p. 150). They are also beginning to read new words by analogy, and starting to use their morphological knowledge to tackle unfamiliar multi-syllabic words.

Essentially, however, while children will still need some systematic instruction to develop skills and strategies at the word level, it is largely through reading connected text that they will reach the consolidated or mature phase of reading.

Consequently, during their third year at school, strategies at the word level take place in the context of reading connected text pitched at students' independent reading level (about 95 per cent accuracy). The aim, now, is to move them from accurate but slow decoding, to fluent and seamless word recognition, so the focus is on comprehending the material being read. Children will need to read in order to allow their sight vocabularies to grow, and they will need to use prediction strategies to confirm the accuracy of words that they have decoded. Nevertheless, as pointed out cogently by Pressley (1998, p. 219), 'good comprehension is not just word-level processing. It involves abstracting the big ideas in a text'. He goes on to say that simply by reading, it is not at all axiomatic that elementary students will discover the comprehension processes necessary to understand these big ideas (p. 220).

Thus the formal reading program suggested for this third critical year has a slightly different format from the one described in the previous sections. I am now proposing a daily component of listening comprehension instruction for about 15 to 20 minutes (shared reading), followed by a reading comprehension segment that also includes word level skill instruction for about 40 minutes (guided reading), and an independent reading segment for about 15 minutes, programmable at any time of the day. In the listening comprehension program, teachers can develop children's comprehension ability through both general and specific cognitive and meta-cognitive instructional strategies. These strategies can then be actively applied in the reading comprehension program where students, in pairs, read literary and factual texts at an appropriate reading level. However, I would not suggest starting this program with students still struggling with word-level skills. For these children, continuing with the format previously described until they reach the full alphabetic phase of reading would probably be a better option.

Literary texts of the narrative type

Most of the elements of the listening comprehension program in the third year of school are simply an extension of the ones discussed in the second school year and will already be familiar. Starting with literary texts of the narrative type, I suggest that a weekly listening comprehension program could contain the following components:

➡   facilitating comprehension (before the story is read)
➡   teaching comprehension (while the story is read)

➡➡ assessing comprehension (after reading the story): story map; teaching grammatical concepts and punctuation conventions
➡➡ extending comprehension: developing higher-order skills; vocabulary extension
➡➡ features of written text
➡➡ joint constructing of text (based on the story just read).

Facilitating comprehension

This, of course, is familiar territory and needs little explanation. It consists of introducing the text, activating prior knowledge with its attendant caveats, effectively developing vocabulary knowledge and providing the motivation for text reading through student predictions about specific aspects of text structure. However, a word about vocabulary development and providing a purpose for reading is relevant here, as both these strategies are treated in more depth than in the first two school years.

With respect to vocabulary development, the objective is, as always, to go beyond mere definitions and to integrate new words with other knowledge (Nagy, 1994). This enables students to assimilate the new information by relating it to concepts already acquired. While this has been advocated before, vocabulary development will be more formally addressed by the use of Nagy's semantic webbing technique in the section on extending comprehension. However, the key word for further detailed discussion is first highlighted during the facilitation of comprehension component.

In regard to the purpose for listening, there will be variability depending on the type of text that is being read, as the purpose for listening is bound inextricably to text structure. For example, with a literary text of the narrative type, the purpose for listening will focus on the specific element of story structure (characters, problem resolution etc.) that is being targetted for discussion.

Teaching comprehension

During the teaching comprehension component, carried out while the text is being read, the focus will be on teaching:

➡➡ inferential comprehension strategies
➡➡ visual imagery strategies
➡➡ text structure
➡➡ meta-cognitive strategies.

Inferential comprehension strategies

Up to this point in our listening comprehension lessons, the emphasis has been on children's literal comprehension of text, or the ability to derive meaning from an author's words in the written text (Durkin, 1988). However, students must also be made aware that in order to fully understand a passage or text they need to go beyond an author's words by active inference making, so the author's implied meaning is also accessible to them.

Oakhill and Yuill (1996) in their work with students having specific comprehension difficulties identified inference making as a critical strategy for successful comprehension. As some students with phonological problems, others with unspecified learning difficulties, and even some competent decoders may have difficulties making inferences during text reading (Oakhill & Yuill, 1996), it makes sense to systematically teach inferential strategies during listening comprehension instruction.

According to Barnes and Dennis (1996, p. 262), 'different types of inferences serve different discourse functions'. For example, the more frequent 'coherence inferences maintain a coherent storyline by adding unstated but important information to explicit text, thus forming a causal link between knowledge and text that helps infer why an event occurred'. Consequently, general world and domain-specific knowledge is critical to successful inferencing, and must not be overlooked in students with poor comprehension skills.

When teaching students to make inferences as they are reading, teachers should point out that, occasionally, the information is text-based, as in the sentence, 'Two girls and their mother were sitting on the sand', with the reader making the inference that the two girls were sisters. More often, however, inference making is a result of an interaction between students' knowledge base and the text information. For example, when reading 'the boy was making a sandcastle', students must activate their own knowledge of this familiar situation in order to flesh out a scene that has only been implied by the author, such as realising in what season of the year the action is taking place, or what clothes the boy would likely be wearing.

While teaching students to make inferences by using examples, first in isolation, then from actual text reading, teachers could show children how to combine their background knowledge with text information in order to answer inferential questions. Students could also be asked additional related questions about each example discussed, in order to develop their critical thinking skills. The complexity of examples chosen by teachers to develop inferential skills will vary directly with the complexity of the passages that children are reading, and with the different elements of text structure that are being highlighted as students progress through the third year.

The importance of understanding inferences was vividly impressed upon for me during a discussion of the book, *The Transit of Venus* (Hazzard, 1981)—it proved to be a matter of life and death! Those of us in the group who had picked up the inferences realised that the two protagonists were fated to die at the end of the book. Those who had not were convinced the hero and heroine were destined to live happily ever after.

Visual imagery strategies

Another strategy that has been found to be useful with students at-risk of comprehension difficulties is the ability to generate a visual image from a text that is being read. It has been suggested that teaching children to construct mental images as they read enhances their ability to generate inferences, make predictions and remember what has been read (Pressley, 1976; Gambrell, 1981; Sadoski, 1985; Gambrell & Bales, 1986). Indeed, poor comprehenders may derive particular benefit from imagery training because it enables or forces them to integrate information contained in a text in a way that they would not normally do (Oakhill & Yuill, 1995). For example, the use of imagery may provide poor comprehenders with an alternative route for integration of passage material by using an additional but non-phonological strategy. This view would be supported by Paivio's (1971, 1991) dual coding theory, which suggests that verbal and non-verbal information are represented and processed in distinct but interconnected sub-systems (Gambrell & Jaywitz, 1993).

However, research (Guttman et al., 1977) also indicates that children under eight years of age have difficulty self-generating visual images when reading text, possibly because of the cognitive overload of decoding and visualising simultaneously. Consequently, some colleagues and I carried out a study (Center et al., 1999) in which visual imagery training, embedded within a listening comprehension program, was provided to a Year 2 classroom (third school year) with most encouraging results for low comprehenders. Compared with matched controls, these students improved significantly on a curriculum-based text of listening comprehension, a standardised test of reading comprehension and a measure of story event structure. I would consider these results encouraging enough to implement a visual imagery training program in regular third-school year classrooms as another way to ensure that no child gets left behind. Consequently, right at the beginning of the listening comprehension program in the third school year, I suggest that children receive direct instruction in generating visual images. In addition, they could be shown how such images help them to remember text and infer meaning not directly stated in the text, since it appears that when children can discuss and reflect upon the use of a specific strategy (meta-cognition), their performance on that strategy is significantly enhanced (Cunningham, 1990).

Visual imagery training can commence using a stimulus picture, of a farm-yard, for example. Teachers can suggest that pupils look carefully at the picture because they will be asked to describe its contents once it has been removed. (If this proves difficult at first, teachers can model the activity for their students.) Several children can then be asked to describe something about the picture they have painted in their mind. Teachers can tell their students that painting mind pictures helps them remember what is in the picture, so that they can clearly understand the reason for employing this particular process.

Another introductory procedure for modelling visual imagery techniques can be through drawing. For instance, teachers could draw a picture that represents the sentence, 'The girl stood on a chair to get the biscuit jar from the shelf.' Using a talk-aloud procedure, as they are drawing a girl standing on a chair, they can begin by saying, 'I can see a girl. She is standing on a chair. Her arm is stretched out as she is reaching up', and continue in this manner until the picture has been completed. After the teacher has talked her students through the drawing, children can be told that this illustration represents the picture the teacher had in mind when she was reading the sentence, and they can now do the same thing while a story is being read. She could also inform the students that each picture either drawn or painted in the mind will vary from individual to individual.

Teachers can explain that a visual image makes it easier to answer both literal and inferential questions about the sentence. For example, if they were to ask the (literal) question, **'Who is getting the biscuits?'** the answer is in the sentence and readily clarified by the drawing. If, however, they were to ask, **'Is the shelf high up on the wall or low down?'**, the answer is not directly located in the text (inferential question), and the students need to use their own knowledge of the situation and the information from the sentence to arrive at an answer. Once again, the picture facilitates the answer.

Visual imagery instruction proceeds from very simple images, modelled by the teacher, to the self-generation of images by students for short passages and stories. As teachers read stories to the class, they could encourage children to practise visualisation strategies, by reinforcing its facilitation effect. In addition, before story reading, sometimes the author's illustrations could be shown up front, if they complement the text, as a model for students, and sometimes they could be withheld until students have generated their own images.

Text structure and meta-cognition strategies

Apart from direct instruction in learning how to go beyond the printed word, and to use visual imagery strategies, students must become familiar with the structure of a text, as difficulties with text structure have also been identified as a characteristic of poor comprehenders (Oakhill & Yuill, 1996). Furthermore, it has been suggested that low progress comprehenders have a less well-developed story event structure than their more skilled classroom peers, and seem unaware that stories consist of a series of causally related events with a climax and consequent resolution (Cain, 1996). It is therefore important for students to have knowledge of story grammars in literary texts, which include realistic fiction, myths, fables, fairy stories, folk tales, and scientific or historic fiction. Such knowledge appears to help children make sense of what is heard or read, by providing them with a schema which increases their comprehension of and memory for the story (Short & Ryan, 1984).

While touched on in the previous section, text structure is more fully explored in this third year of school when the following elements of a story are specifically targeted (Gersten et al., 2001, p. 289):

➡ characters, including their appearance, feelings and development
➡ setting, including time and place
➡ story problem
➡ a series of actions presented in episodes
➡ internal reactions of the characters
➡ attempts to resolve the problem
➡ resolution of problem.

A suggested approach to teaching story structure for a literary text is to introduce, in some detail, each of the elements listed above, when facilitating listening comprehension, so that children can focus more easily on a specific one in turn, during the interactive text reading. This exposition need not necessarily be drawn from the text that is going to be the subject of the week's work, but may involve a short passage from any book relevant to the text structure element being taught.

During the teaching comprehension component, as the story is being read, the teacher could ask both literal and inferential questions that pertain specifically to the story element that is being currently targetted, as well as emphasise the need for students to implement meta-cognitive strategies to facilitate text comprehension.

Then, during the comprehension assessment component, when a story map is jointly constructed and discussed by teacher and students, the specific story element under discussion could readily be considered in more depth and targetted for grammatical analysis. For example, the function of nouns, noun groups, adjectives and adjectival phrases (revision) could accompany a discussion about characters, whereas the role of adverbs and adverbial phrases (new concepts) might be more relevant to a discussion about story setting.

Finally, during comprehension extension, when teacher and students are involved in the joint construction of a text, the particular story element which has been featured can be highlighted in the writing process, using the relevant grammatical concepts introduced in the assessment of comprehension component.

Thus, while inferential, visual imagery and meta-cognitive strategies are typically activated as the text is being read to the children, text structure reinforcement can take place during every component of the listening comprehension program.

Assessing comprehension

In this component, a story map is jointly constructed after the story is read through which the characters, the setting, the sequence of events, problem and resolution are reviewed by means of literal and inferential questions. The drawing of this map is constrained only by the artistic ability of the teacher. In addition, the particular element, highlighted before and during story reading, can be dealt with in more depth.

The story map can also be used as a springboard for teaching punctuation and grammar. For instance, when the characters and sequence of events are drawn onto the story map, children could be encouraged to role-play the different situations encountered by the characters. Teachers can then show their pupils how the characters in a story correspond to function words in a sentence, represented by nouns (revision), noun groups, adjectives and pronouns (new grammatical concepts). For example, using the story map as a base, the wolf in the well-known fairytale can be represented first by a noun in a sentence, amplified by adjectives and adjectival phrases, and subsequently by the pronoun referent 'he' or 'it' (anaphoric reference), to link the story together in a cohesive tie, without constant repetition of the same noun.

Lexical cohesion (new grammatical concept), where a synonym, or near synonym is used to tie text together, for example, 'animal', 'creature', 'beast', referring back to wolf, is another way to encourage variability of spoken and, particularly, written expression. The actions of the characters become the verbs in the sentence, and the goals of the characters turn into objects or predicates. With increase in text complexity, verb tenses can be explored (the continuous present and simple past have already been discussed), as well as different types of verbs representing actions (material processes) and thoughts (mental processes). When verbs are being discussed, adverbs and adverbial phrases (new grammatical concepts) can be introduced, which become particularly relevant when discussing the story element of setting. Furthermore, at an appropriate time, the use of coordinate conjunctions that join two main clauses and subordinate conjunctions which introduce dependent clauses, can also be pointed out to students and discussed. As grammatical concepts are introduced one by one to the students in this section, they can be practised together by teacher and students in the joint construction of text and, eventually, by children independently when they create their own written texts.

Extending comprehension

This component provides a means for developing higher order comprehension skills, extending vocabulary knowledge and encouraging student-constructed questions. During the development of higher order comprehensions skills, the three elements introduced in the second school year at the meaning level (application, elaboration and evaluation) will be revisited, albeit at a more advanced level.

With respect to application, students will not only be required to use the principles of the story and apply them to their own experiences, but could now be taught to distinguish between reality/fantasy and fact/opinion. For example, if children are being read the story of Prometheus in Greek mythology they may be asked to discuss it in terms of its reality value and whether the story has any parallels with their own experiences.

Elaboration activities, at this level, could involve students providing a different problem for the story, or finding an alternative story resolution as a precursor to the joint construction of written text. This segment will also be relevant when students undertake independent writing during the reading comprehension program.

In terms of evaluation, children might be encouraged to give their opinions about the literary text which could involve them in a critical analysis of character development and problem resolution. In this segment, critical analysis could reflect the story element currently being highlighted.

It must be stressed that these are suggestions, only, for developing higher order comprehension skills and teachers will want to use many others. For instance, another approach that has been found useful is the self-questioning procedure developed by Singer and Donlan (1982). While this procedure refers specifically to reading comprehension (Taylor, 1992), it can easily be adapted for younger students during listening comprehension sessions. For example, teachers can show students how to generate and answer questions themselves about different story elements, as they are listening to text. Accordingly, when children are listening to *Little Red Riding Hood*, teachers could replace modelling general questions such as, **'Who is the main character?'** with more story-specific questions such as **'Is Little Red Riding Hood more about the wolf or the little girl?'** when the story element in focus is characterisation. This is a slightly easier procedure than looking at characters from different viewpoints, which is most appropriate for older elementary/primary students.

Extension of vocabulary knowledge is another activity that can be included in this component. The purpose of extending vocabulary knowledge in students is to increase their rapid lexical access (the prompt and effortless recall of meaning) of as many key words as possible. This is because 'the proportion of difficult words in a text is the single most powerful predictor of text difficulty, and a reader's general vocabulary knowledge is the single best predictor of how well that reader can understand text' (Anderson & Freebody, quoted by Nagy, 1994, p. 1). Nagy (1994) proposes semantic webbing as an effective means of extending vocabulary knowledge. In this activity, words grouped in categories which are semantically linked to the vocabulary word chosen for instruction, are used to lock in the meaning of the new word in a fully conceptual way by defining its interrelationships with other words and by relating it to words already known (Nagy, 1994). Word categories include synonyms, antonyms, associated activities and emotions. Think how these categories might enhance learning the meaning of a new word such as 'coward' that has been encountered in a literary text.

While this approach to vocabulary instruction obviously cannot be applied to every word, many critical words in a listening comprehension text can be targetted and assimilated through the process of semantic webbing. This process blurs the distinction between vocabulary instruction and other pre-reading activities (Nagy, 1994, p. 13), as it ties in with other meaning-based approaches to pre-reading, such as discussion of personal experiences.

The critical word to be taught could be briefly discussed first in the facilitation of comprehension component, while the semantic webbing activity would be conducted in much greater depth as a whole-class procedure when extending comprehension. Programming semantic webbing in this manner also permits teachers and students to include the newly acquired word in the joint construction of text, the final component of the listening comprehension program, as well as in independent writing during the reading comprehension instruction program, discussed in the following chapter.

While extending higher order comprehension skills and developing vocabulary knowledge are critical components of extending comprehension, I have also suggested a segment which encourages student-generated questions. This gives children the opportunity to ask each other questions that may be important to them, but may not have been addressed in the teacher-directed component. There is research (Yopp, 1988) to indicate that when students learn to generate questions from text and are provided with a meta-cognitive routine for answering their own questions, their overall comprehension improves. While it is possible that students will not always address the issues that are central to the story map and to enhancement of listening comprehension, this child-directed activity, important in its own right, also gives the teacher, as facilitator, insights into any mismatch between children's and teacher's perception of key story issues. These data notwithstanding, Duke & Pearson (2002) still advocate that student-generated questions should not be encouraged as a regular routine, but as an activity that is intermittently scheduled into guided and shared reading.

Features of written text

As a prelude to the joint construction of text, it is suggested that teachers re-read a section of the literary text studied during the week, to acquaint students with the beauty and diversity of the English language. For instance, they could select a particularly well-written paragraph or sentence, discuss the way it is constructed, and relate it (if possible) to the grammatical concepts that have already been taught. When appropriate, the differences between spoken and written text could also be highlighted.

The different devices employed by both speakers and writers to convey their message can be clearly shown to students. Speakers are able to use pauses, facial expressions, head and hand gestures. They can vary speaking tone (prosody), repeat information, and respond to a listener's question. Writers, however, are limited to the words on the page and punctuation markers with which to engage their readers.

If teachers wish to expose students to the beauty and diversity of written text, they could select a particularly well-constructed passage or sentence from the current literary text under discussion, and draw students' attention to any exceptional literary features. For example, if they were reading *The Elephant's Child* (Kipling, 1996), teachers might point out the author's use of alliteration, onomatopoeia (new grammatical concepts) and choice of vocabulary demonstrated in the following extract: 'and next he was kind to his poor pulled nose, and wrapped it all up in cool banana leaves, and hung it in the great, grey-green greasy Limpopo to cool.' Kipling is also good value when it comes to showing students the literary effect of word repetition, while in *The Wind in the Willows* (Grahame, 1908), the author makes good use of cohesive ties/personal reference (new grammatical concept) in the following passage:

> After some three-quarters of an hour, the door opened, and the Badger reappeared, solemnly leading by the paw a very limp and dejected Toad. His skin hung baggily about him, his legs wobbled, and his cheeks were furrowed by the tears so plentifully called forth by the Badger's moving discourse.

Joint construction of text

In the final component of the listening comprehension program. teachers and pupils could engage in a joint construction of text, based on the story just read, in a similar fashion to that outlined for the second school year. A joint construction of text session can blend the best elements of whole language and traditional instruction through the integration of reading and writing (Spiegel, 1992), an approach that has also been suggested by Graham and Harris (1994). This is to ensure that an over-reliance on child-directed programs, which may hinder the progress of at-risk learners, is balanced by some explicit strategy instruction. Thus, while the objectives of the writing lesson are clearly defined by the teacher and relate to the story elements and grammatical concepts that have been previously taught, children are encouraged to be risk-takers and to work interactively and cooperatively.

The writing program is based on an environmental mode of writing instruction (Hillocks, 1984) which has been shown to be a highly effective form of written expression instruction by establishing a balance between teacher and child input, rather than being exclusively child-oriented or teacher-directed. First, teachers provide introductory teaching and modelling through clear and specific objectives. Then, students work in small groups, with a high level of peer interaction before they proceed to independent work. (At this early stage of written expression instruction, small groups are used to encourage the production of words or ideas associated with the writing assignment.) Finally, the teacher provides feedback criteria through the editing procedure which the class uses to produce the final draft.

As an example of constructing a joint text, let's assume that the class is well advanced in the listening comprehension program, and has already dealt with the story elements of character and character development, setting, problem and resolution. Having worked through both an immediate problem resolution and a delayed one, following a failed resolution attempt, teachers are about to highlight the story element of multiple problems.

In the introductory session, the teacher will have prepared the groundwork for students' comprehension of additional problems, following discussion of a single problem resolution. The students will also have listened to a text dealing with multiple problems, possibly the story of *Cinderella*. Now, during the joint construction of text session, a topic is selected based on the recently read story, which is discussed first in terms of character and setting. A number of problems can then be established as a whole-class exercise and appropriate vocabulary can also be brainstormed, either in small groups or as a whole class. Finally, children are assigned a problem for discussion and resolution in small groups, which is then presented in turn to the whole class, and incorporated into the joint text construction.

When it comes to the joint editing process, teachers can make children aware of the need to edit a text (developing meta-cognition) by explaining that the reader needs to understand the writer's intent, without the latter's access to the devices readily available to a speaker (a notion already familiar to children). First, the writing can be checked for meaning to ensure that it makes sense, that no words have been left out of sentences and that both words and sentences are in the correct order. Then, individual sentences can be made more interesting and accessible, through the use of previously brainstormed vocabulary and recently taught and revised grammatical concepts and punctuation conventions. Finally, when checking spelling, teachers can ensure the words that are already part of the children's spelling lexicon are spelt correctly in the text. An edited copy of the jointly constructed text can then be used as a model for children's independent writing that will take place in the reading comprehension program.

This listening comprehension instructional program, dealing with literary texts of increasing difficulty, can easily extend over the entire third school year. However, as students move into the primary/upper elementary years of school, teachers can begin to increase the complexity of the components outlined. Students' reading comprehension ability will still not match their listening comprehension skills in the fourth school year, so there are more opportunities for discussing richer textual issues in the context of shared reading.

Thus, instruction on all story elements can be extended, as students are taught to become critical readers and are no longer 'glued to print' (Chall, 1983, p. 26). For example, stories can be examined from characters' different viewpoints, to avoid the misconception that there is only a single meaning in the story (Shanahan & Shanahan, 1997). Consider *The Three Little Pigs* or *Little Red Riding Hood* seen from the perspective of the wolf. While this type of instruction may only help children in their third school year think more about the different characters' actions and personalities (Shanahan & Shanahan, 1997, p. 676), it may promote a better understanding of relationships between characters and their actions in older students.

As texts become more complex, the meaning of a text will vary somewhat from reader to reader. The reader response theory, articulated by Louise Rosenblatt (1978), legitimised the teaching of active and interpretive reading, as the meaning of a text involves a transaction between a reader and the text itself (Pressley, 1998, p. 205). Each reader, with his/her particular perspective and prior knowledge responds to texts in slightly different ways, influenced by both personal and cultural experiences (Pressley, 1998). Moreover, students can be taught to respond to certain text features, such as point of view, tone or mood (Duke & Pearson, 2002, p. 229), and to deconstruct texts in order to read for multiple meanings.

The instruction of grammatical concepts and punctuation conventions will also increase in complexity as students are taught the structure of extended noun and verb groups, clause construction, similes, metaphors and idioms, lexical cohesion, paragraphing and passage coherence (grammar), as well as speech punctuation and the use of apostrophes, colons, semicolons, etc. (punctuation) that correspond to the requirements of state and district guidelines.

Factual texts

If schools are to provide authentic learning experiences that relate to children's daily lives outside the classroom, teaching children how to comprehend factual as well as literary texts must be a feature of any listening comprehension program. The difficulty faced by both teachers (teaching listening comprehension) and students (learning reading comprehension) is the dearth of relevant material that is either interesting, well written or easily read by children in their early years (Durkin, 1988). Thus it takes some extra organisation to find a factual text for instructional purposes that is 'considerate', that is, a text where the subsidiary topics clearly relate to the main topic, and where there is an absence of irrelevant content. For the listening comprehension section, the factual text also needs to be above the children's reading level. Once such a text has been obtained, the same procedures, familiar from the section on literary text instruction, are also adopted for instruction in factual texts. However, there are important differences between the two genres which need to be highlighted, so that the purpose and structure of the factual text are clearly differentiated from those of a literary text.

Differentiating factual texts from literary texts

The purpose of this activity is to make students aware that some texts tell a story, whereas others provide information about a topic. Fortunately, we can use students' prior knowledge of literary texts to underscore the similarities and differences between the two genres.

Teachers could begin by choosing a short literary text or prepared passage which features a dog (or any other appropriate subject) as the main character. Before reading this literary text, teachers could facilitate comprehension in the usual way, by activating prior knowledge, discussing relevant vocabulary and articulating a purpose for listening. In the teaching comprehension component, students could be reminded again to employ visual imagery and relevant meta-cognitive strategies as the book is being read. Finally, when the book reading is over, students could be asked to name the main character(s), discuss the sequence of events, and identify the story's problem and resolution.

Now, teachers could introduce a factual text or passage about dogs, indicating that the text about to be read also concerns dogs but differs from the previous one in that it provides information about dogs, rather than a story about them. As teachers facilitate comprehension of this new text, they could initiate a group discussion about dogs, and stress that the purpose for listening to this new type of book is to see what facts can be learnt about dogs. Then while reading the text during the teaching comprehension component teachers could, once again, tell their students to employ monitoring for meaning strategies and to institute fix-up procedures.

While the use of visual imagery techniques to enhance comprehension has been experimentally validated with respect to literary texts (Oakhill &

Yuill, 1995; Center et al., 1999), this has not yet been done for factual texts as far as I am aware. Thus, while it appears an intuitively useful technique when listening to factual texts, it must be remembered that there is no research data on this particular issue.

As the text is being read, the usual summative, inferential and predictive (if appropriate) questions can be asked, but the emphasis now is on factual information garnered from the passage, rather than the characters or sequence of events. Then, once the text reading is finished, teachers could ask their students to compare the two different passages about dogs. For example, pupils could be asked whether the second text would readily conform to a story map framework, with a sequence of events in temporal order, a problem and a resolution. If and when teachers get the desired class response, they could explain that this is a factual passage which provides information about a topic. In this instance, the topic of the factual text is dogs.

During the assessment of comprehension component, students can be informed that to understand and remember material derived from a factual text, it is no longer appropriate to construct a story map. Instead, the information gathered from a factual text is best summarised through a visual representation. Madden and her colleagues (1996) have used the evocative label, 'a fact trap', for this visual representation. As an example, using the simple passage just read, teachers can write the word 'dogs' on the board. Re-read the first part of the passage and ask the students what information about dogs is contained in it. When they (with luck) reply that dogs are animals, they can be encouraged to offer other examples of animals, until your simple visual representation looks something like this:

(Superordinate category)
ANIMALS

dogs   lions   horses   cats   tigers   pigs

Teachers can then tell pupils that, as the text is being re-read, additional information about dogs will be supplied and it will be added to the appropriate column.

According to Duke and Pearson (2002, p. 217), the research suggests that almost any approach to teaching the structure of a factual text improves both comprehension and recall of key text information. A number of plausible explanations are advanced for this finding. One hypothesis is that systematic attention to the underlying organisation of the text helps students relate ideas to one another in ways that make them more understandable and more memorable. Another explanation is that it is actually content knowledge, not text structure facility, that children acquire when they attend to the structural features of text. In summary, the authors conclude that content knowledge and text structure both represent legitimate curricular goals.

Once teachers feel confident that pupils can distinguish the structure of a factual text from that of a narrative, the factual text comprehension program can follow a similar pattern to the one outlined for literary texts with only slight variations:

➤➤ facilitating comprehension (before the text is read)
➤➤ teaching comprehension strategies (during text reading)
➤➤ assessing comprehension (after the text is read): developing a fact trap
➤➤ extending comprehension: extending vocabulary, teaching grammar and punctuation
➤➤ jointly constructing a factual text.

During the facilitation of text component, only the purpose for listening changes. Students must be made aware that they are now listening to the text in order to obtain information about a particular topic. They can be reminded that our topic was 'dogs' in the text just completed.

While important relevant vocabulary can also be discussed in this component, the semantic web to extend vocabulary is replaced by a 'fact trap', because the emphasis is now on the analysis of related words to determine superordinate and subordinate categories. These categories are a prerequisite to developing the concept of a main idea and supporting details that are the structural features of a factual text and are addressed in the assessment of comprehension component.

When teaching comprehension of a factual text, teachers could acquaint their students with the contents page of a particular book. They could then explain that the contents page organises the information in a book into smaller topics in order to facilitate locating, reading and remembering it. Letting children choose what topic they would like to have read to them from the contents page always appears to be a successful strategy.

Generally the same procedures relevant to a literary text apply when reading a factual text, apart from the caveats just discussed. Thus, the significant features of a factual text can be introduced in the facilitation of text and teaching comprehension components, consolidated in the assessment and extension of comprehension components, and practised in the joint construction of text.

For example, students can be made aware they can learn different things about topics. In general, the principal theme of a topic is called the main idea. A passage about dogs that describes dogs as pets or dogs as hunters will have the same topic, but a different main idea. Teachers could explain to students that figuring out the main idea of a passage, once a topic is established, will help them understand and remember the information read to them (activating meta-cognitive strategies). As soon as students demonstrate little difficulty in identifying the main idea of the topic, they can be shown, when listening to appropriate texts, that the number of main ideas varies directly with the complexity of the text. Teachers can then explain that specific information about the main idea(s) can be classified as supporting details. Thus, a more complex fact trap would look something like this:

TOPIC
Frogs

MAIN IDEAS
appearance   habitat

SUPPORTING DETAILS
bulging eyes   all over the world
sticky tongue   not Antarctica
no tail   mostly in tropics

In the extension of comprehension component, vocabulary development is now determined by the fact trap that is being jointly constructed. Returning to our original topic of dogs, and the fact trap previously drawn, children could brainstorm the topic, contributing as much varied information about dogs as possible, which can be added to the fact trap. This information can then provide a springboard for the introduction of novel words associated with different breeds of canines and their eating habits.

When teaching grammatical concepts in this component, the fact that verbs may have different functions can be revised. In factual texts, children are more likely to encounter action rather than introspective verbs denoting thoughts or feelings, which are more characteristic of literary texts. Examples could be found easily from the factual text under discussion and compared with examples from a literary text. Nouns and noun groups that occur in the fact trap could also be discussed, particularly when the supporting details are added to the diagram.

As was discussed in the extension of comprehension section when dealing with literary texts, student-generated questions could be encouraged as an infrequent but regular routine, scheduled into guided and shared reading of a factual text.

Another activity which can improve students' overall comprehension of factual texts is summarisation (Duke & Pearson, 2002). Since summarisation tends to be a difficult task for many children, I suggest that, in this third year of school, teachers could model a set of step-by-step procedures to develop summaries during the extension of comprehension component. Based on the work of McNeil and Donant (1982) and cited by Duke and Pearson (2002, p. 221), these summaries involve deleting unnecessary and redundant material, composing a single word to replace a list of items and individual parts of an action and, finally, selecting a topic sentence for the text in question. These steps can then be translated into group and individual practice during reading comprehension lessons as the linguistic maturity level of the students increases.

In the same way as was done for the literary text, the fact trap structure (and the modelled summary) can be used as a basis for a joint construction of a factual text, perhaps using another animal as the new topic. As the year progresses, joint factual text writing becomes more complex as children's knowledge of text structure, vocabulary and grammatical concepts (prepositions, coordinate and subordinate conjunctions introducing clauses etc.) increases. For teachers needing assistance in the area of teaching grammatical concepts, I suggest *Writing in the Primary School* (O'Brien, 1992).

As was mentioned in relation to literary texts, the model for factual text instruction, outlined here, can be equally serviceable in the upper elementary/primary years, with appropriate adjustments made for more complex factual text material.

Procedural texts

In the sections on developing children's comprehension with respect to literary and factual texts, the strategies taught in the listening comprehension component (above students' reading level) can be practised in the reading comprehension component (at children's reading level). However, with procedural texts, the range of books consonant with children's interests is more limited.

If teachers can access five texts, that are user-friendly, above the students' reading level and outline a procedure that will interest their pupils, then the listening comprehension program using procedural texts can proceed over a five-day period in the manner already outlined for factual texts. If not, then I suggest another procedure be adopted. For instance, teachers could choose any appropriate book for their class, one that is longer than the one they have been typically using for the other genres and that can be read in instalments over five days e.g. *Winnie the Pooh* (Milne, 1926).

The characters from this book can be used to jointly construct a writing activity each day which is procedural in nature. Just as with literary and factual texts, the structure of a procedural text, containing the following elements, will need to be taught:

➻   a purpose or aim (such as learning how to make a cake)
➻   a list of materials and ingredients
➻   a list of steps in temporal order
➻   an optional conclusion (e.g. remembering to wash up the dishes).

You could begin by reading part of the story and discussing it briefly. Then you could tell your students that not only do we want to know what happens to characters in the story, we, like the book characters, may also be concerned with learning how to carry out certain routines. For instance, Pooh Bear may want to know how to:

➻   clean his teeth properly
➻   bake a cake
➻   learn to ride a bike
➻   tidy his room
➻   find his way home from the forest
➻   go to the vet.

Each one of these ideas could form the basis of a joint construction of a procedural text, using the book characters as protagonists, but deriving the relevant procedural information from the children's own experiences and their new knowledge of procedural text structure. Teachers could also explain that, sometimes, other books or people need to be consulted, if the children do not have the relevant information themselves. In this way, although the text read by the teacher is dissimilar from the simple procedural text being read by the students in the reading comprehension lesson, the teacher/pupil reconstruction provides a model for the procedures in which students are individually involved in the reading comprehension component. Furthermore, reading a longer book over an extended period introduces students to a different type of literary text, giving them greater opportunity to make inferences, refine visual imagery skills, learn about character development and event structure, develop additional grammatical concepts and increase their overall motivation for reading (when the teacher stops reading at a vital point in the story).

A suggested listening comprehension program for the third school year appears below.

Listening comprehension program for the third school year

The first 10 weeks
✓ Getting started: Teaching literal and inferential comprehension
✓ Visual imagery training
✓ Emphasising meta-cognition

The second 10 weeks
✓ Literary texts
  – Identifying characters
  – Identifying main characters
  – Describing main characters
  – Identifying and describing the setting
  – Problem and resolution: immediate and delayed
  – Character development
  – Character changes
  – Multiple problems

The third 10 weeks
✓ Factual texts
  – Topic
  – Identifying the main idea
  – Supporting details

The last 10 weeks
✓ Procedural texts

For variety, the teaching of factual and procedural texts could be interspersed throughout the teaching of literary texts.

Summary

This chapter presented strategies for developing listening comprehension ability in young students in their third year at school. A program for improving the listening comprehension of students with respect to literary texts of the narrative type was explored first, followed by a suggested program for factual and procedural texts. Recounts have been omitted in this section as they straddle both literary and factual genres. The strategies, modelled by the teacher, in the context of shared reading, using books at a level above the reading level of most students, can now be practised by the children themselves in the context of guided reading, addressed in the next chapter.

16 Reading comprehension and creative writing

Teaching skills and strategies at the meaning and word level

This chapter extends skills and strategies in the third school year at both the meaning and word level in the context of a reading comprehension program using literary, factual and procedural texts. Strategies for teaching word analysis, spelling, grammatical concepts, punctuation conventions and creative writing are also presented. Finally, a case is made for the inclusion of an independent reading component.

In the listening comprehension program described in the previous chapter, teachers helped students to develop comprehension strategies through interactive text reading. In this chapter, students are taught to apply these strategies independently, as they read literary, factual and procedural texts themselves, at an appropriate reading level. Instruction at the word level is reinstituted but is again embedded within the guided reading session. In addition, the joint construction of text, described in the previous chapter, is replaced by creative writing on the part of the students, although a high level of teacher input is still provided.

The suggested organisation for the reading comprehension program is for each commercial or trade readers to be studied over a two-week period to allow for busy classroom schedules and the probable need for make-up lessons. During the first week of book reading, it is proposed that students work in partner dyads, and learn early meta-comprehension strategies that they can practise individually and in pairs. For additional reading practice and to establish school–home links, the book read in class can be taken home by partners on alternate nights. I also suggest that spelling instruction, as well as grammatical analysis and punctuation conventions, commence in the first week and continue throughout the creative writing component, which is typically scheduled in the second week.

Literary texts of the narrative type

The components of the reading comprehension program with respect to literary texts consist of:

✓ Facilitating reading comprehension
✓ Teaching reading comprehension
✓ Assessing reading comprehension
✓ Teaching spelling: Theory and practice
✓ Extending grammatical and punctuation knowledge
✓ Creative writing: Theory and practice

Facilitating reading comprehension

In the usual fashion in this component, teachers can introduce the new literary text by activating prior knowledge in order to link the story to their pupils' known experiences. As students should already be familiar with the early elements of story structure, it probably makes sense to focus on the story structure feature that has just been discussed in the listening comprehension component. For example, if the listening comprehension lesson has just dealt with the story element, ' the main character', teachers could prime their pupils to identify the main character and closely follow his/her adventures.

Another effective way to prepare students for reading a story is to get them to make predictions about upcoming events (Slavin et al., 1992). Sharing ideas about what might happen in a story engages students and motivates them to read the selected text. However, as I have stressed before, it is important for students to know why they are making predictions about the story, so they can appreciate the importance of such meta-comprehension procedures.

In addition, in this component, a word reading segment, which replaces extending vocabulary knowledge, a feature of the listening comprehension lessons, is included. The aim of this segment is to show students different ways to identify complex words in the context of text reading and to provide enough reading practice for pupils to develop automaticity with both familiar and unfamiliar words.

Ehri and her colleagues (Ehri, 1998; Ehri & McCormick, 1998) have emphasised that reading comprehension cannot be attained unless students develop rapid lexical access (automaticity) during text reading, which depends on the establishment of accurate orthographic representations in memory. If students attempt to read text that contains too many words with unfamiliar letter strings, then cognitive energy will be diverted away from obtaining meaning from print (the ultimate aim of reading) to identifying the printed word (Fleisher et al., 1979). Consequently, to gain more rapid lexical access to an unfamiliar word and facilitate reading comprehension, children will need to be taught a few outstanding graphophonic correspondences and analogies as well as some additional morphemic, semantic and syntactic strategies with which to identify these new words in context and store their orthographic representations in memory.

Instruction in these strategies, at the word level, is now more appropriately situated in reading comprehension lessons, with novel words occurring in context. Once young readers have learnt to analogise, capitalise on the self-teaching principle and extend their morphemic awareness, rapid lexical access of novel words should develop through repeated print exposure during guided and independent reading sessions.

Since students at the beginning of their third school year are moving from the full-alphabetic phase to the consolidated-alphabetic phase of reading, they are still likely to encounter some novel complex regular, exception and multi-syllabic words in text reading that they will need to decode. (This decoding process resembles a mature English-speaking reader struggling with the complex Russian names of too many new characters in a Tolstoy novel.) Thus, when facilitating reading comprehension, about five to seven key words, which occur in the text selected for reading comprehension, could be targetted for identification. I suggest these words be chosen because they are:

➥ critical for text meaning
➥ contain the few still unfamiliar phoneme grapheme translations and analogies
➥ are suitable for structural analysis.

For example, if the selected text is *Where's my Shoe?* (Edwards, 1987), the following procedure could be adopted for the key words listed below:

shoe   yelled   looked   anywhere   find   behind

Obviously, the word 'shoe' is critical for passage comprehension, and it contains a vowel digraph that may not have been explicitly taught in the second year of school. Teachers could thus write the sentence containing the word 'shoe' on the board and explain that there may be an unfamiliar word (perhaps highlighted for ease of identification) in the sentence. Students could be encouraged to read as far as the highlighted word and use their knowledge of letter/sound correspondences to work it out. If they still find it baffling, then they could read to the end of the sentence to see if semantic and syntactic clues will provide the additional help needed. Once the word has been decoded, students should re-read the whole sentence for comprehension.

With a word such as 'shoe', which is a monosyllabic base word, no structural analysis is possible. Furthermore, as the 'oe' has an irregular pronunciation, there is no point in creating a word bank to generalise that particular grapheme/phoneme correspondence. Still, children could use a word like 'shoe' in a number of different sentences to reinforce its pronunciation and meaning (if appropriate). If, however, a key word does contain a new or difficult grapheme/phoneme correspondence, then teachers could create a word chart to generalise the use of that new phonic pattern (for example, 'know', 'knew', 'knob' for the letter combination 'kn').

With the word 'yelled', there is a little more scope. When children see it highlighted on the board in the sentence taken from the text, they can be asked if they can see a smaller word in it, which they can identify. This then gives teachers an opportunity to discuss the base word 'yell', and the inflectional morpheme 'ed', and to revise the simple past tense of a regular verb. Pupils could also be asked to provide examples of other verbs in the simple past tense, and to use them in sentences to extend morphemic knowledge.

The multi-syllabic word 'anywhere' can be broken up into its constituent parts, and children can be encouraged to use that strategy when they encounter a long unfamiliar word in text reading. Examples of similar multi-syllabic words can be discussed and used by the children in sentences. Sometimes, of course, a multi-syllabic word cannot be broken up into smaller meaningful words but must be read through syllabification as in the word 'e/mer/gence'. Ehri and McCormick (1998, p. 155) suggest this could be done by 'locating vowel nuclei and pronouncing each vowel with its adjacent consonants as a separate syllable. Some syllables, of course, can be read by analogy to familiar words'.

The word 'find' gives teachers another opportunity of discussing verbs which are irregular in the past tense as well as the new 'ind' word family. By soliciting words that rhyme with 'ind' from the students, additional items can be included in the word family chart and practised for fluency. Maybe a precocious pupil will give the example of 'behind', the next targeted word. This can then be discussed in terms of its being a multi-syllabic word, consisting of the prefix 'be', attached to the adjective 'hind' in the sense of 'rear'. Somewhat abstruse, I agree, but fun to explore and to check.

When creating word families analogies, teachers could also encourage students to create simple poems that contain words from the word family. While rhymes can often be handled orally, sometimes, in the case of homophones (words that sound alike but are spelt differently) they should be written on the board so that pupils can appreciate the different spelling ('sheet' and 'meat'). All key words could then be read rapidly for fluency practice and used in different sentences to generalise their use. (Spelling the key words is discussed later.)

Finally, after word analysis is completed, teachers could provide students with a purpose for reading the text. Perhaps the fact that the book is geared to a child's reading level is usually motivation enough (the carrot), but the knowledge that literal and inferential questions will also be asked, particularly about a specified story element, may provide additional incentive (the stick).

As the stories chosen for reading comprehension study typically take two days to read, fluency practice of the familiar portion of the text can be undertaken by students working in pairs before commencing the second half of the book. There will also be another group of key words that should be targetted prior to the second day's reading. Facilitating reading comprehension of the second section of the book could follow the same procedures that have just been outlined for the first part.

Teaching reading comprehension

As the prime purpose of both the listening and reading comprehension program in the third school year is to create skilled independent readers, monitoring for meaning by the students themselves becomes the focus of teaching reading comprehension strategies. These procedures were first informally introduced in the second school year in partner dyads, but are now systematically taught so that the children can use self-questioning techniques themselves during text reading. For example, teachers could suggest to students that to check their text understanding, they should stop at the end of a page and ask themselves if they have understood what they have just read. If the answer is in the affirmative, then they can carry on reading the next page. If it is in the negative, they should go back and re-read the page. A 'monitoring for meaning' wall diagram, using a simplified flow chart, can easily be displayed in the classroom.

Teachers could first scaffold their students' meta-cognitive training by asking several children questions at the end of each page to determine whether comprehension has taken place and helping them institute fix-up strategies in the event of a comprehension breakdown. Then they could release control to their pupils, who can continue monitoring their own comprehension during independent reading. As an additional incentive (or precaution), students can be grouped in pairs for guided reading, so that partners question each other orally at the end of the text reading to assess the effectiveness of the monitoring for meaning procedures. However, it is probably also advisable to check individual pupils' comprehension through a written assessment. In addition, to promote improvement in word recognition, fluency and comprehension, the reading comprehension text could be read by partners alternately several times a day throughout the week, as long as teachers feel that time-on-task is not compromised (Fischer et al., 1980).

Teachers can remind students that for a full understanding of a passage, they will also need to go beyond an author's words at times to infer the author's intent. However, while I recommended visual imagery instruction in the listening comprehension component to promote literary text comprehension, I am not advocating this training procedure at this early stage of reading comprehension. There is evidence (Guttman et al., 1977) that visualisation may place an additional cognitive load on young readers as they master accurate and fluent decoding. It appears that only at about the age of eight can children use self-generated images during reading, and so this may not be an appropriate technique in the early part of the third school year.

There is still one additional strategy suggested in the teaching reading comprehension component, and that is a 'working out words' (WOW) strategy. For example, if students come across a word that is not accessed automatically and has not been previously targeted, they could be encouraged to apply all the word strategies learnt in the facilitation of comprehension section to identify it, rather than to skip over it. A WOW chart, strategically placed in the classroom to facilitate word recognition, could look something like this:

✓ Try to sound the word out, looking for parts of the word you know.
✓ If you still can't work it out, read on to the end of the sentence.
✓ Combine the sounds you know and the meaning of the sentence to read the word.
✓ When you have worked out the word, re-read the sentence to get the meaning.

As Adams (1990, p. 153) advises, once children have deciphered the word, they should return to the beginning of the phrase or sentence and re-read it. This is not only valuable for purposes of reinforcing the orthographic structure and meaning of the word; it is necessary for comprehension of the sentence. More generally, repeated reading of text is found to produce marked improvement in word recognition, fluency and comprehension.

At the end of the first day's reading, the confirmation or denial of predictions that were made during the facilitation of reading component can take place. A group discussion like this can reinforce the utility of making predictions in order to understand the events in the story. It can also develop motivation for further text reading on the following day. The same procedures for teaching reading comprehension could apply when the second part of the story is read.

Assessing reading comprehension

This component of the reading comprehension lessons corresponds to the assessment component of the listening comprehension program, although assessment of reading comprehension actually occurs continually throughout the first week of text reading. As a story in the reading comprehension component typically takes two days for students to complete, assessment can already take place at the end of the first day. For instance, after the first day's reading, students, working in dyads, can monitor each other's reading comprehension by orally answering prepared questions from a worksheet that accompanies each text, allowing each child to be both a teacher and learner. Students could then write the answers independently. An example of a worksheet for reading comprehension can be found in the Appendix.

Once the second half of the story has been completed, students in a whole class group can be taught how to summarise the story they have just read using the elements of literary text structure. Reading comprehension is informally assessed by the teacher throughout the week by means of literal and inferential questions, as well as higher order comprehension questions whenever teachers feel the latter are appropriate. By the end of the week, students can complete the story map in their worksheets together, instead of in a whole class group, in order to organise their story understanding and recall.

Assessment for word level skills takes the form of students reading the key words from the entire text with their partners, and then recording the number of correct and incorrect responses on a prepared sheet. This activity can be repeated throughout the week for accuracy and fluency reinforcement.

Teaching spelling

Towards the end of the first week of the reading comprehension program, spelling instruction is introduced. As children are now in their third school year, when morphology takes precedence over phonology, the arguments put forward by Bryant et al. (1997) are particularly cogent. These authors state (p. 236) that:

> Learning to read and write is as much a syntactic problem as a phonological one. No one is properly literate unless he or she has a reasonable understanding of the orthographic patterns that are based on syntactic regularities. Until a child has learned about the conventional spelling for past verb endings and for interrogatives, and knows how to mark possessives with apostrophes, for example, he or she does not really know how to spell.

Just imagine if most secondary and tertiary students had been systematically taught the rules governing the possessive apostrophe and the contracted 's. I'm thinking particularly of **it's food** and **many orange's**. It would obviate the 'satanic sprinkling of redundant apostrophes', so irritating to purists and teachers and so colourfully described by Lynne Truss (2003, p. i) in her book on punctuation, *Eats, Shoots and Leaves*.

Bryant et al. (1997) also postulate a developmental pattern in children's spelling that progresses from the phonetic spelling of word endings (**kisst**) through to the application of conventional 'ed' endings to regular past verbs (**kissed**). However, there is a developmental hiccup along the way, when children also apply the regular 'ed' verb ending, ungrammatically to nouns, as in 'lofed' for 'loft'. Furthermore, before they reach the mature stage of realising that only regular past tense verbs end in 'ed', they over-regularise this ending to irregular verbs in the past tense like 'heared' and 'sleeped' (p. 237).

On this point, I would like to quote a study carried out by Bryant and two colleagues (Bryant et al., 2000) in order to see how much rule teaching can actually benefit children's spelling. If we go back to inflected endings for regular verbs in the past tense, we will find (of course) some exceptions. Verbs like 'kept' and 'heard' are spelt phonetically, which means that even when children know the rule about inflections for past regular verbs, they then have to learn that there are some exceptions. Do children really follow this principle or do they induce the rule that actually governs these exceptions?

Strangely enough, there is a rule that applies to such miscreant verbs (Bryant, 2002, p. 213). Verbs with stems that sound the same in the present and past (**work/worked**) have the 'ed' spelling; words that sound different in the present and past (**hold/held, sleep/slept**) have phonetically spelt endings. Children, according to Bryant, would have to induce this rule because most teachers (as ignorant of it as I was) would not teach it. The results of his study indicated that children, after exposure to appropriate text, were able to learn imperfectly and probably imprecisely the rule governing the spelling of the two different types of verbs. Thus it appears that children certainly have the ability to discover and learn orthographic rules on their own (Bryant, 2002, p. 214).

Does this make them more effective learners as some theorists would like to believe? I'm not sure I can answer this question but I am convinced that, by teaching appropriate rules, the large number of non-inducers will benefit and the inducers will probably learn the rule more quickly and consistently and go on to make more worthwhile inductions. I am happy to adopt Treiman's advice derived from another context, that children may well learn these grammatical structures more rapidly and more completely if they were pointed out to them (Treiman, 1993, p. 172).

With this advice in mind, there is an unprecedented opportunity to pre-empt children's possible spelling difficulties by teaching some of these rules in a spelling segment which could be included towards the end of the first week in the reading comprehension program. Teachers could begin with the entire key word list from the book just read, in which verbs with regular 'ed' endings should feature quite prominently. They could then initiate a lively discussion about the stem and the ending of these verbs and ask students to provide examples of other verbs which behave in the same way. This concept will probably need continual revision because it is a difficult one for children at this age to master. However, Nunes et al. (1997, p. 162) suggest that students, in general, do not spell the correct 'ed' ending on regular verbs until they are over eight years old, although they find the spelling of irregular verbs in the past tense, such as '**found**', relatively easier. However, it is possible that explicit rule teaching may well facilitate the process.

Unfortunately, teachers will always find an exception word that defies (some but not all) phonological and morphological rules, like the verb '**said**'. As only the pronunciation of the vowel digraph in this word is irregular, children could be taught to pay particular attention to its orthographic features, as well as to its phonological ones.

After a word analysis activity like this, which can make spelling learning a much more exciting procedure than just rote learning, children could write the key words into their spelling books for revision purposes before a spelling assessment. At this stage, it is often a good idea for teachers to give their pupils a correct printed spelling list to counteract the colourful attempts that characterise the spelling of some children in their third year at school. Teachers can also supplement word analysis by adopting a procedure something like this:

- ✓ Teachers dictate a word.
- ✓ Students write the word.
- ✓ Teachers write the word on the board.
- ✓ Students check their spelling.
- ✓ Students correct their spelling.

As teachers regularly revise the spelling words before the suggested spelling assessment, they can also emphasise the phonological, orthographic or morphological features associated with each word that may facilitate learning its spelling.

In addition to the key words targetted for spelling assessment, a personal list for pupils can also be compiled. This could contain a number of recalcitrant words from individual students' creative writing, typically scheduled in the second week of reading comprehension instruction. If the class and personal spelling list is too long for students with literacy difficulties, it could be shortened for them. More able students can check each other's spelling, although this tends to become a very time-consuming procedure, since it will still need considerable teacher input.

To encourage school–home links, a spelling list recording form and the suggested procedure for learning spelling could be sent home for practice before the scheduled spelling assessment towards the end of the second week.

Extending grammatical and punctuation knowledge

I have also suggested programming a segment to extend grammatical knowledge and punctuation conventions into the reading comprehension program so that the concepts introduced in the listening comprehension component can be revised.

When the year is just commencing, it could be appropriate to review nouns and noun groups from the book just completed, if these correspond to the ones just taught in the listening comprehension program. Revising capitalisation, full stops, commas, question and exclamation marks could be useful preparation for the upcoming writing segment in the reading comprehension component.

As the year progresses, the complexity of books read and stories written by the children increases, through constant exposure to new vocabulary, grammatical concepts and punctuation conventions. For example, morphemic suffixes marking comparative and superlative adjectival forms (**neat, neater, neatest**), which widen the scope for children's creative writing, are likely to be taught early in the third year. Some time later, connecting multi-syllabic words to their linguistic roots (Anglo-Saxon '**ful**', '**ship**'; Latin, '**tion**', '**rupt**'; Greek, '**graph**', '**ology**', etc.) permits students to learn chunks of letters that recur in different words (Ehri & McCormick, 1998, p. 154). In addition, introducing inverted commas as speech markers and pointing out semi-colons and colons will develop children's under-standing and use of punctuation conventions. With guidance from teachers, these new grammatical concepts and punctuation conventions can be gradually insinuated into children's creative writing throughout the third school year.

Creative writing: Theory and practice

The theory behind the writing procedure suggested here is the same as the one discussed for the joint construction of text in the listening comprehension component, combining the strengths of both a whole language and traditional approach to writing instruction.

The independent writing activity is designed to enable students to connect their own experiences and ideas to the story just read so they can share them with others. I take the approach, adopted by a number of researchers, for example Spiegel (1992), that writing is a process of communication, not just a set of mechanics to be mastered. To be effective writers there must be a balance between teacher and child input in the instructional process (Hillocks, 1984). In this approach, which is 'non-linear and consists of several overlapping sub-processes' (Englert & Raphael, 1988, p. 513), teachers provide introductory teaching by discussing story elements and appropriate vocabulary, and then give clear and specific objectives about the text to be written. At the same time, teachers can help students to create, manipulate and categorise ideas into a cohesive text (planning).

Following planning, students can commence their first draft with a high level of teacher interaction. During this stage, perhaps using the story just read as a model, ideas are translated into coherent written sentences (drafting). Finally, the students edit their own work and the teacher provides feedback criteria about text cohesion, which the students use to produce the final draft (editing).

In summary therefore, during independent writing, students engage in both task-specific strategies and executive control function (Englert & Raphael, 1988, p. 513). Task-specific strategies include children, as writers, planning, monitoring and editing their work to make their communication accessible to an audience. Thus, as writers, they must be aware of different text structures to know what information to include and what grammatical devices and punctuation conventions to employ in order to facilitate and enhance comprehension of the written material. In addition, young writers must exercise control over the writing process so they can monitor and correct inconsistencies, ultimately viewing the completed text as though they were readers.

If we now return to the actual reading comprehension program, the theory outlined above could be applied to the first writing activity. By this time, the children should have completed reading *Where's my Shoe?*, the suggested first story and a possible model for the first piece of creative writing. Once an associated topic has been established, teachers can proceed through the planning stage by deciding on the structure of the text. Ideas can then be brainstormed to create characters, determine the sequence of events and arrive at a suitable conclusion. As appropriate vocabulary is discussed, key words can be written on the board so that children can access them during story writing. Finally, writing a rough draft can conclude the first day's independent writing.

Before continuing with the first draft on the following day, teachers could review grammatical concepts and punctuation conventions, as well as taking children through the class spelling list once more, in preparation for both writing and the spelling assessment. The last three days of the week can be reserved for redrafting, revising, editing and publishing the first story.

When the children are ready for the editing process, they can use any number of strategies. For example, they could re-read their writing to see if their ideas are presented clearly, perhaps consulting a class-editing sheet to facilitate their efforts (*see* Appendix for suggestions on 'A Jointly Constructed Text Editing Chart'). They could also enlist their partner's assistance for what, we hope, is some constructive feedback. Teachers, of course, have many options when responding to their pupils' editing, for example, by:

- giving positive feedback
- volunteering one or two ideas for improving content or expression
- encouraging invented spelling for words not in students' spelling repertoire

➡➡   offering suggestions for the inclusion of appropriate grammatical concepts.

At this early stage of writing, most students will probably not be able to punctuate their work, as they may still be unsure about the structure of a sentence. However, during the editing process, teachers could read the story to pupils individually, pausing at the end of each sentence and instructing them where full stops and capitalisation should be inserted.

As a congenial conclusion to story writing, several children's stories could be published, distributed, displayed or put into a class magazine. Several other students could read their stories to the class with the remaining students providing an interactive audience. In addition, to complement the segment on the beauty and diversity of language in the listening comprehension program, children could be asked to read out their favourite part of the guided reading text at any appropriate time. Pupils could also take home the finished text and discuss their favourite section with caregivers to promote links between school and home.

Factual and procedural texts

The same procedures of facilitating, teaching and assessing reading comprehension, and teaching spelling, just discussed for literary texts, could also be used for factual texts. However, some important differences between the two genres in the instructional procedures should be mentioned. Instead of constructing a story map in the assessment segment, as suggested for literary texts, students are now encouraged to construct a fact trap, to familiarise them with the structure of a factual text. From this visual representation, they can identify the topic, the main idea and the supporting details that are the features of a factual text.

In addition, while extending comprehension to develop vocabulary knowledge was not a component of literary texts in the reading comprehension program, since most of the words read were in the children's spoken vocabulary, this segment reappears when dealing with factual texts. The reason for this re-emergence is that new vocabulary encountered in the main idea and supporting details of a factual text can be taught through words in groups based on related meanings or relationship to a common topic (Nagy, 1994, p. 14). If, for instance, the factual text being read during the reading comprehension lesson is about transport (topic), then the main ideas of the topic might centre on different types of transport, such as cars, trains, ships or even legs. Each of these sub-topics can be further subdivided, with an almost infinite variety of related words that can be created by teachers and students. Just discussing the word 'car' can produce related words such as '**traffic**', '**diesel**', '**dashboard**' etc. When teachers extend children's vocabulary in this manner, they enable students to conceive and express new ideas. After all, as Nagy indicates (1994, p. 21), 'the primary goal of vocabulary instruction, at least after the initial stages of reading, is not to teach students new labels, but to teach them new concepts'.

Once again, as suggested for a literary text, the second week devoted to reading a factual text could also include an independent writing component, using the structure of the text just read as a model in the early stages. As the year progresses, more complex vocabulary, grammatical concepts and punctuation conventions can be incorporated into independent writing as they are covered in the listening comprehension program. The same techniques of facilitating, teaching and assessing comprehension (using procedural text structure) as well as instruction in word analysis, spelling, grammatical concepts and punctuation conventions are also employed for the procedural texts in the reading comprehension program. However, when reading procedural texts, students, working in pairs, could read the procedure, discuss and carry it out with their partners and, finally, write it up individually.

Independent reading

In addition to the listening and reading comprehension program, which could take about 20 and 40 minutes, respectively, I strongly suggest that about 15 minutes be devoted to independent reading on the part of the students at any suitable time during the day. Children could be matched to text (about 95 per cent level of accuracy), and if volunteers or peer tutors are available, make use of them as often as possible. Remember, too, that children's reading accuracy, fluency and comprehension can also be informally assessed during independent reading for benchmarking purposes, as teachers listen to pupils reading individually. Another advantage of children's independent reading is the opportunity it presents for individual students to share their evaluation of a recently completed book with the rest of the class.

A suggested outline of a two-week program for a literary text, which can easily be modified for a factual or procedural text, appears opposite:

Suggested reading comprehension program for the third school year

Day 1
✓ Introducing a book (pre-reading)
  – background knowledge and prediction
  – word reading
  – purpose for reading
✓ Reading the book
  – monitoring for meaning, using fix-up strategies and silent reading
  – answering teacher's questions
✓ Reading round-off for part 1 of book
  – Asking higher order questions, confirming predictions

Day 2
✓ Re-reading part 1 of book
  – rapid reading review
  – partner reading
  – writing the answers to story questions
✓ Reading round-off for part 1 of book
  – reviewing the story (oral)
✓ Introducing part 2 of book
  – predicting part 2
  – word reading
  – purpose for reading
✓ Reading part 2 of book
  – monitoring for meaning and silent reading
✓ Reading round-off
  – confirming predictions

Day 3
✓ Reading the whole book
  – rapid reading review
  – partner reading
  – answering teacher's questions (oral)
  – writing the answer
✓ Reading assessment
  – reading key words with partner
✓ Reading round-off
  – reviewing the story
  – time to share
  – reading at home

Day 4
- ✓ Re-reading the book
- ✓ Reading recall
  - story map
  - story quiz
  - reading at home
- ✓ Assessment
  - reading key words with partner
- ✓ Spelling
  - class spelling list
  - teaching spelling

Day 5
- ✓ Re-reading the book
  - rapid reading review
  - partner reading
- ✓ Reading assessment
  - reading key words with partner
- ✓ Spelling
  - teacher reviews class spelling list
  - spelling at home
- ✓ Extending grammatical knowledge
- ✓ Teaching punctuation conventions

Day 6
- ✓ Spelling
  - teacher reviews class spelling list
  - spelling at home
- ✓ Creative writing
  - planning and drafting
  - topic
  - class conference
  - first draft

Day 7
- ✓ Extending grammatical knowledge
- ✓ Teaching punctuation conventions
- ✓ Spelling
  - teacher reviews class spelling list
  - spelling at home
- ✓ Creative writing
  - writing the story

Days 8–10

✓ Spelling assessment

✓ Spelling
  - personal spelling list

✓ Creative writing
  - redrafting, revising, editing and publishing
  - author's editing
  - partner's response
  - author's response
  - publication
  - celebration of writing

Summary

This chapter presented strategies for extending skills at both the meaning and word level for young students in their third year at school. A two-week program for improving the reading comprehension of students with respect to literary texts of the narrative type, factual and procedural texts was outlined first. Teaching word analysis, spelling, grammatical concepts, punctuation conventions and creative writing also became a feature of the reading comprehension program. In addition, a case was made for the inclusion of independent reading in the formal literacy program in the third school year.

ASSESSMENT
and *intervention*

Assessing prevents guessing:

Assistance prevents

resistance

17 Assessment and intervention

This chapter presents suggested assessment and intervention procedures for both meaning and word level skills in the first three years of school. A case study of a reluctant reader in his third school year is also discussed to highlight assessment and intervention techniques.

Skill and strategy attainment, both at the meaning and word level, needs to be assessed regularly to inform teachers about the success of their instruction, and to identify those students who need either intervention or extension. Thus, suggested assessments and intervention procedures from the beginning of the school year, as well as for the first, second and third school years are presented in this chapter.

Assessment and intervention for the beginning of the first school year

Meaning level assessment/intervention

I have suggested using individual retell forms from the end of the third week of interactive text reading in the first year to identify any children who may be having trouble with narrative text structure. (*See* panel on page 223 for an example of one of these for the book *A Friend for Little Bear*.) Intervention for meaning-level skills for any low-progress children could take place, in a small group, a couple of times a week for a short period of time. Such small-group intervention should be instituted at different times of the day so that children already at-risk are not taken out of the same class lesson.

Ideally, the first intervention session, after all the children have been assessed, could recap the four essential elements of narrative text using the first story studied to consolidate concepts learned. These four elements are:

➤ story introduction
➤ story reading
➤ story review
➤ story retelling.

If possible, the second intervention session could precede the second weekly story telling (to prepare students for the upcoming text). Individual retells could be administered at the end of each week of intervention, so the teacher can decide when one student should be discontinued from intervention, and another included.

The reasons for children failing to develop listening comprehension strategies are many and complex, and this simple intervention program may seem to be minimising such complexity. For example, if a child comes from a non-English background (NESB), it is of course possible that she cannot as yet access the language of the text and is having understandable difficulty with retelling the story.

In practice, however, we have found that small group story retelling intervention works even better for many of these children than does decontextualised withdrawal with a specialist teacher. This is possibly because, in this type of intervention, children with limited English language skills are receiving exposure to both language and comprehension strategies which parallel the classroom program (*see* chapter 18 for more information on this issue).

If, however, you are faced with a native English speaker having retelling problems, which is suggestive of a slow learner or a child with poor listening comprehension, more intensive practice with narrative text structure, that is, setting, characters, problem, resolution, is usually the best option (*see* also chapters 11 and 15 for more strategies on teaching listening comprehension).

Word-level assessment/intervention

Assessment for word-level skills, at the beginning of the school year, could probably take place at the end of each new group of lexical awareness concepts taught (i.e. the concept of a word, identical words, long and short words). To specifically test phonological awareness skills, teachers could use a standardised test such as the Phonological Abilities Test (Muter et al.,

Individual retell example

A FRIEND FOR LITTLE BEAR

Name _____   Name _____

A little while ago your teacher read you a story called A Friend for Little Bear.

1. Where was Little Bear?   *On a desert Island.*

2. Did he have anyone to play with?   *No.*

3. What did he play with when he was alone?
   A stick.   He drew pictures in the sand.

4. What came floating by after the stick?
   A bottle, then a wooden horse.

5. How did they play together?   *They played chasings, hidings, drew pictures and filled the bottle.*

6. What else did Little Bear want?   *A cup.*

7. When he got the cup what happened to the rocking horse?   *He fell into the sea and floated away.*

8. What did Little Bear do when he realised the horse had gone?   *He realised he needed a friend, not a cup and cried.*

9. What happened in the end?   *He pulled the horse out of the sea again and they danced.*

10. What was your favourite part of the story?

1997), a criterion-referenced test such as the Phonological Awareness Assessment Instrument (Adams et al., 1998) or easily devise an assessment of their own using objects and pictures that are different from those employed in teaching routines.

Small group intervention sessions for word-level skills could also take place two to three times a week for a short period of time. These sessions could provide more opportunities for at-risk students to practise lexical and phonological awareness concepts. Different teaching procedures involving games like Bingo picture cards, or any appropriate teacher-created activities to reinforce the concepts, could also be used. In addition, task analysis (*see* Glossary) of the teaching activities to make them simpler for difficult-to-teach students can be employed. If, however, a large number of students in the classroom are having trouble with the concepts taught, you may need to pace whole-class lessons a little more slowly.

Assessment and intervention for the first year of formal schooling

Meaning-level assessment/intervention

As the interactive text reading program continues from school entry throughout the first year of school, the assessment procedures are the same as the ones just outlined. However, as teachers may be introducing different text types into the listening comprehension program after the first few months, individual retell forms will need to reflect the different structure of such texts. For example, for a factual/information text, children will need to be asked relevant questions about the main topic and supporting details rather than about the characters, setting, problem and resolution that are features of a narrative text. Remember that a temporal sequence, vital for recalling a narrative with event structure, is not necessarily appropriate in a factual text. However, knowledge of a temporal sequence might be completely appropriate when retelling a procedural text dealing with preparations for planning a birthday party, for example. It is obviously less relevant when the routine involves setting the table.

In dealing with intervention for meaning-level skills, a similar format to the one outlined for intervention at the beginning of the school year could be instituted. However, as it is extremely important to ensure that word-level skills intervention takes place regularly, one of the sessions suggested for interactive text reading assistance might need to be sacrificed.

Word-level assessment/intervention

Assessment at the word level in the first school year could take place during the first review week, typically scheduled after the introduction of about four new sound/symbol correspondences. This is primarily to organise class restructuring for the word-level program. However, regular assessment should take place in subsequent review sessions to ensure student regrouping occurs at reasonable intervals, so children who are either progressing quickly or who are struggling are not left in inappropriate classes.

At this early stage, assessment takes the form of reading words in connected text in order to obtain an accuracy and fluency score for the children. I have suggested a curriculum-based measure (Deno et al., 1982) for this purpose, rather than a standardised test, because the former is sensitive to small changes in achievement, is easy for teachers to administer and displays high correlations with comprehension scores derived from standardised tests (Davidson, 2001).

As an example, the first assessment in the first review week takes the form of an unfamiliar short passage based on the characters and words that children have encountered in their 'little readers' (or any appropriate text) up to this point. A running record of their reading is taken and an accuracy score is computed for each child. Accuracy scores should reach 95 to 100 per cent since text comprehension would be jeopardised if the score were any lower. However, since all the words in the assessment passage either contain sounds that have already been taught or are familiar exception words, these accuracy scores should be anticipated. If it appears that children are having difficulty with word identification, a reputable word attack skills test, such as the Woodcock Reading Mastery Series (Woodcock, 1987) or the Macquarie University Word Attack Skills Test (1983), could be used to pinpoint the exact source of sound/symbol correspondence difficulty.

Fluency scores are generated by counting the number of words read in a minute and norms for fluency are generally considered to be 30 to 70 words per minute (wpm) (first school year), 60 to 90 wpm (second school year) and 80 to 120 wpm (third school year). In practice, fluency scores would probably only be computed after the first or second assessment.

If, for example, a student obtained an accuracy score below 90 per cent for an early reading passage, fluency and thus text comprehension would be seriously compromised. Such a child would need to be re-taught the phoneme/grapheme correspondence of sounds already covered, either in small group or in one-on-one intervention. If, however, a child achieved 100 per cent accuracy, but fluency levels were about 10 words per minute, such a student would need more practice reading texts containing taught sounds to increase his/her speed of reading (*see* section on fluency building discussed later in this chapter).

The second phase of the assessment examines the spelling of taught decodable words that are presented to students within a sentence. With children whose motor skills are still developing at this early stage, letter blocks can be used. As spelling reveals a student's explicit knowledge of the alphabetic system, I would also suggest using a developmental spelling marking procedure for this assessment (see Tangel & Blachman, 1992, p. 259).

For students who have been assessed as having minor difficulties in either reading or spelling perhaps through illness or school transfer, peer or volunteer tutoring could be organised. For students who have been found to have major problems, small group intervention (a class of about six to eight students) could be arranged, although an individual program, based on the classroom program, would be an excellent option if personnel were available.

As struggling students proceed into their second year of school, individual tutoring is, generally, the intervention of choice although, of course, it is the most costly (*see* chapter 18 for more information on this issue). If, however, the whole class is having difficulties with reading/spelling specific words or with other concepts taught, this would indicate inappropriate pacing on the part of the teacher and would suggest that whole class re-teaching needs to take place.

Assessment and intervention for the second year of formal schooling

Meaning-level assessment/intervention

In the second school year, as teachers introduce different text types into the interactive reading program, such as factual description/information reports and procedural texts, individual retell forms will need to reflect the different structure of these texts from literary ones (see meaning-level assessment for the first school year). In dealing with intervention for meaning-level skills, a similar format to the one outlined for first year intervention could be instituted. Assessment of reading comprehension skills with the introduction of more complex 'little readers' is also included in the regular assessment.

Word-level assessment/intervention

In the second school year, assessment still takes the form of reading words in connected text in order to obtain an accuracy and fluency score for the children, as has already been discussed for first year word-level assessment. At this stage also, a standardised test like the Test of Word Reading Efficiency, (TOWRE) (Torgesen et al., 1999), appropriate word reading sub-tests from the Woodcock Reading Mastery Series (Woodcock, 1987), or a criterion-referenced test like the Macquarie University Word Attack Skills Test (1983) should also be employed to see whether children can read real words in isolation as well as pseudo (non) words in order to assess decoding skills and identify possible sources of sound/symbol correspondence difficulty.

Children are also assessed on their spelling progress, although the use of letter blocks will probably have been discontinued for most children in their second school year. Assessment is first restricted to testing familiar decodable words, but the range of spelling words can be extended with the introduction of morphology instruction. Once again, a developmental spelling rating scale should be used (Tangel & Blachman, 1992, p. 259), rather than a simple correct/incorrect procedure, to determine students' phonological and morphological maturity.

Small-group placement was suggested for children having major difficulty with word-level concepts in their first school year (mainly because of lack of trained personnel available for kindergarten children) and still remains an option in the second year of school. However, individual tutoring has been generally found to be the most effective form of intervention for children at-risk of difficulties in learning to read (Wasik & Slavin, 1993; Juel, 1998; *see also* chapter 18).

Research undertaken by my colleagues and me (Center et al., 2001) indicates that if Reading Recovery operates in a school, such intervention works even better with a structured early program as described here, than it appears to do with a program which has a less explicit focus. However, an individual intervention program which parallels the class program and is carried out by a regular class teacher familiar with the program as often as possible during the week, has also been shown to be cost-effective in the U.S. (Slavin et al., 1992).

An example of a reading words in context assessment is presented on the following page.

Reading words in context

Assessment for the first and second school year (based on 'little readers').

Assessor: 'Today, I would like you to read me this story which is about Russ and his pet Flash.'

> Russ and Flash are on top of a hill. They can see a big fat duck. The duck likes to sit in the hot sun and pick at the rubbish from the bin.
> Flash sees the duck and runs to it.
> 'Yap! Yap!' went Flash.
> 'Hush,' said Russ. 'Come back to me.'
> The duck sees Flash, jumps into the pond and swims to the rocks.
> 'Come back here, Flash! You are a bad pup! Do not rush at the duck.'

Number of words read correctly in one minute . . .
Number of words read correctly . . .
Number of words in passage (80).
Accuracy score . . .
Fluency score . . .
Comments

Spelling

Assessment for the first and second school year

All words to be used in a sentence before the assessment

run	yap
shop	dish
jam	

Assessment and intervention for the third year of formal schooling

Meaning and word-level assessment/intervention

Students could be continually assessed informally during the story quiz, word reading and spelling sections of their worksheets in their third year of school. In addition, formative evaluation of accuracy, fluency and reading comprehension by teachers could also take place during the daily 15-minute independent reading sessions. However, formal individual assessments of students' reading and listening comprehension of literary, factual and procedural texts, as well as word-level skills, are also recommended approximately every term or ten weeks.

Assessments are used primarily to see whether instruction has been successful for the whole class. If the majority of the class is having difficulty with specific words or strategies, some whole class re-teaching may need to take place. It also allows the teacher to indentify those individual students who may need either assistance or extension. A formal assessment may take several hours of class time to administer, but I believe it is time well spent. However, to accelerate the procedure, assistance from either a support teacher or teaching assistant is strongly recommended.

The first assessment, dealing with both listening and reading comprehension of literary texts, as well as word-level skills, could contain the following components:

➡ listening comprehension assessment of an unfamiliar passage at a Year 2 level using an individual retell procedure, which could include recall, inferential and higher order comprehension questions (here, an additional pair of hands is invaluable)

➡ individual oral reading assessment of both accuracy and fluency using a one-minute sample taken from two familiar literary texts (follow up with a Word Attack Skills Test if necessary)

➡ whole-class assessment of some of the spelling words taught in the first ten weeks

➡ whole-class assessments of some of the grammatical concepts taught in the first ten weeks

➡ whole-class assessment of some of the punctuation conventions taught in the first ten weeks

➡ individual assessment of comprehension strategies to use before, during and after text reading (story map knowledge), using an unfamiliar literary text at the students' independent reading level.

The second assessment could contain the following components:

➡ individual oral reading assessment of both accuracy and fluency using a one-minute sample taken from two familiar factual texts (follow up with a Word Attack Skills Test if necessary)

➤ whole-class assessment of some of the spelling words taught in the second ten weeks
➤ whole-class assessments of some of the grammatical concepts covered in the second ten weeks
➤ whole-class assessments of some of the punctuation conventions covered in the second ten weeks
➤ individual assessment of comprehension strategies to use before, during and after text reading (fact trap knowledge), using an unfamiliar factual text at the students' independent reading level
➤ individual writing of an unfamiliar procedure.

The third assessment could focus on literary texts and writing knowledge. Teachers could use a similar assessment to the first one outlined in order to assess text comprehension (using a more complex literary text), as well as oral reading and spelling. In this assessment, students could also be asked to produce a written literary passage on a set topic, completed over a number of days, to allow for drafting and editing. Story map knowledge, grammatical concepts, punctuation conventions and written expression can be assessed through these individual scripts.

The fourth assessment could focus on reading comprehension ability (using a literary and factual text at an appropriate reading level), and on spelling knowledge. Students could again be asked to produce a written factual passage, so that text structure, grammatical concepts, punctuation convention and written expression can be assessed. In addition, this assessment could also focus on word-level activities to test students' knowledge of base words, comparatives and superlatives, and homonyms/antonyms covered in the lessons to date. Standardised and criterion-referenced tests suggested in word-level skills for the second school year should also be employed in this assessment to test students' ability to read real words in isolation as well as pseudowords.

Assessment and intervention: An individual case study

Recently, I received an interesting query from the teacher of a very articulate boy (whom I shall call Max) in Year 2 (the third school year). As far as the teacher was concerned, Max exhibited no reading problems and was in fact in one of the higher class reading groups. However his mother, a highly trained professional, complained that her son, while an avid listener, refused to read on his own. She asked the teacher for assistance and the teacher sought my advice. We talked the problem through and came up with a number of hypotheses. The teacher, convinced of Max's reading ability, suggested that the books provided in the classroom and at home did not interest him enough. She had come across many boys for whom reading was an anathema, and suggested that his mother look for texts that matched his interests. While agreeing that this was a very plausible explanation, I still felt that we could investigate further, particularly as the mother had also reported that Max's father had a history of reading difficulties. The teacher was very willing to probe a little deeper but was somewhat at a loss, since Max was able to read all the books in the early Year 2 series reading program. Surely the mother was being overanxious?

I suggested a course of action to her that she could pursue while she listened to children read individually. She could first choose a graded Year 2 passage that Max had not seen before, without any illustrations. She would then ask him to read the passage silently, telling him that there would be questions on the text when he had completed it. If he had no difficulty answering her questions (about 75 per cent correct, graded for an early Year 2 level), then her first hypothesis would be validated. Max could obviously read well enough, but didn't want to do it. More motivational books would need to be found. However, if he did have difficulty answering the questions, then there were four possibilities: Max might have a comprehension problem, a fluency problem, a word recognition problem, or any combination of these three problems.

To eliminate the first possibility, his teacher would read the same passage to him, and ask him the same questions. If he exhibited the same difficulties with the questions when the passage was read to him, then he certainly did have a comprehension problem. Of course, this would not exclude a fluency or word recognition problem as well which should also be checked. To counteract an identified comprehension difficulty, an intensive tutorial program (one-on-one) could be instituted, based on the classroom comprehension program (*see* chapters 11 and 15), after a comprehension assessment had revealed Max's specific areas of difficulty. However, should there be a discrepancy between his reading and listening comprehension, revealed if Max exhibited no difficulty answering questions when the passage was read to him (as we would expect), then the problem was probably located in the word recognition rather than the comprehension area (reading = decoding x comprehension). Thus Max could have either a fluency difficulty (slow but accurate decoding) or an accuracy/word recognition problem (difficulty with some phoneme/grapheme translations, suggesting reading development at a partial alphabetic stage).

The investigative process commenced, and the teacher found that Max could answer comprehension questions correctly, but only when the passage was read to him, not when he was obliged to read the text himself. Thus, more probing was necessary to pinpoint the exact source of his reading difficulty, since listening comprehension difficulties had been eliminated.

Assessment was thus continued, with Max's teacher timing his reading on a grade appropriate passage. She found that his fluency was indeed compromised (30 words per minute instead of the acceptable 60 to 90 wpm for early Year 2). This result could entail two possibilities, the first being that Max was a slow but accurate decoder who needed fluency training in order to achieve speedy and fluent word retrieval, or that, in fact, Max actually had basic difficulties in the area of word recognition.

According to Kuhn and Stahl (2000), if indeed Max were found to have a fluency problem, then he would be an excellent candidate for fluency training, since fluency intervention works best for children 'who have some entering knowledge about words' (p. 23). They recommend remedial approaches that involve the re-reading of text, either through assisted reading or repeated reading, although there does not seem to be a difference in effectiveness between repeated readings of a small number of texts and non-repeated readings of a larger number. While a more recent study (Kuhn et al., 2004/2005) appears to give non-repeated readings a slight edge, particularly for higher performing children in their third school year, the critical issue appears to be the amount of time spent reading connected text, and the use of classroom practices that scaffold reading texts aloud. However, Kuhn's latest study (Kuhn, 2004, p. 343), targetting struggling students, seems to suggest that a repeated-reading strategy may be more effective for students who need to improve the mechanics of reading (automaticity or prosody). A wide-reading approach, on the other hand, appears to benefit those struggling readers who need to improve their comprehension as well as word recognition and expression.

In addition, research has not yet established the level of connected text to which students should be exposed. While some investigators, quoted by Kuhn and Stahl (2000, p. 25), maintain that reading easy text (95 per cent difficulty level) improves fluency, others have argued equally convincingly for text pitched at children's frustrational level, provided there is strong support. More research needs to be directed to this issue, and Max's teacher would have to experiment with both easy and difficult text material.

Max's primary difficulty turned out not to be his dysfluent decoding. What his teacher discovered, when she presented him with an appropriate unseen passage to read, was that the cause of Max's slow reading was his inability to fully sound out long or unfamiliar content words that carry the text message, although he was able to easily read common function words. In other words, Max's basic difficulty was with word recognition, not fluency. Thus, in class, through repeated readings and contextual assistance, Max had learnt to distinguish a fair number of words in his readers based on incomplete representations of sight words (e.g. the first and last letter of the word), but this semi-logographic system of word recognition broke down in the presence of novel words when he was presented with an unfamiliar passage.

This diagnosis was confirmed when the teacher took some of the more complex and less familiar words out of Max's class reader and presented them to him in isolation. This proved a very difficult task for him and without the help of context, position in text and illustrations he made many errors. Max should also have been given a test of pseudo (non) words to read, because such a test precludes a child from reading well-learned words from memory (Jenkins et al., 2004), since no pseudoword has ever been encountered previously in text reading.

In summary, Max's problem was that he was only at a partial alphabetic phase of reading development. According to Ehri and McCormick (1998, p. 140) this is characterised by having only a rudimentary working knowledge of the alphabetic system, particularly with respect to vowels. Max's high intelligence, his verbal skills and his ability to store a large number of familiar whole words in memory, without completely knowing how the graphemes symbolised the individual phonemes, had enabled him to slip through the net, at least until Year 2.

Unfortunately, this is not an atypical story. Recently published American data (Shaywitz & Shaywitz, 2002) indicates that 37 per cent of fourth graders are not able to read basic materials proficiently, and that struggling children are often not recognised until they are in the third grade or even later. Furthermore, the research suggests that if they are not caught early, for example, by the age of nine, they will continue to have problems until adulthood (p. 520). One should never underestimate the insight of parents, nor the power of assessment.

Max would now need the administration of any appropriate word attack skills test to locate his specific difficulties in letter/sound translations in order to implement a tutorial program. This program should consist of explicit instruction in those letter/sound correspondences that have eluded Max, possibly short vowels and consonant clusters (with emphasis on the more difficult second sound in the cluster), and a word-building program

(McCandliss et al., 2003). These novel sound/symbol combinations should then be practised in connected text, a procedure suggested by Ehri and McCormick (1998) and a core component of the second school year program. These authors also suggest that partial-alphabetic readers engage in writing activities, so that invented spelling of unfamiliar words is attempted (p. 147). This gives children like Max the opportunity to fully analyse words in order to spell them and, at the same time, gives teachers the opportunity to intervene and scaffold their pupils' learning. In addition, during writing activities teachers can make students aware that 'each word has a unique, prescribed sequence of letters that constitutes the word's identity and that distinguishes it from similarly spelled words' (p. 148). It was ignorance of this principle that was directly implicated in Max's reading difficulty.

Ehri and McCormick (1998, p. 148) describe how Gaskins and colleagues at Benchmark School employ a multiple-step strategy to help struggling readers establish words in memory as fully analysed forms. First the teacher pronounces the word, and then stretches out the pronunciation, so that the word can be segmented into its sounds. This step, before the spelling of the word was presented, was found to be necessary by Benchmark teachers, to get the children to attend to sounds rather than to the letters. After segmentation, the spelling of the word is presented, and a discussion ensues if there is a discrepancy between the number of sounds and letters in the target word e.g. 'late'. Children can then suggest other words, from word family lists, for example, that exhibit a similar pattern.

Ehri and McCormick (1998, p. 146) also discourage the use of analogies at this stage in order to read unfamiliar words because sight words are not represented in memory in sufficient detail to recognise similar patterns between known and unknown words. Teaching children to read new words by analogy is more appropriate at the full alphabetic phase of reading.

While word-level skills and strategies are being implemented, both literary, factual and procedural texts should be read to Max, and recorded on tape at school and at home, so that he does not miss out on the general knowledge, vocabulary and conceptual development that other students are acquiring through individual reading.

This case study underscores the importance of classroom and support/resource/remedial teachers' knowledge of assessment procedures to pinpoint the locus of reading difficulties and their ability to institute intervention procedures within the classroom setting. A review of research on individual intervention programs for children at-risk of literary difficulties is presented in the next chapter.

Flow chart for teacher-directed assessment

A flow-chart for teacher-directed assessment to identify difficulties once children are reading connected text, could look something like this:

✓ Using two parallel passages, check first for specific listening comprehension difficulties by determining whether a disparity exists between listening comprehension and reading comprehension ability

✓ If no disparity exists and scores are below grade level on both passages treat as a comprehension problem, keeping in mind that word-level difficulties may also be implicated.

✓ Identify the source of the comprehension difficulties. Using the class program as a guide, implement a more intensive individualised program in listening and reading comprehension strategies.

✓ Also check for possible fluency and accuracy difficulties.

✓ If disparity exists, with no comprehension difficulties evident when the text is read to the student, treat as either a fluency or an accuracy problem.

✓ To check for fluency, use grade norms available for the number of words accurately read per minute (60 to 90 wpm for Year 2, 30 to 70 wpm for Year 1) using a grade- appropriate reader.

✓ If fluency check reveals that reading is slow but accurate, institute individual fluency training program.

✓ If fluency check reveals that the problem is with accurate word recognition (as in Max's case above), use any appropriate word-attack skills test to locate area of phoneme-grapheme difficulties. Then commence an individualised word recognition program. (See Stahl et al., 1998) for additional suggestions.)

✓ Ensure the child still has access to literary, factual and procedural texts, either orally or on tape, to maintain comprehension, general knowledge and vocabulary skills.

Summary

This chapter examined assessment and intervention procedures for both meaning and word-level skills for the formal reading program in the first three years of school. In addition, a case study of a reluctant reader in his third school year was presented in order to highlight general individual assessment techniques that can be applied at any time a difficulty with a particular child arises, or when a new student needs profiling.

18 Individual intervention: Research and practice

This final chapter presents some current research data on individualised early intervention programs, using trained teachers, volunteers and peers. The components of successful intervention programs are also outlined, and a brief section on teaching reading to specific groups of children at-risk of literacy difficulties is included.

If the ultimate aim of this book is to provide effective literacy instruction to all children, then it is not enough to focus exclusively on exemplary classroom teaching. While classroom reading practices, based on scientifically proven reading research, are a sine qua non of effective literacy instruction, there will always be a number of students who will need additional support during the first three critical years to avoid reading failure.

Formative and summative assessment for skills at both the word and meaning level, to identify students who may need some form of intervention, was discussed in the previous chapter. However, as converging research data indicates that individual intervention is more effective than instruction given in small groups (Cohen et al., 1982; Glass et al., 1982; Bloom, 1984; Wasik & Slavin, 1993), the emphasis in this chapter is on individual intervention.

The effectiveness of one-on-one tutoring, using a trained teacher, results from the fact that tutors have the opportunity to give constant, immediate feedback to a student and adjust instruction to the pupil's needs. Furthermore, because tutors spend considerable time with individual children, they can determine their strengths and weaknesses and can present components of the class program in the most pedagogically appropriate manner, for example, by using task analytic procedures (*see* Glossary) or by increasing motivation and changing attitudinal perspectives.

Wasik and Slavin (1994, p. 145) have argued that Vygotsky's theory of cognitive development provides a framework for explaining why the individual tutoring model may be particularly effective for children experiencing difficulties in regular classrooms. According to Vygotsky's theory, children can often complete tasks when working with another person that they could not complete on their own (Vygotsky, 1978). The distance between the child working alone and with one-on-one assistance has been called the zone of proximal development. (However, for a different perspective on this view, see Gredler and Shields, 2004.)

Wasik and Slavin (1994, p. 145) go on to say that with a group of 25 to 30 children with varying levels of cognitive ability, it is very difficult to teach within each student's zone of proximal development. While the majority of children can generally make the necessary accommodations, there will (unfortunately), always be a few children who slip through the net (for example, Max). Some children, because of phonological difficulties, cognitive impairment, cultural differences, itinerant parents or illness, will always need additional assistance, either for the short term or longer. While we have to accept this as a reality, we need to ensure that it does not occur through ineffective classroom instruction.

Currently, the most popular individualised intervention program, certainly in Australia, New Zealand, the UK, and in the United States, is Reading Recovery, developed by Marie Clay in New Zealand. This daily early intervention program is designed to bring struggling readers who have failed to benefit from twelve months of classroom reading tuition to the level of their peers. Children who are developmentally delayed or from a non-English-speaking background are usually not candidates for Reading Recovery intervention. Reading Recovery teachers, who undergo intensive training, are generally assigned to the program for about 50 per cent of the school day. As they tutor only four students at a time, their typical case load is eight children over the course of a year (Juel, 1998). For a full overview of the program, *see* Shanahan and Barr (1995).

Although Reading Recovery is not considered by its practitioners to have a whole language orientation, it does emphasise the constructive as well as the strategic process involved in extracting meaning from print during early reading acquisition. Klein et al. (1997, p. 163) in their chapter on Reading Recovery state that beginning readers 'learn to read by reading and writing, and an environment that engages young children in a rich array of literacy activities supports children taking on the behaviours of good readers and writers'. They further quote Clay (1991) who says, 'Writing is an analytic activity that requires close attention to print. It is through writing that children learn about the conventions of print, visual features of print, and how the sounds of speech are coded in print.' Further in the same chapter, the authors indicate that 'in literacy learning, too, children construct their own understandings, but lean on the social context to weave meaning around their first interactions with written language' (p. 169).

It has been also clearly stated (Smith-Burke & Jagger, cited in Hiebert & Taylor, 1994, p. 81) that Reading Recovery is only enhanced and supported in those schools in which Reading Recovery teachers and classroom teachers share a common theoretical perspective on literacy development.

While its benefits in whole-language oriented classrooms have been well documented in the United States (DeFord et al., 1991), there have been some divergent American voices, for example Elbaum et al., 2000 who, in a recent meta-analysis of one-to-one reading interventions, concluded that:

> Overall, the findings of this meta-analysis do not provide support for the superiority of Reading Recovery over other one-to-one reading interventions. Typically, about 30 percent of students who begin Reading Recovery do not complete the program and do not perform significantly better than control students. As indicated in the meta-analysis, results reported for students who do complete the program may be inflated due to the selective attrition of students from some treatment groups and the use of measures that may bias the results in favour of Reading Recovery students. Thus it is particularly disturbing that sweeping endorsements still appear in the literature (p. 617).

The widely documented benefits of Reading Recovery have also been questioned by Australasian researchers (Center et al., 1995; Chapman et al., 2001). Center et al. (1995) concluded that Reading Recovery was only specifically effective for about 35 to 40 per cent of the students it targetted, since 30 per cent of students were unsuccessful, while the remaining 30 per cent of matched students would have 'recovered' spontaneously without any intervention. Chapman et al. (2001) found that the Reading Recovery program did not meet its stated goal of accelerating the progress of struggling six-year-old children to average levels of reading performance. Indeed, Tunmer and Chapman (2003), in an overview of the program, concluded that: 'Reading Recovery in its present form is not the most effective approach to preventive early intervention. It is not as good as it gets.'

Apart from the reported lack of efficacy and cost-effectiveness, perhaps the most significant outcome of both studies was the finding that those children who did not benefit from Reading Recovery intervention were precisely those struggling students who were deficient in meta-linguistic skills prior to entering the program. It seems that participation in the

Reading Recovery program did not eliminate or reduce phonological processing deficits in these students. Support for these results has also been provided by the earlier research of Iversen and Tunmer (1993), who found that the inclusion of explicit code instruction in the Reading Recovery program allowed participants to achieve criterion performance more quickly than children in the standard condition (quoted by Snow et al., 1998).

In view of this finding, it could be instructive to examine the impact of Reading Recovery on at-risk students selected from classes where an explicit phonologically based, rather than a psycholinguistic, program was in operation. A study in New South Wales, Australia, conducted by Center et al. (2001), examined the effects of Reading Recovery intervention on the reading proficiency of regular and low-progress Year 1 students in six classrooms where two different early literacy instructional programs were used.

The first program was meaning-oriented, while the second program, a code-oriented one, was implemented in the same six Kindergarten and Year 1 classrooms one year later, when the three target schools decided to change their early literacy program. The code-oriented program, known as Schoolwide Early Language and Literacy or SWELL (Center & Freeman, 1996a; 1996b; 1997; 2000a; 2000b; 2000c; Center et al., 1998) and adapted from Success for All (Slavin et al., 1992), stressed the explicit instruction of phonological awareness and the alphabetic code in context. The meaning-oriented programs tended to have a 'whole language' perspective, so that teachers favoured the use of syntactic, semantic and pragmatic information in surrounding text as the primary means of initial printed word recognition.

All students, including both regular and Reading Recovery students, in the six non-SWELL classrooms were tested on four early literacy measures at the end of Year 1 when they had completed two years of schooling (comparison group). At the end of the following year, all Year 1 students in the six SWELL classrooms were tested on the same early literacy measures, when they had completed two years of schooling (experimental group).

The results of the study indicated that all regular and Reading Recovery students in SWELL classes significantly outperformed their regular and Reading Recovery counterparts in non-SWELL classes on tests measuring pseudoword decoding, reading connected text, invented spelling and a standardised reading measure at the end of Year 1. However, Reading Recovery students, as a group, whether in SWELL or non-SWELL classes, did not reach the average level of their peers on any of the four literacy measures used.

While this latter result supports the use of phonologically based programs in the early school years and is significant in its own right, it was not the main focus of the study. More importantly for classroom practitioners, the results also revealed that those low progress children receiving Reading Recovery in SWELL classes outperformed their at-risk peers in non-SWELL classes in the same way as their regular classmates, on all the four measures used. In addition, Reading Recovery students from SWELL classes needed less time to be discontinued successfully from the Reading Recovery program than their counterparts from the more 'meaning' oriented classrooms.

As the theoretical orientation of the Reading Recovery program tends to be more psycholinguistic than that of SWELL, there was always the possibility that the low progress students from the SWELL classes would be at a disadvantage during intervention, relative to their low progress peers from the more psycholinguistically oriented classrooms (Smith-Burke & Jagger, cited in Hiebert & Taylor, 1994, p. 81). However, the results of this study seem to contradict current views often held about the incompatibility of Reading Recovery and structured programs (like SWELL in Australia or Success for All in the US) which stress phonemic awareness and phonological recoding in the early years of school. Moreover, the findings support those of Iversen and Tunmer (1993) in their modified Reading Recovery intervention, and confirm the hypothesis that children with reading problems will be remediated more quickly if they receive systematic instruction in sound/symbol relatedness. In the study cited above, this training was incorporated into the Reading Recovery intervention. In our evaluation study, this instruction was a part of the regular SWELL classroom program.

It does not seem to be adventitious that the Reading Recovery students from phonologically based classrooms, where phonemic awareness and the cracking of the alphabetic code are explicitly taught both in isolation and context, significantly outperformed students from classrooms where these prerequisites to literacy are not taught in this way.

The most recent research on literacy acquisition for hard-to-teach students has indicated the need for explicit instruction in these skills as a necessary but not sufficient condition for both regular classroom instruction (Tunmer et al., 1998) and for remediation (Torgesen et al., 1997). A number of successful early intervention programs have already included such instruction (Slavin et al., 1992; Vellutino et al., 1996). Shanahan and Barr (1995, p. 992), in their comprehensive review of Reading Recovery, have also suggested that the program should consider modifying its strategies to encompass those that have been found to enhance early literacy acquisition.

It is perhaps unduly optimistic to believe that children with specific phonological difficulties and those with a combination of phonological and general cognitive deficiencies, who are typical candidates for Reading Recovery, can be returned to their classrooms as 'full participants' after a single period of intervention (see also Ross et al., 1995). There is no doubt that some students who are experientially impoverished will only need a 'quick fix' in order for them to rejoin their peers successfully. Others, however, with problems of a more constitutional origin will need ongoing individualised intervention to avoid 'Matthew effects' (Stanovich, 1986; *see* Glossary). Our results and those from other recent studies (Chapman et al., 1998; 1999) particularise the point made by Shanahan and Barr (1995, p. 990) when they suggest that it would be an unwise strategy to shift all resources for remediation to Reading Recovery since some students are likely to require additional support.

So what effective alternatives remain for struggling students in mainstream classrooms who need additional literacy assistance? We already know, from our own research, that if a school wishes to implement Reading Recovery, then students will be discontinued more rapidly and with greater success if they experience a structured, code-oriented program, prior to their admission to this early intervention. We also know that trained teachers, who support students in one-on-one tutorial sessions which complement the objectives taught in regular phonologically based classrooms have enjoyed significant remedial success (Slavin & Madden, 2001). Indeed, a comparison between early intervention programs based on Success for All (SFA) principles, in SFA schools, and Reading Recovery intervention programs in matched non-SFA schools recorded a substantial effect size (*see* Glossary) in favour of low progress students in SFA schools (Ross et al., 1996).

As cost is always a critical issue, what about cheaper tutorial models, using trained volunteers, rather than trained teachers, when cost precludes the use of the latter? Wasik (1998, p. 282), in her overview of this type of program, found that in order for such an intervention program to be successful, the following four features need to be observed:

➨ the presence of a designated coordinator who is knowledgeable about reading instruction
➨ the use of structure and inclusion in each session of
   – a new book reading
   – a familiar book reading
   – word analysis and letter/sound relationships
   – writing activities that include composing activities
➨ training provided to volunteers which involves the use of scaffolding and explicit modelling of word reading and writing strategies

➤➤ coordination between the volunteer program and classroom instruction, exemplified by the use of controlled vocabulary readers, if the class uses basal readers.

While Wasik (1998) clearly endorses the potential of well-designed volunteer tutoring, she warns of the dangers to struggling children of inadequately trained volunteers. For a fuller description of a successful volunteer training program, it would be instructive to read *What Kind of One-on-one Tutoring Helps a Poor Reader?* (Juel, 1998).

Finally, a no-cost and a win-win solution to tutorial models involves the use of peer or cross-age tutors, since it appears that both are likely to benefit from such interactions (Cohen et al., 1982). I have already alluded to the mutual benefits of learning in partner (peer) dyads. There is also evidence that when cross-age tutors, who are below grade average, help low progress students, both improve. However, if students are assisted by above average cross-age tutors, it appears, logically enough, that gains are restricted to the former (Stahl & Kuhn, 2000).

Teaching reading to specific groups of at-risk students

And, now, a word about teaching reading to students who may be at-risk of reading difficulties because of cultural differences; for example, children whose first language is not English on school entry, or who do not belong to the dominant culture serviced by the school system.

According to Snow et al. (1998), children from a non-English background should not be taught to read in English until they have achieved a certain level of proficiency in speaking the English language. This is because proficiency in spoken English not only enables children to 'support subsequent learning about the alphabetic principle through an understanding of the sub-lexical structure of spoken English words', but also allows them to 'understand the language and content of the material they are reading' (p. 324). It is very difficult, for instance, to attempt to correctly identify the word 'yacht' (even in context) on first exposure, if it is not already in a person's spoken lexicon.

This is one of the reasons that we have found that non-English-speaking children benefit significantly from being included in classrooms that employ both an early interactive text reading program and a structured language program. If, however, these children arrive at a school, where reading is also taught in their native tongue, they can be taught reading immediately in their first language, while acquiring oral proficiency in English at the same time. As Snow et al. (1998, p. 324) observe, 'being able to read and write in two languages confers numerous intellectual, cultural, economic and social benefits', and is probably the way of the future. Indeed, a study undertaken by Bialystok et al. (2005) found that bilingual children learning to read in both languages in the first year at school were more advanced than mono-lingual children, provided both languages used an alphabetic script.

Children from the non-dominant indigenous culture (such as native American children in North America, Maori children in New Zealand or Aboriginal children in Australia) may also be at risk of literacy difficulties on school entry, if they have not been exposed to the pre-school phonological activities which foster effective literacy development.

A study by Tunmer et al. (2003) compared two groups of children in Year 1 (second school year) classrooms, all containing a mix of non-indigenous and Maori pupils. Students in control classrooms received standard whole language literacy instruction. However, for the experimental group of students, the major components of three commercially available packages, designed to explicitly teach phonemic awareness, rhyme and analogy, as well as sound/symbol translations were incorporated into the classroom program over four school terms (Tunmer et al., 2002, p. 22).

While there were no differences between the two groups of children at school entry on any literacy measure, the difference between the two groups, by the end of the second school year, was a mean reading age of 14 months, in favour of the students who had received the phonologically enhanced classroom program. In addition, of significant interest was the fact that despite initial differences on school entry between Maori and European children, favouring the latter, the gap between the two cultural groups had vanished by the end of Year 2 (the third school year) in the experimen-tal classrooms, but had widened in the traditional whole-language classrooms. While there is no doubt that culturally accommodated instruc-tion promotes student participation (Snow et al., 1998, p. 243), the results of this study should have important curriculum implications for school authorities in other multicultural societies.

Finally, what about that small but seemingly intractable group of children, without sensory problems, who do not appear to respond to the best efforts of parents at home and teachers in regular and tutorial class-rooms? According to Olson (2004, p. 122), it is important to understand that there are 'specific genetic mechanisms that constrain learning rates for reading and related skills'. He goes on to say that Byrne et al. (2002) have demonstrated that preschoolers' phoneme identity learning rates are significantly influenced by genes although, as yet, only one gene 'has been tentatively identified that may account for a small percentage of genetically influenced reading disabilities' (Taipale et al., 2003, cited by Olson, 2004). It has generally been unfashionable to suggest that reading difficulties may have a genetic origin, on the grounds that this explanation may absolve parents and teachers from instructional responsibilities. However, Olson suggests that, on the contrary, it is important to have such knowledge, so that the need for 'extraordinary environmental intervention' and 'significantly more reading practice' is recognised, in order to obviate the otherwise inevitable Matthew effects (see Glossary) for such children.

Summary

This final chapter presented some current research data on individualised early intervention programs, using both trained teachers, volunteers and peers. The components of successful intervention programs were also outlined and a brief section was included on teaching reading to the atypical children that teachers will almost certainly find in their regular classrooms at school entry.

This review of research and practice relevant to individual intervention for atypical students in regular classrooms completed the literacy instructional program during the first three critical years of school. Teachers' implementation of effective literacy classroom and intervention practices, derived from their pedagogical skills and knowledge of converging research data, ensured the best possible environment for all their students who started school, eager to learn to read and write, three years ago. Their literacy fledglings are now ready to fly!

Afterword

I am well aware that a book that attempts to provide literacy instructional practice based on converging literacy research may invoke a certain amount of criticism at a time when the 'Reading Wars' are still being waged.

I imagine one such criticism will be directed at the ostensibly reductionist view of reading taken in this text, exemplified by the simple view that reading is a product of decoding and listening comprehension. 'Progressive' detractors of what they consider an essentially 'conservative' educational approach have argued that 'reading is more than phonics, and literacy is more than the reading and writing of print' (Walsh, 2003).

One of the best responses to this criticism has been articulated by Keith Stanovich (2000, p. 387), when he says that 'we must stop creating a progressive politics where to be of the left you must oppose science'. Science has shown us, unequivocally, that knowledge of phonological processes is the key to deciphering print. It has also shown us, convincingly, that children who are culturally, cognitively and phonologically at-risk of inducing the alphabetic code need explicit instruction in phonological processes, in the first three years of school, to avoid literacy failure. As poor reading skills contribute in large measure to social and economic inequity, socially progressive educators should be supporting rather than attacking research-based literacy programs.

A second criticism may be levelled at the possible over-prescriptive nature of the literacy instructional processes suggested in the book. Surely such scripting is offensive to teachers who believe that structure and creativity are mutually exclusive? For mature teachers in regular classrooms from which children at literacy risk are excluded, this proposition may be tenable. As this ideal situation rarely occurs, I believe that both experienced and novice teachers in today's inclusive classes generally 'need the guidance of a relatively scripted, or at least moderately prescriptive curriculum of predesigned activities. This view would suggest that under-generalisation is potentially less disruptive to students' opportunity to learn than over-extensions and over-generalizations' (Snow, 2001, p. 6) and need not compromise the creativity of teachers'.

Appendices

1 Verbal *cue phrases* for letter formation

The purpose of verbal cue phrases is to provide a repetitive, rhythmic verbal sequence to assist the students in remembering the steps for forming each letter. Practise each letter prior to presenting it and determine the rhythm of that particular pattern. You may have a different way of teaching the letter, so feel free to make your own cue phrase.

Letter	Suggested Verbal Cue
a	Around, up and down.
b	One stroke down, half-way back up, right around.
c	Around and stop.
d	Circle left, right up, back down.
e	Cross left to right 'C' curve around.
f	Curve left, straight down, lift and cross.
g	Circle left, up, right down, hook left.
h	One stroke down, half-way back up and a bump.
i	One short stroke down, lift and dot.
j	One stroke right down, hook left, lift and dot.
k	One stroke down, back up a bit, around and kick out.
l	One stroke down and stop.
m	One short stroke down, back up, a bump and a bump.
n	One short stroke down, backup and a bump.

Letter	Suggested Verbal Cue
o	Whole circle left, around and close.
p	One stroke right down, back up and around.
q	Circle left, up, right down, hook right.
r	Short stroke down, back up, half a bump.
s	Around, across and around.
t	One stroke down, lift and cross.
u	One short stroke down, curve up, straight down.
v	Short slant right, slant up.
w	Short slant right and slant up and down and up.
x	Short slant right, lift, cross left.
y	One short stroke down, curve up, all the way down and hook.
z	Zig right, zig left, zig right.

(Source: Slavin et al., 1992)

2 Visual *vowel* cues

Alphie Apple

Izzy Insect

Olive Octopus

Eggbert Egg

Uppity Umbrella

(Source: adapted from Madden et al., 1996)

3   *A Big Bad Bug*: a little reader

Author   Yola Center
Illustrator Davida Strasser

I see a bug
sit on a rug.

Get up from that rug
you big, big bad bug.

Can you not see
that rug is for me?

My mum gets a mug
to trap that big bug.

That bug is not dim
That mug is for him.

From the rug he will run
and sit in the sun.

4 Readles
example

Readles are iconic representations of words: these provide clues to help the student decode the word.

happy

sad

ice cream

Sam

bike

bat

basket

door

pizza

school

chair

water

spider
spider web

5 Worksheets for *The hat trick* in the Bangers and Mash series

The hat trick

Story Retell

Students divide into pairs and take it in turns asking each other the following questions. The answers do not have to be written down. Teacher circulates to make sure that the students are asking and answering the questions properly.

Is Bangers big?

What gets stuck on Banger's head?

Who puts the jam on his head?

What does Mum do to Mash?

Story Writing

Pairs discuss the following topic together and then write a story by themselves.

What do you think Bangers and Mash will do with the box?

The hat trick

Story Quiz

Answer these questions in a full sentence.

1) Who does Mash play with in the 'The hat trick'?

2) Who puts the box on his head?

3) Does Mash have a red hat?

4) Does Mum get the box off Banger's head?

5) Who rubs the jam off Mash's nose?

6 Reading comprehension worksheets for *Where's my shoe?*

Where's my shoe?

Take turns with your partner reading and answering these questions.

1. Who was playing with John's shoe?

2. Where did he find her?

3. What was she doing with the shoe?

4. What time of day was it in the story?

Write down the answers to these questions.

Who was playing with John's shoe?

Where did he find her?

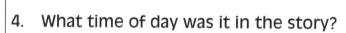

What was she doing with the shoe?

_____

What time of day was it in the story?

_____

Where's my shoe?

With your partner complete the following Story Map.

Title

Main
Character

Other
Characters

What happened in this story?

Where's my shoe?

Let's see how words work in sentences.

a)   **The girl played with the shoe.**

Draw a circle around the 2 words that tell us who played with the shoe.

Draw a circle around the 2 words that tell us what the girl played with.

b)   Fill in the missing words.

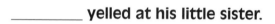

      under the bed   the boy
         in the kitchen

_____ **yelled at his little sister.**

c)   Think of some words to complete this sentence.

John looked for _____

Put in the capital letters and full stops where they belong.

a)   the shoe is not under John's bed

b)   the shoe was not in the bedroom

c)   he looked in the dog's bed

d)   it was in the bathroom sink

7 Jointly constructed *text editing chart*

Let's check what we have written for meaning.

Does this writing make sense?
Have any words been left out?
Are the words in the correct order?
Are the sentences in the correct order?

Let's make the sentences more interesting.

Can we add or change any words to make the sentences more interesting?
In each lesson attention should be drawn to the specific concept being
taught.

Let's check the punctuation.

Are there capital letters in the correct places?
Have full stops and question marks been used properly?
In each lesson attention should be drawn to the specific concept being
taught.

Let's check for spelling.

Can you see any words that may not be spelt correctly?
How should these words be spelt?

Glossary

Auditory discrimination The ability to hear similarities and differences in phonemes and words, e.g. do Sam and Pam sound the same?

Coda/peak A monosyllabic word such as 'dog' can be divided into its onset /d/ and its rime /og/. A rime must contain a peak or vowel nucleus, in this case /o/, and may also contain a consonantal coda, in this case /g/. In a word like 'tree', the rime has the obligatory peak, /e/, but no coda.

Effect size This is calculated as the difference in performance between the results of students in an experimental condition and those in a comparison condition, divided by the comparison group's standard deviation. An effect size of about .5 is regarded as moderate.

Graphemes These are units of written language and represent phonemes in the spelling of words e.g. the written word 'go' has two graphemes, while the written word 'check' has five graphemes.

Guided reading Small-group reading of instructional level text by students that is facilitated by teachers.

Kindergarten In this text, refers to the first year of compulsory formal schooling.

'Matthew' effects Terminology proposed by Keith Stanovich (1986) to describe incremental literacy differences that develop between individuals who have advantageous early educational experiences and those who do not (adapted from the biblical text, 'the rich get richer and the poor get poorer').

Meta-analysis A statistical approach for summarising the results of many studies which have investigated a similar problem. Given a number of studies, this procedure provides a numerical way of expressing 'average' results.

Meta-cognitive Cognition (knowledge) about cognition (knowledge), e.g. knowing that making a summary will assist retention of information.

Meta-comprehension Monitoring one's own comprehension about text being read, so fix-up strategies can be employed if the meaning is not clear.

Meta-linguistic ability The ability to bring knowledge of the spoken language to bear upon written language; this requires the ability to reflect on the structural features of spoken language.

Morpheme The smallest meaning units into which a word can be divided, e.g. 'dog'. However 'dogs' has two morphemes—'dog' and 's', representing the plural form.

Onset In a one-syllable word, the part that precedes the vowel and any following consonants, e.g. the onset in 'hat' is 'h'. In 'at', there is no onset.

Orthographic processor/knowledge Knowing how a word looks in print.

Orthography The writing system of a language, ie knowing how a word looks in print.

Peak *See* Coda.

Phonemes The smallest units in spoken language that change the meaning of words, e.g. /h/ and /b/ in 'hat' and 'bat'. As phonemes represent the sounds in words, the spoken word g/o has two phonemes, while the spoken word ch/e/ck has three phonemes.

Phonemic awareness The ability to deal explicitly with the smallest unit in the spoken word, the phoneme, i.e. the ability to subdivide 'dog' into its three phonemes /d/ /o/ /g/.

Phonetics The study of the speech sounds that occur in languages, including the way these sounds are articulated, e.g. the first sound in 'pie' is bilabial—it is made with both lips. It is useful for students of foreign languages.

Phonics Teaching reading and spelling through sound/symbol correspondences (decoding; phoneme/grapheme translations), e.g. the sound /buh/ is represented by the symbol 'b'.

Phonological awareness Sensitivity to the sound structure rather than to the meaning of speech, i.e. recognising that 'cat' and 'hat' rhyme.

Phonology The study of the unconscious rules governing speech-sound production, e.g. children unconsciously learn the rules of admissible consonants and vowels when uttering words (cat versus cta).

Pseudowords Regularly spelled non words, e.g. 'lim'.

Rime In a one-syllable word, the part that includes the vowel and any following consonants, e.g. the rime in both 'hat' and 'cat' is 'at'.

Scaffold Teacher-provided assistance when students falter, e.g. prompting students to use recently learnt vocabulary when drafting a new text.

Shared reading Teacher-directed text read to promote children's listening comprehension, generally above children's independent reading levels.

Task analysis A range of different strategies that attempts to simplify instructional tasks by breaking them down into teachable steps, e.g. highlighting the initial phoneme in a written word when teaching sound/symbol correspondence.

References

Aarnoutse, C. (1994), 'Reading comprehension instruction: Where is it and can we improve it?' in E.M.H. Assink (ed.), *Literacy acquisition and social context*, New York: Harvester Wheatsheaf, pp. 176–98.

Adams, M.J. (1990), *Beginning to read: Thinking and learning about print*, Cambridge, MA: MIT Press.

—— (1991), 'Why not phonics and whole language?' in W. Ellis (ed.), *All language and the creation of literacy*, Baltimore, MD: Orton Dyslexia Society, pp. 40–52.

—— (1999), 'The science and politics of beginning reading practices' in J. Oakhill & R. Beard (eds), *Reading development and the teaching of reading*, Oxford, UK: Blackwell Publishers Ltd, pp. 213–17.

——, Foorman, B.R., Lundberg, I. & Beeler, T. (1998), *Phonemic awareness in young children*, Baltimore, Maryland: Paul H. Brookes Publishing Co.

Allen, P. (1990), *Who sank the boat?*, New York: Coward-McCann.

Allington, R.L. (2001), *What really matters for struggling readers*, New York: Longmans.

Andrews, S. (1990), 'What children need to know in order to learn to read', *STIR*, Sydney: NSW Department of School Education.

Appleton-Smith, L., *Books to Remember* series, Lyme N.H.: Flyleaf Publishing.

Banville, J. (2000), *Eclipse*, Picador.

Barnes, M.A. & Dennis, M. (1996), 'Reading comprehension deficits arise from diverse sources: Evidence from readers with and without developmental brain pathology' in C. Cornoldi & J. Oakhill (eds), *Reading comprehension difficulties*, Mahwah, NJ: Lawrence Erlbaum & Associates, pp. 251–78.

Baumann, J.F., Hoffman, J.V., Duffy-Hester, A.M. & Moon Ro, J. (2000), 'The first R yesterday and today: U.S. elementary reading instruction practices reported by teachers and administrators' in *Reading Research Quarterly*, vol. 35, no. 3, pp. 338–77.

Beck, I.L. (1989), *Reading today and tomorrow*, Teachers' editions for grades 1 and 2, Austin, TX: Holt.

—— & Hamilton, R. (2000), *Beginning reading module*, Washington, DC: American Federation of Teachers (original work published 1996).

—— & Juel, C. (1992), 'The role of decoding in learning to read' in S.J. Samuels & A.E. Farstrup (eds), *What research has to say about reading instruction*, Newark, Delaware: International Reading Association, pp. 101–23.

—— & McKeown. M.G. (2001), 'Text talk: Capturing the benefits of read-aloud experiences for young children' in *The Reading Teacher*, vol. 55, no. 1, pp. 10–20.

——, McKeown, M., Sandora, C., Kucan, L. & Worthy, J. (1996), 'Questioning the author: A yearlong classroom implementation to engage students with text' in *Elementary School Journal*, no. 96, pp. 385–414.

——, Perfetti, C.A. & McKeown, M.G. (1982), 'The effects of long-term vocabulary instruction on lexical access and reading comprehension' in *Journal of Educational Psychology*, vol.. 74, pp. 506–21.

Bialystok, E., Luk, G. & Kwan, E. (2005), 'Bilingualism, biliteracy and learning to read: Interactions among languages and writing systems' in *Scientific Studies of Reading*, vol. 9, no. 1, pp. 43–61.

Blachman, B. (2000), 'Phonological Awareness' in M.L. Kamil, P.B. Mosenthal, P.D. Pearson & R. Barr (eds), *Handbook of reading research*, Mahwah, NJ: Lawrence Erlbaum Associates, vol. 3, pp. 483–502.

Bloom, B.S. (ed.) (1956), *Taxonomy of educational objectives. Handbook 1: Cognitive domain*, New York: David McKay.

Bloom, B.S. (1984), 'The 2 sigma problem: The search for methods of group instruction as effective as one-to-one tutoring' in *Educational Researcher*, vol. 13, pp. 4–6.

Board of Studies NSW (1998), *English K–6 syllabus*, NSW, Australia: Board of Studies.

Borman, G.D., Hewes, G.M., Overman, L.T. & Brown, S. (2003), 'Comprehensive school reform and achievement: A meta-analysis' in *Review of Educational Research*, vol. 73, no. 2, pp. 125–30.

Bos, C., Mather, N., Dickson, S., Podhajski, B. & Chard, D. (2001), 'Educators' perceptions and knowledge of early reading' in *9th Annual Meeting of the Society for the Scientific Study of Reading*, Boulder: Colorado.

Bosman, A.M.T. & Van Orden, G.C. (1997), 'Why spelling is more difficult than reading' in C.A. Perfetti, L. Rieben & M. Fayol (eds), *Learning to spell. Research, theory and practice across languages*, Hillsdale, NJ: Lawrence Erlbaum Associates, pp. 173–94.

Bowers, P.G. & Newby-Clark E. (2002), 'The role of naming speed within a model of reading acquisition' in *Reading and Writing: An Interdisciplinary Journal*, vol. 15, pp. 109–26.

—— & Wolf, M. (1993), 'Theoretical links among naming speed, precise timing mechanisms and orthographic skill in dyslexia' in *Reading and Writing: An Interdisciplinary Journal*, vol. 5, pp. 69–85.

Bowey, J. (1994), 'Grammatical awareness and learning to read: A critique' in E.M.H. Assink (ed.), *Literacy acquisition and social context*, New York: Harvester Wheatshaff, pp. 122–49.

—— (2000), 'Early onset-rime sensitivity training in at-risk children' in N.A. Badian (ed.), *Prediction and prevention of reading failure*, Baltimore, Maryland: New York Press, pp. 217–46.

Bryant, P.L. (2002), 'Children's thoughts about reading and spelling' in *Scientific Studies of Reading*, vol. 2, pp. 199–216.

—— & Cavendish (2001), 'On revisiting an old hypothesis about phonology and reading', *9th Annual Meeting of the Society for Scientific Study of Reading*, Boulder: Colorado.

——, Nunes, T. & Bindman, M. (1997), 'Children's understanding of the connection between grammar and spelling' in B. Blachman (ed.), *Foundations of reading acquisition and dyslexia*, Mahwah, NJ: Lawrence Erlbaum Associates, pp. 219–40.

——, Nunes, T. & Pretzlik, U. (2004), 'Does it help to be explicit about morphology?', *Eleventh Annual Meeting of TripleSR*, June 27–30, Amsterdam: Holland.

——, Nunes, T. & Snaith, R. (2000), 'Children learn an untaught rule of spelling' in *Nature*, vol. 403, pp. 157–58.

Burns, M.S., Griffin, P. & Snow, C.E. (1999), *Starting out right*, Washington DC: National Academy Press.

Byrne, B. (2002), 'The process of learning to read: A framework for integrating research and educational practice' in *Learning and Teaching Reading, Monograph Series*, vol. 11, no. 1, The British Psychological Society.

——, Delaland, C., Fielding-Barnsley, R., Quain, P., Samuelsson, S. & Hoien, T. (2002), 'Longitudinal twin study of early reading development in three countries. Preliminary results' in *Annals of Dyslexia*, vol. 52, pp. 49–74.

—— & Fielding-Barnsley, R. (1989), 'Phonemic awareness and letter knowledge in the child's acquisition of the alphabetic principle' in *Journal of Educational Psychology*, vol. 81, pp. 313–21.

—— & Fielding-Barnsley, R. (1991), *Sound foundations: An introduction to prereading skills*, Sydney: Peter Leyden Educational.

—— & Fielding-Barnsley, R. (1993), 'Evaluation of a program to teach phonemic awareness to young children: A 1-year follow-up' in *Journal of Educational Psychology*, vol. 85, pp. 104–11.

Cain, K. (1996), 'Story knowledge and comprehension skill' in C. Cornoldi and J. Oakhill (eds), *Reading comprehension difficulties*, Hillsdale, NJ: Lawrence Erlbaum & Associates, pp. 167–92.

Calfee, R. (1998), 'Phonics and phonemes: Learning to decode and spell in a literature-based program' in J.L. Metsala & L.C. Ehri (eds), *Word recognition in beginning literacy*, Mahwah, NJ: Lawrence Erlbaum Associates, pp. 315–40.

Cardoso-Martins, C. & Pennington, B.F. (2004), 'The relationship between phoneme awareness and rapid serial naming skills and literacy acquisition: The role of developmental period and reading ability' in *Scientific Studies of Reading*, vol. 8, no. 1, pp. 27–52.

Carle, E. (1989), *The very hungry caterpillar*, Philomel Books.

Carlisle, J.F. (1995), 'Morphological awareness and early reading achievement' in L.B. Feldman (ed.), *Morphological aspects of language processing*, Hillsdale, NJ: Lawrence Erlbaum & Associates, pp. 198–209.

Castiglioni-Spalten, M.L. & Ehri, L.C. (2003), 'Phonemic awareness instruction: Contribution of articulatory segmentation to novice beginners' reading and spelling' in *Scientific Studies of Reading*, vol. 7, no. 1, pp. 25–52.

Castles, A. & Coltheart, M. (2004), 'Is there a causal link from phonological awareness to success in learning to read?' in *Cognition*, vol. 91, no. 1, pp. 77–111.

Catts, H., Hogan, T.P., Barth, A.E. & Adlof, S.M. (2003), 'The simple view of reading. Changes over time', poster presented at the *13th Annual Meeting of the Society for the Scientific Study of Reading*, Boulder: Colorado.

Center, Y. & Freeman, L.B. (1996a), *Towards literacy competence manual*, NSW: Macquarie University.

—— & Freeman, L.B. (1996b), *The SWELL tutor manual*, NSW: Macquarie University.

—— & Freeman, L.B. (1997), 'A trial evaluation of SWELL (Schoolwide Early Language and Literacy Program for at risk and disadvantaged children) in *International Journal of Disability, Development and Education*, vol. 44, pp. 21–39.

—— & Freeman, L. (2000a), *Schoolwide early language and literacy: supporting emergent literacy manual*, Sydney: Macquarie University.

—— & Freeman, L. (2000b), *Schoolwide early language and literacy: Becoming literate—kindergarten manual*, Sydney: Macquarie University.

—— & Freeman, L. (2000c), *Schoolwide early language and literacy: Becoming literate—year 1 manual*, Sydney: Macquarie University.

——, Freeman, L.B. & Robertson, G. (1998), 'An evaluation of Schoolwide Early Language and Literacy (SWELL) in six disadvantaged schools' in *International Journal of Disability, Development and Education*, vol. 45, pp. 143–72.

—— Freeman, L. & Robertson, G. (2001), 'The relative effect of a code-oriented and a meaning-oriented early literacy program on regular and low progress Australian students in Year 1 classrooms which implement Reading Recovery' in *International Journal of Disability, Development and Education*, vol. 48, no. 2, pp. 207–32.

—— Freeman, L., Robertson, G. & Outhred, L. (1999), 'Visual imagery training and comprehension' in *Journal of Research in Reading*, vol. 22, pp. 241–56.

——, Wheldall, K., Freeman, L., Outhred, L. & McNaught, M. (1995), 'An evaluation of Reading Recovery' in *Reading Research Quarterly*, vol. 30, pp. 240–63.

Chall, J. (1983), *Stages of reading development*, New York: McGraw-Hill.

Chapman, J.W., Tunmer, W.E. & Prochnow, J.E. (1998), *Success in Reading Recovery depends on the development of phonological processing skills*, New Zealand: Massey University.

——, Tunmer, W.E. & Prochnow, J.E. (1999), *An examination of the effectiveness of Reading Recovery: A longitudinal study*, New Zealand: Massey University.

——, Tunmer, W.E. & Prochnow, J.E. (2001), 'Does success in the Reading Recovery program depend on developing proficiency in phonological processing skills? A longitudinal study in a whole language instructional context' in *Scientific Studies of Reading*, vol. 5, pp. 141–76.

Chiappe, P., Siegel, L.S. & Wade-Woolley, L. (2002), 'Linguistic diversity and the development of reading skills: A longitudinal study' in *Scientific Studies of Reading*, vol. 6, no. 4, pp. 369–400.

Clay, M.M. (1985), *The early detection of reading difficulties*, second edition, Auckland, NZ: Heinemann.

Clymer, T. (1996), 'The utility of phonic generalizations in the primary grades' in *The Reading Teacher*, vol. 50, no. 3, pp. 182–87 (originally published in *RT*, vol. 16, 1963).

Cohen, P., Kulic, J. & Kulic, C.L. (1982), 'Educational outcomes of tutoring: A meta-analysis of findings' in *American Educational Research Journal*, vol. 19, pp. 237–48.

Connor, C., Morrison, F.J. & Katch, L.E. (2004), 'Beyond the Reading Wars: Exploring the effect of child-instructional interactions on growth in early reading' in *Scientific Studies of Reading*, vol. 8, no. 4, pp. 305–34.

Corballis, M.C. (2004), 'The origins of modernity: Was autonomous speech the critical factor?' in *Psychological Review*, vol. 111, no. 2, pp. 543–52.

Cunningham, A.E. (1990), 'Explicit versus implicit instruction in phonemic awareness' in *Journal of Experimental Child Psychology*, vol. 50, pp. 429–44.

——, Perry, K.E., Stanovich, K.E., Stanovich, P.J., Rodriguez, L. & Chappell, M. (2002), 'How teachers spend their time teaching language arts: The mismatch between policy and practice', *12th Annual Conference of the Society for the Scientific Study of Reading*, Chicago: USA.

Davidson, M. (2001), 'Validity and reliability of oral reading fluency measures', *11th Annual Meeting of the Society for the Scientific Study of Reading*, Boulder: Colorado.

Deford, D.E., Lyons, C.A. & Pinnell, G.S. (eds) (1991), *Bridges to literacy: Learning from reading recovery*, Portsmouth, NH: Heinemann.

De Lemos, M. (2002), *Closing the gap between research and practice: Foundations for the acquisition of literacy*, Victoria: Australian Council for Educational Research.

Deno, S.L., Mirkin, P.K. & Chiang, B. (1982), 'Identifying valid measures of reading' in *Exceptional Children*, vol. 49, pp. 36–45.

Duke, N.K. & Pearson P.D. (2002), 'Effective practices for developing reading comprehension' in A.E. Farstrup & S.J. Samuels (eds), *What research has to say about reading instruction*, Newark, Delaware: IRA, pp. 205–42.

Dunn, L.M., Smith, J.O. & Dunn, L.M. (1981), *Peabody language development kits—Revised*, Circle Pines, MN: American Guidance Service.

Durkin, D. (1988), *Teaching them to read*, Boston: Allyn & Bacon.

Dymock, S. & Nicholson, T. (2001), *Reading comprehension: What is it? How do you teach it?*, New Zealand Council for Educational Research.

Edwards, P. (1987), *Where's my shoe?*, Eureka Treasure Chest, Longman: Australia.

Ehri, L.C. (1987), 'Learning to read and spell words' in *Journal of Reading Behaviour*, vol. 19, pp. 5–31.

—— (1991), 'Development of the ability to read words' in R. Barr, M.L. Kamil, P.B. Mosenthal & P.D. Pearson (eds), *Handbook of reading research*, White Plains, NY: Longmans, vol. 11, pp. 383–417.

—— (1998), 'Grapheme-phoneme knowledge is essential for learning to read words in English' in J.M. Metsala & L.C. Ehri (eds), *Word recognition in beginning literacy*, Mahwah, NJ: Lawrence Erlbaum Associates, pp. 3–40.

——, Deffner, N. & Wilce, L. (1984), 'Pictorial mnemonics for phonics' in *Journal of Educational Psychology*, vol. 76, pp. 880–93.

—— & McCormick, S. (1998), 'Phases of word learning: Implications for instruction with delayed and disabled readers' in *Reading & Writing Quarterly: Overcoming Learning Difficulties,* vol. 14, pp. 135–63.

——, Nunes, S., Stahl, S. & Willows, Q. (2001), 'Systematic phonic instruction helps students learn to read: Evidence from the National Reading Panel's meta-analysis' in *Review of Educational Research*, vol. 71, no. 3, pp. 393–447.

——, Nunes, S.R., Willows, D.M., Schuster, B., Yaghoub-Zadeh, Z. & Shanahan, T. (2001), 'Phonemic awareness instruction helps children learn to read: Evidence from the national Reading Panel's meta-analysis' in *Reading Research Quarterly*, vol. 36, no. 3, pp. 250–87.

—— & Saltmarsh, J. (1995), 'Beginning readers outperform older disabled readers in learning to read words by sight' in *Reading and Writing: An Interdisciplinary Journal*, vol. 7, pp. 295–326.

—— & Sweet, J. (1991), 'Finger-pointing of memorized text: What enables beginners to process the print' in *Reading Research Quarterly*, vol. 26, no. 4, pp. 442–62.

—— & Wilce, L.S. (1980a), 'Do beginners learn to read function words better in sentences or in lists?' in *Reading Research Quarterly*, vol. 15, pp. 451–76.

Elbaum, B., Vaughn, S., Hughes, M. & Moody, S. (2000), 'How effective are one-to-one tutoring programs in reading for elementary students at risk for reading failure? A meta-analysis of the intervention research' in *Journal of Educational Psychology*, vol. 92, pp. 605–19.

Engelman, S. & Osborn, J. (1999), *Language for learning*, Columbus, OH: Presentation Book Co., SRA/McGraw-Hill.

Englert, C. & Raphael, T.E. (1988), 'Constructing well-formed prose: Process, structure and meta-cognitive knowledge' in *Exceptional Children*, vol. 54, pp. 513–20.

Fischer, C.W., Berliner, D.C., Filby, N.N., Marlianve, R., Cahen, S.L. & Dishaw, M.M. (1980), 'Teaching behaviours, academic learning time, and student achievement: An overview' in C. Denham & A. Lieberman (eds), *Time to learn*, Washington, DC: National Institute of Education, pp. 7–32.

Fleisher, L., Jenkins, J. & Pany, D. (1979), 'Effects on poor readers' comprehension of training in rapid decoding' in *Reading Research Quarterly*, vol. 15, pp. 30–48.

Foorman, B.R. (1995), 'Research on the "great debate". Code-oriented versus whole language approaches to reading instruction' in *School Psychology Review*, vol. 24, pp. 376–92.

——, Francis, D.J., Fletcher, J.M., Schatschneider, C. & Mehta, P. (1998), 'The role of instruction in learning to read. Preventing reading failure in at-risk children' in *Journal of Educational Psychology*, vol. 90, pp. 37–55.

——, Francis, D.J., Davidson, K.C., Harm, M.W. & Griffin, J. (2004), 'Variability in text features in six Grade 1 basal reading programs' in *Scientific Studies of Reading*, vol. 8, no. 20, pp. 167–97.

Gambrell, L.B. (1981), 'Induced mental imagery and the text prediction performance of first and third graders' in J.A. Niles & L.A. Harris (eds), *New inquiries in reading research and instruction: Thirty-first yearbook of the National Reading Conference*, Rochester, NY: National Reading Conference, pp. 131–35.

—— & Bales, R. (1986), Mental imagery and the comprehension monitoring performance of fourth- and fifth-grade poor readers' in *Reading Research Quarterly*, vol. 11, pp. 454–64.

—— & Jawitz, P.B. (1993), 'Mental imagery, text illustrations, and children's story comprehension and recall' in *Reading Research Quarterly*, vol. 28, pp. 265–73.

Gersten, R., Fuchs, L., Williams, J.P. & Baker, S. (2001), 'Teaching reading comprehension strategies to students with learning disabilities: A review of research' in *Review of Educational Research*, vol. 71, no. 2, pp. 279–320.

Gipstein, M., Brady, S.A. & Fowler, A. (2000), 'Questioning the roles of syllables and rimes in early phonological awareness' in N.A. Badian (ed.), *Prediction and prevention of reading failure*, Baltimore, Maryland: New York Press Inc, pp. 179–217.

Glass, G., Cahen, L., Smith, M.L. & Filby, N. (1982), *School class size: Research and Policy*, Beverly Hills: Sage Publications.

Goodman, K.S. (1986), *What's whole in whole-language: A parent-teacher guide*, Portsmouth, NH: Heinemann.

—— (1993), *Phonic Phacts*, Portsmouth, NH: Heinemann.

Goswami, U. (1995), *Rhyme and analogy*, Oxford: Oxford University Press.

—— (2000), 'Phonological and lexical processes' in M.L. Kamil, P.B. Mosenthal, P.D. Pearson, R. Barr (eds), *Handbook of Reading Research*, Mahwah, NJ: Lawrence Erlbaum Associates, vol. 3, pp. 251–67.

—— & Bryant, P. (1992), 'Rhyming, analogy and children's reading' in P.B. Gough, L.C. Ehri & R. Treiman (eds), *Reading Acquisition*, Hillsdale, NJ: Lawrence Erlbaum Associates, pp. 49–64.

Gough, P.B. (1993), 'Context, form and interaction' in K. Rayner (ed.), *Eye movements in reading*, New York: Academic Press, pp. 203–11.

—— (1999), 'The New Literacy: Caveat Emptor' in J. Oakhill & R. Beard (eds), *Reading development and the teaching of reading*, Oxford, UK: Blackwell Publishers Ltd, pp. 1–11.

——, Hoover, W.A. & Peterson, C.L. (1996), 'Some observations on a Simple View of Reading' in C. Cornoldi & J. Oakhill (eds), *Reading comprehension difficulties: Processes and intervention*, Mahwah, NJ: Lawrence Erlbaum & Associates, pp. 1–13.

—— & Tunmer, W. (1986), 'Decoding, reading and reading disability' in *Remedial and Special Education*, vol. 7, pp. 6–10.

—— & Wren, S. (1999), 'Constructing meaning: The role of decoding' in J. Oakhill & R. Beard (eds), *Reading development and the teaching of reading*, Oxford, UK: Blackwell Publishers Ltd, pp. 59–78.

Graham, S. & Harris, K.R. (1994), 'Implications of constructivism for teaching writing to students with special needs' in *The Journal of Special Education*, vol. 28, no. 3, pp. 275–89.

Grahame, K. (1908), *The Wind in the Willows*, N.Y.: Charles Scribner's Sons.

Gredler, M. & Shields, C. (2004), 'Does no one read Vygotsky's words?' in *Educational Researcher*, vol. 33, pp. 21–5.

Green, L., McCutchen, D., Schwiebert, C., Quinlan, T., Eva-Wood, A. & Juelis, J. (2003), 'Morphological development in children's writing' in *Journal of Educational Psychology*, vol. 95, no. 4, pp. 752–61.

Groves P. (1989), Bangers and Mash (comprises two series of 'little readers'—*see* p. 165), Hong Kong: Longman Group.

Guttman, J., Levin, J. & Pressley, M. (1977), 'Pictures, partial pictures and young children's oral prose learning' in *Journal of Educational Psychology*, vol. 69, pp. 473–80.

Hazzard, S. (1981), *The Transit of Venus*, New Zealand Ltd: Penguin Books.

Hiebert, E.H. & Taylor, B.M. (eds) (1994), *Getting reading right from the start*, Boston: Allyn & Bacon.

Hillocks, Jr, G. (1984), 'What works in teaching composition: A meta-analysis of experimental treatment studies' in *American Journal of Education*, November, pp. 133–70.

Hoover W. & Gough, P. (1990), 'The simple view of reading' in *Reading and Writing: An Interdisciplinary Journal*, vol. 2, pp. 127–60.

House of Representatives Standing Committee on Employment, Education and Training (1992), *The literacy challenge: A report on strategies for early intervention for literacy and learning for Australian children*, Canberra, ACT: Australian Government Printing Service.

Hutchins, P. (1978), *Happy Birthday, Sam*, New York: Greenwillow Books.

Invernizzi, M. & Hayes, L (2004), 'Developmental-spelling research. A systematic imperative' in *Reading Research Quarterly*, vol. 39, pp. 216–28.

Iversen, J.A. & Tunmer, W.E. (1993), 'Phonological processing skills and the Reading Recovery program' in *Journal of Educational Psychology*, vol. 85, pp. 112–25.

Jenkins, J.R., Peyton, J.A., Sanders, E.A. & Vadasy, P.F. (2004), 'Effects of reading decodable texts in supplemental first-grade tutoring' in *Scientific Studies of Reading*, vol. 8, no. 1, pp. 53–85.

Juel, C. (1988), 'Learning to read and write. A longitudinal study of fifty-four children from first through fourth grade' in *Journal of Educational Psychology*, vol. 80, pp. 437–47.

—— (1994), *Learning to read and write in one elementary school*, New York: Springer-Verlag.

—— (1998), 'What kind of one-on-one tutoring helps a poor reader?' in C. Hulme & R.M. Joshi (eds), *Reading and spelling: Development and disorders*, Mahwah, NJ: Lawrence Erlbaum & Associates, pp. 449–71.

——, Griffith, P.L. & Gough, P.B (1986), 'Acquisition of literacy: A longitudinal study of children in first and second grade' in *Journal of Educational Psychology*, vol. 78, pp. 243–55.

Karweit, N. (1989b), 'The effects of a story-reading program on the vocabulary and story comprehension skills of disadvantaged pre-kindergarten and kindergarten students' in *Early Education and Development*, vol. 1, p. 2.

Kemp, D. (2000), 'Ministerial statement on teaching early reading' in *Sydney Morning Herald*, Sydney: Australia.

Kerr, B.M. & Mason, J.M. (1994), 'Awakening literacy through interactive story reading' in F. Lehr & J. Osborn (eds), *Reading, language, and literacy*, Hillsdale, NJ: Lawrence Erlbaum Associates, Publishers, pp. 133–48.

Kipling. R. (1996), *The Just So Stories*, William Morris.

Klein, A.F., Kelly, P.R. & Pinnell, G.S. (1997), 'Teaching from theory: Decision making in reading recovery' in S.A. Stahl & D.A. Hayes (eds), *Instructional models in reading*, Mahwah, NJ: Lawrence Erlbaum & Associates, pp 161–79.

Kuhn, M.R. (2004/2005), 'Helping students become accurate expressive readers: Fluency instruction for small groups' in *The Reading Teacher*, vol. 58, no. 4, pp. 338–44.

——, Schwanenflugel, P.J., Morris, R., Woo, D., Meisinger, B., Morrow, L.M. & Stahl, S. (2004), interactive paper presented at the *Eleventh Annual Meeting of TripleSR*: Amsterdam, Holland.

—— & Stahl, S.A. (2000), *Fluency: A review of developmental and remedial practices*, University of Michigan, Ann Arbor: Center for the Improvement of Early Reading Achievement.

Liberman, A.M. (1997), 'How theories of speech affect research in reading and writing' in B. Blachman (ed.), *Foundations of reading acquisition and dyslexia*, Mahwah, NJ: Laurence Erlbaum Associates, pp. 3–19.

—— & Mattingly (1985), 'The motor theory of speech perception revised' in *Cognition*, vol. 21, pp. 1–36.

Liberman, I.Y. & Liberman, A.M. (1992), 'Whole-language versus code-emphasis: Underlying assumptions and their implications for reading instruction' in P.B. Gough, L.C. Ehri & R. Treiman (eds), *Reading acquisition*, Hillsdale, NJ: Lawrence Erlbaum & Associates, pp. 343–66.

Lloyd, S. (1998), *The phonics handbook* (3rd ed.), Chigwell, England: Jolly Learning.

Lyster, S.H. (2002), 'The effects of morphological versus phonological training in kindergarten on reading development' in *Reading and Writing: An Interdisciplinary Journal*, vol. 15, pp. 261–94.

Maclean, M., Bryant, P. & Bradley, L. (1987), 'Rhymes, nursery rhymes, and reading in early childhood' in *Merrill-Palmer Quarterly*, vol. 33, no. 3, pp. 255–81.

Macquarie University Word Attack Skills Test (1983), NSW, Australia: Macquarie University Special Education Centre.

Madden, N.A., Slavin, R.R., Farnish, A.M., Livingstone, M.A., Calderon, M. & Maxns, R.J. (1996), *Reading wings: Teacher's manual*, Baltimore: Johns Hopkins University.

Manis, F.R. (1985), 'Acquisition of word identification skills in normal and disabled readers' in *Journal of Educational Psychology*, vol. 77, pp. 78–90.

Mason, J.M. (1992), 'Reading stories to preliterate children: A proposed connection to reading' in P.B. Gough, L.C. Ehri & R. Treiman (eds), *Reading acquisition*, Hillsdale, NJ: Lawrence Erlbaum & Associates, pp. 215–41.

McCandliss, B., Beck, I.L., Sandak, R. & Perfetti, C. (2003), 'Focusing attention on decoding for children with poor reading skills: Design and preliminary tests of the word building intervention' in *Scientific Studies of Reading*, vol. 7, no. 1, pp, 75–104.

Menon, S. & Hiebert, E.H. (2005), 'A comparison of first graders' reading with little books or literature—based on basal anthologies' in *Reading Research Quarterly*, no. 40, pp. 12–38.

Milne, A.A. (1926), *Winnie the Pooh*, London: Methuen.

Muter, V. (2000), 'Screening for early reading failure' in N.A. Badian (ed.), *Prediction and prevention of reading failure*, Baltimore, Maryland: New York Press, pp. 1–30.

——, Hulme, C. & Snowling, M. (1997), *The phonological awareness test*, London, UK: Psychological Corporation Europe.

Nagy, W.E. (1994), *Teaching vocabulary to improve reading comprehension*, Newark, Delaware: International Reading Association.

NICHD Early Child Care Research Network (2002), *American Educational Research Journal*, vol. 39, no. 1, pp. 133–64.

Nicholson, T. (2000), *Reading the writing on the wall*, Palmerston North, New Zealand: Dunmore Press.

—— (2005), *The phonics handbook*, London: Whurr.

Nunes, T., Bryant, P. & Bindman, M. (1997), 'Spelling and grammar—the necsed move' in C.A. Perfetti, L. Rieben, M. Fayol, (eds), *Learning to spell*, Mahwah, NJ: Lawrence Erlbaum Associates, pp. 151–70.

Oakhill, J.V. & Yuill, N.M. (1995), 'Learning to understand written language' in E. Funnell & M. Stuart (eds), *Learning to read*, Oxford, UK: Blackwell.

—— & Yuill, N.M. (1996), 'Higher order factors in comprehension disability: Processes and remediation' in C. Cornoldi and J. Oakhill (eds), *Reading comprehension difficulties*, Hillsdale, NJ: Lawrence Erlbaum & Associates, pp. 69–92.

O'Brien, D. (1992), *Writing in the primary school*, Melbourne: Longman Chesire, Pty Ltd.

Olson, R.K. (2004), 'SSSR, environment and genes' in *Scientific Studies of Reading*, vol. 8, no. 2, pp. 111–24.

O'Shea, L.J., Sindelar, P.T. & O'Shea, D.J. (1985), 'The effects of repeated readings and attentional cues on reading fluency and comprehension' in *Journal of Reading Behaviour*, vol. 17, pp. 129–42.

Paivio, A. (1971), *Imagery and verbal processes*, New York: Holt, Rhinehart, & Winston.

Paivio, A. (1991), 'Dual coding theory: Retrospect and current status' in *Canadian Journal of Psychology*, 45, pp. 255–87.

Pearson, P.D. & Gallagher, M.C. (1983), 'The instruction of reading comprehension' in *Contemporary Educational Psychology*, vol. 8, pp. 317–44.

Perfetti, C.A. (1997), 'The psycholinguistics of spelling and reading' in C.A. Perfetti, L. Rieben & M. Fayol (eds), *Learning to spell: Research, theory and practice across languages*, Hillsdale, NJ: Lawrence Erlbaum Associates, pp. 21–38.

—— (1999), 'Cognitive research and the misconceptions of reading education' in J. Oakhill & R. Beard (eds), *Reading development and the teaching of reading*, Cornwall: Blackwell Publishers, pp. 42–58.

—— (2003), 'The universal grammar of reading' in *Scientific Studies of Reading*, vol. 7, no. 1, pp. 3–24.

Plourde, L. (1995), *Classroom listening and speaking (CLAS)*, Tucson, AZ: Psychological Corporation.

Pressley, G.M. (1976), 'Mental imagery helps eight-year-olds remember what they read' in *Journal of Educational Psychology*, vol. 68, pp. 335–59.

Pressley, M. (1998), *Reading instruction that works: The case for balanced instruction*, New York: Guilford Press.

—— (2002), 'Metacognition and self-regulated comprehension' in A.E. Farstrup & S.J. Samuels (eds), *What research has to say about reading instruction*, Newark, Delaware: IRA, pp. 291–309.

Rayner, K., Foorman, B.R., Perfetti, C.A., Pesetsky, D. & Seidenberg, M.S. (2002), *Scientific American*, March, pp. 71–77.

Read, C. (1975), *Children's categorization of speech sounds*, NCTE Research Report no. 17, Urbana Il: National Council of Teachers of English.

Reitsma, P. (1983), 'Printed word learning in beginning readers' in *Journal of Experimental Child Psychology*, vol. 36, pp. 321–39.

—— (1989), 'Orthographic memory and learning to read' in P.G. Aaron & R.M. Joshi (eds), *Reading and writing disorders in different orthographic systems*, Dordrecht/Norwell, MA: Kluwer Academic, pp. 51–73.

Roberts, C. & Salter, W. (1995), *The phonological awareness test*, East Moline, Il: Lingui Systems.

Rosenblatt, L.M. (1978), *The reader, the text, the poem: The transactional theory of the literary work*, Carbondale, Il: Southern Illinois University Press.

Ross, S.M., Nunnery, J. & Smith, L.J. (1996), *Evaluation of title 1 reading programs: Amphitheater public schools, year 11, 1995–1996*, Memphis TN: University of Memphis.

——, Smith, L.J., Casey, J. & Slavin, R.E. (1995), 'Increasing the academic success of disadvantaged children: An examination of alternative early intervention programs' in *American Educational Research Journal*, vol. 32, pp. 773–800.

Sadoski, M. (1985), 'The natural use of imagery in story comprehension and recall: Replication and extension' in *Reading Research Quarterly*, vol. 20, pp. 658–67.

Samuels, S.J. (2002), 'Reading fluency: Its development and assessment' in A.E. Farstrup & S.J. Samuels (eds), *What research has to say about reading instruction*, Delaware, USA: International Reading Association, pp. 166–83.

Schatschneider, C., Francis, D., Forman, B., Fletcher, J. & Mehta, P. (1999), 'The dimensionality of phonemic awareness: An application of item response theory' in *Journal of Educational Psychology*, vol. 91, pp. 439–49.

Scott, J. & Ehri, L.C. (1989), 'Sight word reading in pre-schoolers: Use of logographic vs alphabetic access routes' in *Journal of Reading Behaviour*, vol. 22, pp. 149–66.

Senechal, M., Thomas, E. & Monker, J. (1995), 'Individual differences in 4-year-old children's acquisition of vocabulary during story book reading' in *Journal of Educational Psychology*, vol. 87, no. 2, pp. 218–29.

Seuss, Dr (2003), *The Cat in the Hat*, UK: HarperCollins Children's Books.

—— (2003), *Hop on Pop*, UK: HarperCollins Children's Books.

—— (2003), *One fish, two fish, red fish, blue fish*, UK: HarperCollins Children's Books.

Shanahan, M. & Barr, R. (1995), 'Reading Recovery: An independent evaluation of the effects of an early instructional intervention for at-risk learners' in *Reading Research Quarterly*, vol. 30, no. 4, pp. 958–96.

Shanahan, T. & Shanahan, S. (1997), 'Character perspective charting: Helping children to develop a more complete conception of story' in *The Reading Teacher*, vol. 50, no. 8, pp. 668–77.

Share, D.L. (1995), 'Phonological recoding and self-teaching: Sine qua non of reading acquisition' in *Cognition*, vol. 55, pp. 151–218.

—— (1999), 'Phonological recoding and orthographic learning: A direct test of the self-teaching hypothesis' in *Journal of Experimental Child Psychology*, vol. 72, pp. 95–129.

——, Jorm, A.F., Maclean, R. & Matthews, R. (1984), 'Sources of individual differences in reading acquisition' in *Journal of Educational Psychology*, vol. 5, pp. 35–44.

—— & Stanovich, K.E. (1995), 'Cognitive processes in early reading development: Accommodating individual differences into a model of acquisition' in *Issues in Education: Contributions from Educational Psychology*, vol. 1, pp. 1–57.

Shaywitz, S.E. & Shaywitz, B.A. (2002), 'Science informing policy: The National Institute of Child Health and Human Development's contribution to reading' in *Pediatrics, Commentaries*, vol. 109, pp. 519–21.

Short, E.J. & Ryan, E.B. (1984), 'Meta-cognitive differences between skilled and less skilled readers: Remediating deficits through story grammar and attribution training' in *Journal of Educational Psychology*, vol. 76, pp. 225–35.

Singer, H. & Donlan, D. (1982), 'Active comprehension: A problem-solving schema with question generating for comprehension of complex short stories' in *Reading Research Quarterly*, vol. 17, pp. 166–86.

Slavin, R.E., Karweit, N.L. & Wasik, B. (1994), *Preventing early school failure*, Boston: Allyn and Bacon.

—— & Madden, N.A. (2001), *Success for All: Research and reform in elementary education*, Mahwah, NJ: Lawrence Erlbaum Associates, Inc., Publishers.

——, Madden, N.A., Karweit, N.L., Dolan, L. & Wasik, B.A. (1992), *Success for all: A relentless approach to prevention and early intervention in elementary schools*, Arlington, VA: Educational Research Service.

Snow, C.E. (2001), 'Knowing what we know: Children, teachers, researchers' in *Educational Researcher*, vol. 30, no. 7, pp. 3–9.

——, Burns, M.S. & Griffin, P. (eds) (1998), *Preventing reading difficulties in young children*, National Research Council Washington, DC: National Academic Press.

Spiegel, D. (1992), 'Blending whole language and systematic direct instruction' in *The Reading Teacher*, vol. 46, pp. 38–44.

Stahl, S.A., Duffy-Hester, A. & Stahl, K.A. (1998), 'Theory and practice into research: Everything you wanted to now about phonics (but were afraid to ask)' in *Reading Research Quarterly*, vol. 33, pp. 338–62.

—— & Murray, B. (1998), 'Issues involved in defining phonemic awareness and its relation to early reading' in J.L. Metsala & L.C. Ehri (eds), *Word recognition in beginning literacy*, Mahwah, NJ: Lawrence Erlbaum & Associates, pp. 65–88.

Stanovich, K.E. (1980), 'Toward an interactive–compensatory model of individual differences in the development of reading fluency' in *Reading Research Quarterly*, vol. 16, pp. 32–71.

—— (1984), 'The interactive-compensatory model of reading: A confluence of developmental, experimental and educational psychology' in *Remedial and Special Education*, vol. 5, pp. 11–19.

—— (1986), 'Matthew effects in reading: Some consequences of individual differences in the acquisition of literacy' in *Reading Research Quarterly*, vol. 21, pp. 360–407.

—— (1992), 'Speculations on the causes and consequences of individual differences in early reading acquisition' in P.B. Gough, L.C. Ehri & R. Treiman (eds), *Reading acquisition*, Hillsdale, NJ: Lawrence Erlbaum Associates, pp. 307–42.

—— (2000), *Progress in understanding reading: Scientific foundations and new frontiers*, New York: The Guilford Press.

—— & Stanovich, P.J. (1999), 'How research might inform the debate about early reading acquisition' in J. Oakhill & R. Beard (eds), *Reading development and the teaching of reading*, Cornwall: Blackwell Publishers, pp. 12–41.

Stedman, L.C. & Kaestle, C.E. (1987), 'Literacy and reading performance in the United States from 1880 to the present' in *Reading Research Quarterly*, vol. 22, pp. 8–46.

Swan, N. (2002), *The Health Report*, radio program, Australia: Australian Broadcasting Commission.

Tangel, D.M. & Blachman, B.A. (1992), 'Effect of phoneme awareness instruction on kindergarten children's invented spelling' in *Journal of Reading Behaviour*, vol. 26, no. 2, pp. 233–61.

Taylor, B. M. (1992), 'Text structure, comprehension, and recall' in S.J. Samuels & A.E. Farstrup (eds), *What research has to say about reading instruction*, Newark, Delaware: International Reading Association.

Torgesen, J.K. (2000), 'Individual differences in response to early interventions in reading: The lingering problem of treatment resisters' in *Learning Disabilities Research and Practice*, vol. 5, no. 1, pp. 55–64.

—— & Bryant (1994), *The phonological awareness test*, Austin TX: Pro-Ed.

——, Wagner, R.K. & Rashotte, C.A. (1997), 'Prevention and remediation of severe reading disabilities: Keeping the end in mind' in *Scientific Studies of Reading*, vol. 1, pp. 217–34.

——, Wagner, R.K. & Rashotte, C.A. (1999), *Test of word reading efficiency*, (TOWRE) Austin, TX: ProEd.

——, Wagner, R.K., Rashotte, C.A., Burgess, S. & Hecht, S. (1997), 'Contributions of phonological awareness and rapid automatic naming ability to the growth of word-reading skills in second- to fifth-grade children' in *Scientific Studies of Reading*, vol. 1, pp. 161–95.

Trieman, R. (1993), *Beginning to spell: A study of first-grade children*, New York: Oxford University Press.

—— (1998a), 'Beginning to spell in English' in C. Hulme & R.M. Joshi (eds), *Reading and spelling development and disorders*, Mahwah, New Jersey: Lawrence Erlbaum & Associates, pp. 371–93.

—— (1998b), 'Why spelling?' in J.L. Metsala & L.C. Ehri (eds), *Word recognition in beginning literacy*, Mahwah, NJ: Lawrence Erlbaum Associates, pp. 289–314.

Truss, L. (2003), *Eats, shoots and leaves*, London: Profile.

Tunmer, W.E. & Chapman, J.W. (1998), 'Language prediction skill, phonological recoding ability and beginning reading' in C. Hulme & M. Joshi (eds), *Reading and spelling: Developmental disorders*, Hillsdale, NJ: Lawrence Erlbaum & Associates, pp. 33–87.

Tunmer, W.E. & Chapman, J.W. (2003), 'The reading recovery approach to preventive early intervention: As good as it gets' in *Reading Psychology*, vol. 24, pp. 337–60.

——, Chapman, J.W., Greaney, K.T. & Prochnow, J.E. (2002), 'The contribution of educational psychology to intervention research and practice' in *International Journal of Disability, Development and Education*, vol. 49, no. 1, pp. 11–29.

——, Chapman, J.W. & Prochnow, J.E. (2003), 'Preventing negative Matthew effects in at-risk readers: A retrospective study' in B. Foorman (ed.), *Preventing and remediating reading difficulties: Bringing science to scale*, Timonium: York Press, pp. 121–63.

——, Chapman, J.W., Ryan, H.A. & Prochnow, J.E. (1998), 'The importance of providing beginning readers with explicit training in phonological processing skills' in *Australian Journal of Learning Disabilities*, vol. 3, pp. 4–14.

——, Herriman, M.L. & Nesdale, A.R. (1988), 'Metalinguistic abilities and beginning reading' in *Reading Research Quarterly*, vol. 23, pp. 134–58.

—— & Hoover, W.A. (1992), 'Cognitive and linguistic factors in learning to read' in P.B. Gough, L.C. Ehri & R. Treiman (eds), *Reading acquisition*, Hillsdale, NJ: Lawrence Erlbaum & Associates, pp. 175–214.

Uhry, J.K. (2002), 'Finger-point reading in kindergarten: The role of phonemic awareness, one-to-one correspondence, and rapid serial naming' in *Scientific Studies of Reading*, vol. 6, no. 4, pp. 319–42.

Van Kraayenoord, C., Elkins, J., Palmer, C. & Rickards, F.W. (2000), *Literacy, numeracy and students with disability*, vol. 1, Australia: Department of Education, Training and Youth Affairs.

Vellutino, F.R., Scanlon, D.M., Sipay, E.R., Small, S.G., Pratt, A., Chen, R. & Denckla, M.B. (1996), 'Cognitive profiles of difficult-to-remediate and readily remediated poor readers: Early intervention as a vehicle for distinguishing between cognitive and experiential deficits as basic causes of specific reading disability' in *Journal of Educational Psychology*, vol. 88, pp. 601–38.

Venezky, R.L. (1998), 'An alternative perspective on Success for All' in K.K. Wong (ed.), *Advances in educational policy: Perspectives on the social functions of schools*, Stamford, Connecticut: JAI Press Inc, pp. 145–65.

Verhoeven, L. & Perfetti, C. (2003), 'Introduction to this special issue: The role of morphology in learning to read' in *Scientific Studies of Reading*, vol. 7, no. 3, pp. 209–17.

Vinson Report (2001), *Public Education Enquiry*, NSW: Australia.

Vygotsky, L.S. (1978), *Mind in society: The development of higher psychological processes*, Cambridge, MA: Harvard University Press.

Wagner, R., Torgesen, J.K. & Rashotte, C. (1997), *Comprehensive test of phonological processing (CTOPP)*, Austin, TX: ProEd.

Walsh, M. (8 December 2003), 'When it comes to literacy it's not as simple as ABC' in *Sydney Morning Herald*, Sydney: Australia.

Waring, S., Prior, M., Sanson, A. & Smart, D. (1996), 'Predictors of "recovery" from reading disability' in *Australian Journal of Psychology*, vol. 48, no. 3, pp. 160–66.

Wasik, B.A. (1998), 'Volunteer tutoring programs in reading: A review' in *Reading Research Quarterly*, vol. 33, no. 3, pp. 266–91.

—— & Slavin, R.E. (1993), Preventing early reading failure with one-to-one tutoring: A review of five programs' in *Reading Research Quarterly*, vol. 28, pp. 179–200.

——, & Slavin, R.E. (1994), 'Preventing early reading failure with one-to-one tutoring: A review of five programs' in R.E Slavin, N.L. Karweit, B.A. Wasik (eds), *Preventing early school failure: Research, policy and practice*, Boston: Allyn & Bacon, pp. 143–74.

Wendon, L. (1993), 'Literacy for early childhood: Learning from learners' in *Early Childhood Development and Care*, vol. 86, pp. 11–22.

Whitehurst, G.J., Arnold, D.S., Epstein, J.N., Angell, A.L., Smith, M. & Fischel, J.E. (1994), 'A picture-book reading intervention in day care and home for children from low-income families' in *Developmental Psychology*, vol. 30, no. 5, pp. 679–89.

Williams, J.P. (2002), 'Reading comprehension strategies and teacher preparation' in A.E. Farstrup & S.J. Samuels (eds), *What research has to say about reading instruction*, Newark, Delaware: IRA, pp. 243–60.

Wolf, M., Bowers, P.G. & Biddle, K. (2000), 'Naming-speed processes, timing, and reading: A conceptual review' in *Journal of Learning Disabilities*, vol. 33, no. 4, pp. 387–407.

Wolf, M., Miller, L. & Donnelly, K. (2000), 'The retrieval, automaticity, vocabulary elaboration, orthography (RAVE-O): A comprehensive fluency-based reading intervention program' in *Journal of Learning Disabilities*, vol. 33, pp. 375–86.

Woodcock, R.W. (1987), *Woodcock reading mastery tests—Revised: Examiner's manual*, Circle Pines, MN: American Guidance Service.

Xue, Y. & Meisels, S.J. (2004), 'Early literacy instruction and learning in kindergarten: Evidence from Early Childhood Longitudinal Study—Kindergarten Class of 1998–1999' in *American Educational Research Journal*, vol. 41, no. 1, pp. 191–229.

Yopp, R.E. (1988), 'Questioning and active comprehension' in *Questioning Exchange*, vol. 2, pp. 231–38.

Zion, G. (1956), *Harry the Dirty Dog*, UK: HarperCollins.

Index